Stories and Minds

Frontiers of Narrative

SERIES EDITOR

David Herman *Ohio State University*

Stories
and Minds

Cognitive Approaches to Literary Narrative

EDITED BY LARS BERNAERTS, DIRK
DE GEEST, LUC HERMAN, AND BART VERVAECK

University of Nebraska Press | Lincoln and London

Library of Congress Cataloging-in-Publication Data
Vervaeck, Bart, editor of compilation.
Stories and minds: cognitive approaches to literary narrative/ edited by Lars Bernaerts, Dirk De Geest, Luc Herman, and Bart Vervaeck.
p. cm. — (Frontiers of narrative)
Includes bibliographical references and index.
ISBN 978-0-8032-4481-8 (pbk.: alk. paper)
1. Narration (Rhetoric) 2. Cognitive science—Philosophy. 3. Psycholinguistics. I. Bernaerts, Lars, 1980–, editor of compilation. II. Geest, Dirk de, 1957–, editor of compilation. III. Herman, Luc, editor of compilation.
PN212.S763 2013
401.41—dc23   2012045559

Set in Minion Pro by Laura Wellington.

Contents

Illustrations

Stories and Minds

Introduction

Cognitive Narrative Studies: *Themes and Variations*

LARS BERNAERTS, DIRK DE GEEST,
LUC HERMAN, AND BART VERVAECK

The present collection of essays offers a sample of cutting-edge research
in the field of cognitive narrative studies. The workings and effects of literary narratives provide the main focus, but the collection also reflects
upon the relations between hermeneutic and empirical tendencies as they
increasingly affect the study of cognition and narrative. In particular, the
chapters in this volume will show how speculative research on readers'
positions can supplement empirical inquiries. In the remainder of our
introduction, we first summarize some of the trends in the cognitive study
of literature against the background of literary theory. We start off with a
phenomenon that has been thoroughly examined in literary theory and
that is approached with new tools in several of the chapters in this volume: the gappy nature of literary narratives. At the end of our introduction, we provide a synopsis of the separate chapters.

Minds, Narrative, and the Pursuit of Gappiness

One of the sections in B. S. Johnson's *The Unfortunates* (1969), a book
published in the form of twenty-seven unbound chapters in a box, starts
with a reflection on narrativization and style. How will the narrator, who
is a sports journalist, report on the local soccer derby? He considers using
the bald spots on the field as a metaphor in his article: "The pitch worn,
the worn patches, like   There might be an image, there, if I can
think of one, at this stage of the season, it might too stand for what these
two teams are like, are doing.   If I can think of one" (Johnson 1969,
1). While the character-narrator is thinking about these worn patches,
they already materialize in front of the reader's eyes. The bald spots in
Johnson's text echo the narrator's thoughts as well as the narrator's thinking. His mind and his narrative are full of gaps and sudden shifts, and

therefore the text is gappy. The fact that the chapters of the novel are loose and presented in a book-shaped box reinforces this idea and further transposes it into the reader's experience. As the author explains himself (in a BBC documentary broadcast in 1969), the physical and typographical presentation of the text is a metaphor for the mind of the narrating protagonist. In addition, it is a metaphor for the mind of the reader. *Albert Angelo* (1964), another novel written by Johnson, demonstrates that gaps in a narrative text not only require an additional effort of the reader but also *enable* him or her to see something else and to make new narrative connections. The holes cut in the pages (1964, 149–52) of *Albert Angelo* function as windows on the further course of the narrative.

Far from being mere places of emptiness, void of significance, gaps like the ones Johnson foregrounds in his texts provide access to some of the key concerns of this volume. In particular, as we discuss in what follows, there are various kinds and levels of narrative gaps discussed in narrative theory. By going into these theoretical constructs, we can show some of the constants appearing in cognitive approaches to narrative, and in this book in particular.

Minding the Gap

Bridging gaps and filling holes is what readers do all the time when they are comprehending or interpreting narratives. In literary theory, this process of gap-filling is widely recognized and linked to the reader's cognitive efforts. From Gérard Genette's paralipsis to Meir Sternberg's informational gaps, from Wolfgang Iser's *Leerstellen* to Lubomir Doležel's and David Herman's deliberations on gaps and action representations, the idea of narrative lacunae has been prominent in theories of the narrative.[1] The reader mobilizes his or her knowledge and experience to supplement what is left unsaid. More particularly, models of fictional minds such as Alan Palmer's stress the importance of gap-filling activities undertaken both by fictional characters and by real readers.

A similar line of reasoning can be found in the philosophy of mind (which has, in fact, inspired narrative scholars like Palmer), in cognitive science, and in neurological approaches to literature and art. Daniel Dennett's and Galen Strawson's views on consciousness, as taken up by Palmer (2009, 292–93) in his model of fictional minds, chime with the notion of lacunae-driven narrativization. In *Consciousness Explained*, Dennett stresses the "gappy and sparse" (1991, 366) nature of consciousness, on the one hand, and the narrative constitution of the self, on the other hand. The self is no more than "the center of narrative gravity"; our minds and selves are the "product [of narratives], not their source" (418).

On yet another level of minds and narrative, there is an "explanatory gap" (Herman 2009, 146) between qualia, or the felt experience of subjective awareness, and neurophysiological descriptions of mental functioning. Up to now, the neurological repertoire—offering explanations in terms of neurons, synapses, and electrochemical transactions—remains partly unsatisfactory in accounting for the ways in which we experience the world through our consciousness. Because of its fragmented narrative structure, B. S. Johnson's *The Unfortunates* can impose a feeling of disorientation on the reader. While this feeling is meaningful in the reader's subjective experience, it might be insignificant or even barely distinguishable in a neurological description of that reader's brain. Although they both theorize the mind, there is still quite a gap between phenomenological (subjective) and neurological (objective) inquiries. To give one more example, Ellen Spolsky's *Gaps in Nature* (1993) characterizes the activity of compensating for lacunae as inherent not just in literary interpretation and literary historiography but also in the modular processing that goes on in our brains. It is not the smooth cooperation of modules (e.g., the senses) that generates new meanings, but the gaps and seams between them: "They are the sites of innovations resulting from the incommensurability between modules" (1993, 31).

Although there are significant differences as to the level and function of the "gaps" in these theories, they arise from a shared interest in minds and narrative, or what Herman (2009) terms the "nexus of narrative and mind" (137–60). The dynamics and interpretation of narratives depend on the absence of information and on discrepancies between the reader's knowledge and the knowledge possessed by narrators and characters. As narrative theory teaches us, narratives come into being through the interaction between minds and narrative gaps. In brief, there is a profound awareness among theorists of mind as well as theorists of narrative that the construction and interpretation of narratives as coherent wholes paradoxically require gaps, empty spaces, and hidden information. The inquiry into minds and narrative has often taken the shape of pinpointing these gaps and describing how we fill them. In what follows we first offer a thumbnail history of some of these approaches to narrative gaps. In that way, some of the theoretical affiliations connecting the history of literary theory to the current cognitive approaches will become apparent. Against that background, we will then focus on the novelties associated with cognitive approaches in particular.

Traditions in Narrative and Cognition

Narrative theorists have always shown interest in the relation between minds and narrative. But though this continuity is striking, there are some noticeable shifts in method and actual focus—shifts that, again, the issue of narrative gaps can help throw into relief. To clarify both continuity and shifts, we will simplify matters and present the evolution of thinking about minds and texts in three steps: the hermeneutic phase associated with phenomenology (largely preceding narratology), the structuralist stage of classical narratology, and the cognitive, postclassical approach.

Generally speaking, the hermeneutic tradition tries to integrate the objective, philological dimension of the text and the subjective processing of the text. In Schleiermacher's (1998, 9–18) terminology, the grammatical and psychological aspects must merge into one. This presupposes an endless back-and-forth movement between the "actual" text and the reader's interpretation of it. In this movement—which takes the form of the famous hermeneutic circle—the text becomes ever more meaningful and the reader continually learns more and more. Ideally, this would lead to a "complete" interpretation, but in practice there is always something left to be interpreted—a gap.

The tradition of hermeneutics and, more broadly, of phenomenology offers an explanation for these gaps. Thus, Roman Ingarden stresses that every interpretation or "concretization" (1973, 162) centers around "spots of indeterminacy" (246 ff.) that can never be fully determined as the literary text itself is necessarily indeterminate on all levels, for example, on the level of spatiotemporal representations and descriptions. In a novel such as B. S. Johnson's *The Unfortunates* these indeterminacies are foregrounded typographically and thematically, but they are an integral part of each work of fiction and every act of reading. The evocation of a story can never be exhaustive, and a quasi-exhaustive account of a fictional world would probably be unreadable. The excess of information would kill the story.

Before the emergence of narratology and cognitive theory, Ingarden's discussion of the textual organization and the readerly filling out of blanks already deals with issues taken up by recent cognitive approaches. Hans-Georg Gadamer, another key figure in the hermeneutic tradition, uses the term "horizon" to frame the meeting between the mind of the reader and the demands of the text. As it is part of a larger textual and cultural tradition, the text "expects" a certain knowledge of its reader, who, in his or her turn, comes to the text with his or her own tradition and prejudices. Interpretation is the complex meeting point of the textual horizon with the readerly horizon. A good interpretation is the result of a "fusion of horizons" (1979, 306) that implies a "self-forgetfulness" (122) and aims at a specific truth. Such a complete fusion and forgetfulness is presented as an ideal. In many interpretations, this ideal is never attained.

The idea of horizons meeting and, especially, clashing is omnipresent in the reception theory of Hans-Robert Jauss and Wolfgang Iser. They tend to contest the hermeneutic belief in a perfect interpretation and integration. Their interest lies less in situating literary works in a tradition than in identifying the mechanisms that underlie literary dynamics. To them, openness and conflict define the literary quality of a text, and therefore literature is incompatible with a perfect fusion of horizons or a complete filling in of blanks. Jauss (1970, 187) takes Gadamer to task for the latter's belief in a final reconciliation of minds and texts. As an alternative, Jauss defines literature in terms of the "aesthetic distance" between the horizons of the reader and the text. This distance is never bridged in literary works of art.

As Jauss corrects Gadamer, so Iser (1978, 274 ff.) corrects Ingarden. The gaps—or *Leerstellen* in Iser's terminology—can be filled in many ways (there is not one final and correct reading) and, indeed, will always remain open to some extent: "one text is potentially capable of several different realizations, and no reading can ever exhaust the full potential, for each individual reader will fill in the gaps in his own way, thereby excluding the various other possibilities; as he reads, he will make his own decision as to how the gap is to be filled. In this very act the dynamics of reading are revealed" (Iser 1972, 285). In its material presentation *The Unfortunates* underlines this fact: individual readers are invited to freely choose the order in which they read the chapters, thereby creating new gaps and filling them in very different ways. As the order of the chapters changes, readers will interpret the events and the narrator's memories differently. The idea of "different realizations" becomes very palpable in the case of Johnson's novel.

Not unlike cognitive studies, Iser's reception theory offers a model for the understanding of the reader's mental response. That is why his ideas are often integrated in that context. Iser's approach, however, operates on a more abstract level of theorization than the cognitive approach. Instead of dealing with concrete cognitive processes or empirical readers, he adopts a broad phenomenological view—this is the term he himself (1978, 274) uses—on the reader's experience. The same goes for the other hermeneutic and phenomenological thinkers we mentioned: they introduce an idealized and abstract reader, not going into concrete cognitive processes involved in the idealized process of minds meeting narratives.

Structuralist and formalist theories tend to ignore subjectivity and instead emphasize the distribution and structure of textual gaps. For his part, Gérard Genette uses the term "paralipsis" to indicate information that is needed but absent in the narration (1980, 194). His classification is concerned with the surface structure of narrative texts, rather than a deep structure situated in the human mind. Similarly, when the French structuralists A. J. Greimas and J. Courtès examine "The Cognitive Dimension of Narrative Discourse" (1976), they are dealing with gaps in the distribution of knowledge. They suggest, for example, that "a *gap* or disjunction is produced between the acting subject (the *subject of doing*) and the knowing subject (the *cognitive subject*), a gap the sudden destruction of which can constitute an event of a different order, a cognitive event with repercussions and peripeteias" (1976, 439). For Greimas and Courtès, a cognitive imbalance exists on several levels, between characters as well as between the reader and the text.

There is, in formalist and structuralist thought, an undercurrent of thinking about narrative and literature in terms of minds. Structuralism is obviously built on linguistic foundations and textual features, but the universal underlying systems it discriminates are situated in the human mind. In Culler's seminal study on structuralism, *Structuralist Poetics* (1975), this becomes particularly clear when he discusses literary competence, convention, and naturalization. Culler's notion of "naturalization" stems from the Russian formalists' concept of "motivation" and the structuralist idea of "vraisemblablisation" (Culler 1975, 161). Readers tend to recuperate textual material by placing it in a "discursive order" that is already familiar to them. The style and structure of *The Unfortunates*, for example, might strike us as unconventional and odd at first. However, if we consider the text as a mimetic and verbalized evocation of the narrator's thought processes, we can easily naturalize the textual fragmentation. Another mechanism already involved here is that of "literary competence": readers can use literary frames of reference to make sense of Johnson's novel and read it as "experimental fiction." More recently, the concept of "naturalization" has been expanded and revised in Monika Fludernik's "natural" narratology (1996) and revitalized in schema-theoretical approaches to narrative texts. Likewise, David Herman systematically does justice to the structuralist tradition when he recalibrates narratological concepts (Herman 2002).

"Motivation" is not the only formalist or structuralist term adumbrating the current cognitive models of minds and narrative. Shklovsky's concept of defamiliarization ("ostranenie") and Mukařovský's foregrounding ("aktualisace") also entail hypotheses about the reader's mental functioning. The reader's perception of reality is presumed to be affected by the reading of literary texts. In the empirical study of literature, these explicit and implicit claims about the reader's mind have been tested. Willie van Peer's *Stylistics and Psychology* (1986) is a classic example, on which a number of other scholars have built (see Miall 2006, 112–13). Focusing on foregrounding, van Peer's study provides empirical data for literary-theoretical hypotheses developed by Mukařovský. In that way, the empirical study of literature tackles the problem of the reader's position—a problem that remains tacit in structuralist approaches. As Marisa Bortolussi and Peter Dixon indicate, structuralism seems to approach readers as "universal, aggregate, hypothetical entities responding in unison" (2003, 6), whereas empirical studies factor in the (individual) responses of real readers. Instead of divining the reader's response to *The Unfortunates*, we could set up an experiment. We can, for example, empirically test whether the reader's image of the characters is affected by the order in which he or she reads the chapters. One group of readers can be asked to read the chapters in a certain order, and their reading experiences (documented on the basis of a questionnaire) can be compared with those of another group.

Another prominent model of narrative gaps is developed in Meir Sternberg's *Expositional Modes and Temporal Ordering in Fiction* (1978). According to Sternberg, the dynamics of reading arise from the informational gaps between the represented time and the communicative time. In *The Unfortunates*, the particular succession of these gaps—which, in turn, lead to surprise/suspense/curiosity—depends on the order in which the reader processes the text. For example, information about the narrator's relationship with his passed-away friend can be announced but withheld in one chapter and then disclosed in the next one. If the latter chapter is read first, then the effect might be "surprise" rather than "curiosity."

For their part, more recent cognitive approaches[2] to narrative systematically relate such textual patterns to the workings of a human mind keyed to information processing. For the sake of clarity, we can distinguish between the terms "cognitive" and "cognitivist" here. The former is a generic term used for a broad variety of approaches directly affected by the cognitive turn, ranging from cognitive narratology to evolutionary, neurological, and empirical studies of literature. "Cognitivist" is the term we use in a strict sense for those forms of inquiry that focus not on the reader's subjective experience but on the mental operations required to comprehend narratives. The main goal is to describe these cognitive responses (e.g., the activation of memory patterns). While phenomenology deals with minds and narrative in intentionalist terms and neurology in biological, materialist terms (cf. Hogan 2003, 31), cognitivist research often hovers between those two poles. When we use the term "empirical," we draw attention to a particular *method* in the examination of readers' minds.

Moving beyond structuralist emphases on the grammar of gapping, cognitivist, empirical, and neuropsychological views on narrative sense-making situate the gap-filling process in both the brain (the computer) and the mind (the software). Simplifying these positions, we can say that the cognitivist reading ends when the mental processes have been described, whereas the structuralist reading ends when the rules that govern the narrative have been reconstructed. Meanwhile, more traditionally hermeneutic approaches address empty spaces in a particular narrative by following the hermeneutic circle. In that sense, the hermeneutic reading *never* ends, since the hermeneutic circle entails an endless feedback loop between the content of the narrative and the consciousness of the interpreter.

Empirical studies of literature may focus on surface phenomena such as eye movements and speed of reading, but they may also try to explain these behavioral phenomena in terms of mental patterns behind them. In their empirical approach to aspects of the narrative, for example, Marisa Bortolussi and Peter Dixon (2003) pay particular attention to the way textual cues are processed by readers on the basis of their convictions and prior knowledge. In sum, the way minds and narrative are conceptualized depends on the research object the researcher has in mind: the deep structure of the narrative for structuralism, the cognitive processes that make up narrative comprehension for cognitivist studies, the concrete text as a whole for hermeneutics, or the patterns of the reader's behavior for the empirical study of literature.

Narrative Studies and Cognitive Theory

The cognitive turn has reinforced the empirical basis of narrative studies and strengthened the connection with other disciplines (such as artificial intelligence, discursive psychology, evolutionary biology, philosophy of mind, cognitive linguistics, neuroscience, etc.). Whereas the first wave of cognitive approaches to narrative mainly imported insights from the cognitive sciences, the second wave has displayed a stronger awareness of the unique qualities of (literary) narratives and their potential value for cognitive research. In other words, second-wave cognitive narrative studies can see more clearly how the study of narratives can enrich theories of the mind.

We can find several versions of this development in cognitive literary studies. Mark Turner situates the roots of typical human mental functioning in "literary" processes. The way we think is based on literary, narrative devices such as "metaphor," "story," and "parable" (Turner 1996). In her accounts of sociocognitive complexity in literature, Lisa Zunshine (2006) suggests that levels of intentionality can be multiplied in narrative fiction, so that readers are challenged and tested in their ability to read the minds of others. In *Basic Elements of Narrative*, David Herman (2009, 143–53) explains the interconnection between narratives and qualia, stressing the unique capacity of narratives to create "an environment in which versions of what it was like to experience situations and events can be juxtaposed, comparatively evaluated, and then factored into further accounts of the world (or *a* world)" (151). In the same vein, Uri Margolin, who also touches upon the importance of qualia (2003, 286–87), considers literature as "probably the most eloquent and differentiated non-scientific mode of describing specific instances of the mind in action" (288).

For all these reasons, narrative texts and literary reading can be of special interest to cognitive theorists. Or to put it differently, if philosophers and psychologists claim that our self and our mind are fundamentally the product of narrativization, it would follow that a discipline with decades of expertise in the theory and interpretation of narrative can contribute to the understanding of narrative self-construction. The succession of a narrative and a cognitive turn has made narrative theory into a privileged partner for other disciplines. It is the logical consequence of the work of, for example, Jerome Bruner, Daniel Dennett, and Daniel Hutto. Bruner, who states that "we organize our experience and our memory of human happenings mainly in the form of narrative" (1991, 4), recognizes the expertise of literary theory in this respect (5). Commenting on Hutto's hypothesis about the narrative foundations of our thinking, Herman also makes this logical consequence explicit: "further work on the NPH [Narrative Practice Hypothesis] would itself stand to benefit from a fuller integration of ideas developed by scholars of story" (2008, 512). Narrative theory and literary studies in general can enrich the cognitive study of artistic creations. They have a strong tradition of accounting for linguistic deviation, semantic density, narrative complexity, and interpretive layeredness.

As this overview suggests, cognitive studies of minds and narrative can indeed benefit from a strong awareness of the work done in literary theory from Aristotle to Russian formalism, reception theory, reader-response criticism, and so on. This is recognized and put into practice by many scholars in the field—for example, by Peter Stockwell, who states in his *Cognitive Poetics* that the old insights from literary theory are "useful starting points" for a cognitive analysis that allows us "to conceptualise things differently" (2002, 6). After the cognitive turn, familiar questions (What is literature? Why do we read fiction?) can be conceptualized in new ways, the reader's consciousness can be theorized on various levels (from intentionalist to neurological), and the evocation of fictional consciousness can be analyzed accordingly.

Threats and Opportunities of Cognitive Approaches

While we do not doubt the relevance of a cognitive approach, we should not be blind to criticism that has been leveled against it. Possible threats surfacing in comments on cognitive literary studies are its blindness to tradition, the potential backfire of eclecticism, a new essentialism based on naive positivistic optimism, and a reductionist teleological thinking. First, for Meir Sternberg, who discusses the "cognitivist fortunes" at length, blindness to the theoretical traditions we just sketched is one of the reasons why interdisciplinarity after the cognitive turn has remained largely unsuccessful (2003, 314). In the same vein, Marie-Laure Ryan recently stressed that cognitive approaches to narrative often confirm what narrative theory already knows. They are not yet able to be more precise or to surprise narrative theorists with less obvious findings (2010, 471–2).

Second, cognitive approaches may become so eclectic that they lose the quality of sharing a repertoire of terms and models, which is one of the major benefits of cognitive studies. The benign image used by H. Porter Abbott for cognitive literary studies is that of a group of pirates: "scholar-pirates who plunder for their purposes troves of hypotheses, bright ideas, and yes, rigorous scientific work" (2006, 714). The loot hauled in by these pirates can be very diverse. In an essay on blending theory and narratology, Monika Fludernik observes that a lot of cognitive literary studies display this "strong eclecticism." Scholars select a diversity of "perhaps not compatible" cognitive tools to renew literary theory (2010, 3). For example, prototype theory, schema theory, and blending theory (cf. Turner 1996; Stockwell 2002) approach narrative phenomena in different ways because they start from different accounts of cognitive representations and mental functioning. Arguably, the appropriateness of the model depends on the task we are describing (e.g., building fictional spaces or understanding irony), but how do we decide which model is preferable?

Third, the cognitive turn threatens to elicit essentialist or reductionist thinking. Researchers might suggest that evolutionary or neurological readings reveal the "essence" of literature—which may become reduced to its cognitive dimension—or that ultimate explanations of literary texts spring from these readings. We do not need postmodern ruminations to show that in essentialist thought the interpretive potential of literature is denied. In neurological and evolutionary theories of literature in particular, the belief that the new paradigm will be able to provide conclusive answers to a variety of age-old questions is striking. In this way, one of the major benefits of cognitive approaches, namely, the promise of an empirical basis (i.e., biological materialism), can become the instigator of positivistic optimism. What is problematic is not the conviction that our interpretations can be described as cognitive and neurological processes, but rather the idea that these processes are the be-all and end-all.

We can find this type of reasoning, for example, in Brian Boyd's version of literary Darwinism (a term he himself rejects), in which evolutionary criticism is presented as the solution to the mistakes made by critical theory (2009, 384–92): "[Capital-T theory] has isolated literary criticism from the rest of modern thought and alienated literary studies even from literature itself. A biocultural or evolutionary approach to fiction can reverse these trends" (384). However, Boyd explicitly states that evolutionary criticism "does not limit itself to scientific reduction" (390). Even though his approach has a proclivity toward essentialism, it rejects the kind of reductionism with which cognitive literary studies are sometimes associated.

What is sometimes overlooked is not so much the interpretive power of literature but the extent to which observations and explanations are based on interpretive acts. When literary Darwinists formulate literature's adaptive functions (see Carroll 2008, 119–28), they are *interpreting* the features of literature and the meaning of literature within a constrained explanatory framework and an a priori system of assumptions (e.g., that literature has an adaptive function). In sum, different interpretations of literature as adaption are put forward, but the interpretive act and the ideology underlying these activities are not always acknowledged.

Finally, reductionism in cognitive approaches can take the shape of speculative and teleological thinking. Alan Richardson (2004, 4), for example, criticizes Turner's propensity to stress continuities and universalities. In his approach to "the literary mind," Turner does not do justice to cultural differences and to the specificity of literature and literary reading. Richardson also notes that the empirical evidence for a lot of the claims in cognitive literary studies is rather poor, a criticism that has been seconded by David Miall (2006, 35–46). Teleological reasoning can be found, for example, in straightforward Darwinistic underpinnings such as Boyd's claim that "our minds reflect evolution's design" (2009, 25), as if the evolution of mind is goal-oriented. As Richardson indicates, the generalizing claims of evolutionary literary studies are often speculative and, until now, lack an empirical basis (2004, 13).

As we have suggested in the previous sections, the cognitive turn has a lot to offer. The possibility of a dialogue across disciplinary boundaries and the promise of an empirical basis are of great value. What is more, there seems to be an increasing awareness of the aforementioned risks, and a lot of cognitive literary studies provide integrative models (e.g., Spolsky 1993; Herman 2002; Palmer 2004; Herman 2009). Rather than turning away from structuralist narratology, cognitive narratologists such as David Herman and Alan Palmer build on the insights from structuralism and combine them with cognitive studies. When Ellen Spolsky applies cognitive theory to literary criticism in *Gaps in Nature*, she consistently integrates ideas from a range of literary theories: New Criticism, deconstruction, poststructuralism, feminism, and so on. More recently, Spolsky (2002) demonstrates that both cognitive theory and poststructuralism acknowledge the fuzziness of categories and the instability of meanings. In that respect, Spolsky suggests, Darwin and Derrida are compatible. In brief, these studies bridge the space between disciplines (cognitive sciences, literary studies) and between subdisciplines (structuralist narratology, poststructuralism, cognitive narratology).

An Outline of the Chapters

The same conviction that narratives thrive on gappiness underlies some of the central questions of this book: How do gaps in our *memory* for texts shape our comprehension of a given narrative? How does the stylistic control of the reader's *attention* create and remedy the gappiness of the narrative? What makes us capable of filling the lacunae in visual representations, the portrayal of bodily experiences, or the figuring of fictional minds? Why do we fill some of the empty spaces and ignore others? Why do we pursue this gappiness and at the same time try to resolve it? New cognitive research on narratives is brought together here to investigate these and related questions, with a focus on the real mind of the reader as well as the fictional minds of characters.

On the one hand, this collection brings together inquiries into fictional minds and the examination of the reader's mind. On the other hand, it stages a dialogue between the three orientations mentioned earlier on—the interpretive (hermeneutic), the empirical, and the cognitive. Issues such as the gappiness of fictional minds and their transparency or opacity are brought up, questioned, and examined in new ways (Mäkelä, Sommer). Several aspects of the reader's mind are explored in the essays, ranging from the moral component of folk psychology (Keunen) to the way the reader mobilizes his or her perceptual and bodily experiences (Auyoung, Caracciolo, Kuzmičová). Several modules of processing, such as memory (Bortolussi and Dixon) and attention (Emmott, Sanford, and Alexander) are specified.

In the opening section of the book, authors who are well known for the way they integrate narratology, stylistics, and empirical study present new research. Two chapters in this section work in tandem, examining two compatible concepts: memory and attention for narratives. In their study of memory for the literary text, Marisa Bortolussi and Peter Dixon first show that the extant research on this topic is far from extensive. Neither literary theory nor psychology has produced in-depth studies of the ways literature uses and tests the memory capacity of readers. Bortolussi and Dixon first map the research on the three levels of memory representation distinguished by cognitive psychology and discourse analysis—namely, the surface structure, the semantic content, and the situation model. Next, they distinguish what is characteristic about memory for *literary* texts. They introduce three blank spots in this domain, which they term the surface-structure puzzle, the distal-coherence puzzle, and the extended-text puzzle. In order to solve the first puzzle, they present the results of their own experiments, which show the relatively poor quality of the memory for the literary surface structure. In their conclusion, Bortolussi and Dixon discuss ways in which this research could and should affect our teaching.

It can be said that our memory is sharpened when the literary text uses stylistic devices to draw our attention. Catherine Emmott, Anthony J. Sanford, and Marc Alexander test the plausibility of this proposition, exploring how narrative texts can capture the reader's attention through stylistic and narratological devices. The authors conducted several experiments within the framework of the STACS (Stylistics, Text Analysis, and Cognitive Science) Project in order to identify the rhetorical strategies that control the reader's attention. In their chapter, they summarize the work in cognitive psychology and discourse analysis on such related issues as attention, change blindness, depth of processing, and text change detection. The results of the recent STACS experiments reveal the wide variety of textual strategies (e.g., mini-paragraphs, italics, cleft sentences, pre-announcements) that can be used to draw the reader's attention. The authors' narrative-continuation experiment shows how the attention of the reader is focused differently if scenario-dependent characters (as opposed to principal characters) behave in unexpected ways. Finally, the authors go into four distinct strategies characteristic of detective fiction. Burying and revealing information, distractors, and false reconstructions typically manipulate the reader's attention in detective fiction, so that the reader is efficiently guided from ignorance through suspicion to recognition and surprise.

In the third chapter of this section, Elaine Auyoung analyzes the paradoxical nature of reading. On the one hand, reading entails the ongoing combination of smaller units (sentences, words, even letters) into a larger, more comprehensive whole. This process is often described as the shift from surface information to in-depth processing. On the other hand, readers are often confronted with partial—sometimes even minimal— cues that nevertheless are sufficient to prompt recognition. Auyoung discusses this intriguing phenomenon by making recourse to both literary and psychological theories. In her reading of Tolstoy's *Anna Karenina*, two levels of inferencing are examined: the level on which characters decipher each other's actions, and the level on which the reader of the novel displays similar behavior. Auyoung shows that blanks need not be filled in—contrary to what Ingarden assumed—and that themes and stylistic devices often exploit this lack of definiteness. She links this tolerance for gaps with our everyday way of coping with incomplete cues.

The second part of the book deals with readers' experiences from a philosophical viewpoint. Marco Caracciolo bridges the study of minds and the study of narratives by integrating narratological and philosophical models. His central claim is that the consciousness the reader "finds" in narrative texts is not represented or projected but enacted in the reader's imagination. He takes issue with Fludernik's conception of experientiality in narrative texts and proposes to lay more weight on the reader's consciousness. He takes his departure from Fludernik's "experientiality" as well as Herman's focus on qualia. In the philosophy of mind, and more specifically in "enactivist" research, Caracciolo finds the appropriate concepts to specify the reader's mental engagement with the literary work. According to enactivist theories, human experience amounts to an active and embodied interaction with the world. When we are reading, experiences are simulated in our imagination. By implementing philosophical thought into literary theory and applying it to Saramago's *Blindness*,

Caracciolo elucidates the implications of enactivism for the understanding of the reading experience.

The contribution by Anežka Kuzmičová ties in with Caracciolo's enacted consciousness as she focuses on the "embodied mind of the reader." She starts from a phenomenological approach, which studies narrative as a verbal presence (inducing the reader to experience things via descriptions) and as a direct presence (inducing the reader to experience, more immersively, the imaginary world described). By elaborating on the second aspect, she tries to fill one of the gaps in narratology, namely, the relative lack of attention paid to the reader's sensorimotor participation in the imaginary storyworld. As a case study, Kuzmičová analyzes the sensorimotor details in Flaubert's *Madame Bovary* and Robbe-Grillet's *Jealousy*. She pays special attention to motor imagery and movement descriptions, linking those narrative elements to the reader's experience not only by combining narratology with phenomenology but also by using findings from experimental psychology, neuroscience, anthropology, and the history of reading. This enables her to draw some general conclusions about the sensorimotor effects of narrative texts and to indicate some of the problems that need to be tackled before this approach can really fill these lacunae in narrative theory.

In linking narrative fiction with real minds and worlds one may downplay the literariness of fiction, and this may lead to "serious literary theoretical losses." Maria Mäkelä wants to redirect the general cognitivist attention to the specific literariness of texts and readerly responses to them. She points to the dangers of reducing "literary experientiality" to everyday experience and offers a way out of this impending reductionism. Literary narratives evoke a sense of cognitive familiarity *and* estrangement. The familiar and the other are intertwined more closely and more intricately in literary texts than in everyday life. They go together with a multilayered narrative construction demanding "a multi-level cognitive performance" that refuses the smooth "naturalization" of regular experientiality and that sets great store by uncertainty, unreliability, foregrounding, self-reflexiveness, and lack of closure. Mäkelä scrutinizes all these aspects in two short stories by Richard Ford, showing that much can be gained if one does not reduce literary *constructions* to familiar forms of communicative (or informational) *transmission*.

The final section of the book puts some of the questions raised in the earlier chapters in a broader cultural and anthropological perspective. Roy Sommer adds an important dimension to the understanding of interactions between the reader and the narrative text. In theorizing intercultural aspects of reading, he draws our attention to the narrative gaps emerging from cultural difference and to our ways of filling them. In Sommer's exploration of these issues, cognitive, hermeneutic, stylistic, and empirical methods are nicely geared to one another. Cognitive concepts such as "narrative empathy," "inferencing," and "categorization" are adopted in an intercultural reading of Ajub Khan-Dhin's play *East Is East* and Ben Okri's novel *The Famished Road*. Sommer's interpretation of empathy in *East Is East* shows how the interactions between the characters stage their subjectivity and provide scaffolds for narrative empathy. In the last part of the essay, Billy Clark's method of sophisticated inferentialism is used to analyze the way a group of students reads the opening of Ben Okri's intercultural novel. The students' responses enable Sommer to distinguish between several cognitive strategies for resolving intercultural gaps.

Bart Keunen places the reading mind in the broader frame of folk psychology, which tends to ascribe intentions to subjects and objects alike. This is done not only to make sense of them but also to evaluate them in terms of moral principles. In addition, this activity always involves the construction and the influence of a specific social and cultural context. Thus, the social-cultural context and moral heuristics are essential aspects of our reading activity, whereas these two dimensions hardly come into the purview of existing cognitive narrative studies. In order to accommodate these aspects of literary interpretation, Keunen develops a functional frame for narrative practices that avoids reductionism as it stresses the literary nature of the discussed functions. He shows that literature deals with "thick moral concepts" (complicated, multilayered concepts such as loyalty and courage) rather than thin concepts such as "right" and "wrong." These thick moral concepts imply complex action models and multilayered ("maximalist") causality attributions. Modernist novels exhibit these narrative complexities, whereas myths and moralistic stories tend to simpler forms of models and attributions. The functional frame developed by Keunen not only fills a gap in the "narrative practice hypothesis" of folk psychology theory but also enables us to distinguish between various forms of narrativity and literariness.

This collection of essays provides the reader with fresh theoretical perspectives as well as insightful literary analyses in the field of cognitive narrative studies. As a whole, it also shows the tensions and the complementary nature of different methodological strands. Interpretive and empirical research can and should join forces to improve our understanding of stories and minds. In addition, the volume reflects upon the nature of literary narratives from the point of view of cognitive theory. Finally, its chapters demonstrate that cognitive narrative studies offer added value for general cognitive theory. In sum, we are convinced this volume helps to fill gaps in theory and in reading, but we also hope it exposes new explanatory lacunae worth filling in the future.

Acknowledgments

We would like to thank the Research Foundation Flanders (FWO) for financially supporting the OLITH conference that provided the basis for this collection. OLITH is an international research group uniting researchers from the universities of Ghent, Leuven, Liège, Vienna, and Groningen. Special thanks to David Herman for putting his shoulders under the project right from the start and for all his support in the process of compiling and editing this book.

Notes

1. Significantly, the *Routledge Encyclopedia of Narrative Theory* has a separate entry on "gapping" (Spolsky 2005, 193–94; see also the entry on "indeterminacy" by Emma Kafalenos).
2. Since several surveys of cognitive literary studies have been published in recent years, we are only briefly touching upon some developments here. See, for example, Crane and Richardson (1999), Richardson (1999), Richardson and Steen (2002), Richardson (2004), Richardson and Steen (2002), Herman (2010), and Zunshine (2010).

References

Abbott, H. Porter. 2006. "Cognitive Literary Studies: The 'Second Generation.'" *Poetics Today* 27 (4): 711–22.

Bortolussi, Marisa, and Peter Dixon. 2003. *Psychonarratology: Foundations for the Empirical Study of Literary Response.* Cambridge: Cambridge University Press.

Boyd, Brian. 2009. *On the Origin of Stories: Evolution, Cognition, and Fiction.* Cambridge: The Belknap Press of Harvard University Press.

Bruner, Jerome. 1991. "The Narrative Construction of Reality." *Critical Inquiry* 18 (1): 1–21.

Carroll, Joseph. 2008. "An Evolutionary Paradigm for Literary Study." *Style* 42 (2/3): 103–35.

Crane, Mary Thomas, and Alan Richardson. 1999. "Literary Study and Cognitive Science: Toward a New Interdisciplinarity." *Mosaic* 32 (2): 123–40.

Culler, Jonathan. 1975. *Structuralist Poetics*. London: Routledge.

Dennett, Daniel. 1991. *Consciousness Explained*. London: Penguin.

Fludernik, Monika. 1996. *Towards a "Natural" Narratology*. London: Routledge.

———. 2010. "Naturalizing the Unnatural: A View from Blending Theory." *Journal of Literary Semantics* 39 (1): 1–27.

Gadamer, Hans-Georg. 1979. *Truth and Method*. London: Sheed and Ward.

Genette, Gérard. 1980. *Narrative Discourse*. Oxford: Blackwell.

Greimas, Algirdas Julien, and Joseph Courtès. 1976. "The Cognitive Dimension of Narrative Discourse." *New Literary History* 7 (3): 433–47.

Herman, David. 2002. *Story Logic: Problems and Possibilities of Narrative*. Lincoln: University of Nebraska Press.

———. 2008. "Narrative and the Mind of Others." *Style* 42 (4): 504–16.

———. 2009. *Basic Elements of Narrative*. Malden: Wiley-Blackwell.

———. 2010. "Narrative Theory after the Second Cognitive Revolution." In *Introduction to Cognitive Cultural Studies*, ed. Lisa Zunshine, 155–75. Baltimore: John Hopkins University Press.

Hogan, Patrick Colm. 2003. *Cognitive Science, Literature, and the Arts: A Guide for Humanists*. London: Routledge.

Ingarden, Roman. 1973. *The Literary Work of Art: An Investigation of the Borderlines of Ontology, Logic, and Theory of Language*. Evanston: Northwestern University Press.

Iser, Wolfgang. 1972. "The Reading Process: A Phenomenological Approach." *New Literary History* 3 (2): 279–99.

———. 1978. *The Implied Reader: Patterns of Communication in Prose Fiction from Bunyan to Beckett*. Baltimore: Johns Hopkins University Press.

Jauss, Hans Robert. 1970. *Literaturgeschichte als Provokation der Literaturwissenschaft*. Frankfurt am Main: Suhrkamp.

Johnson, B. S. 1964 [2004]. *Albert Angelo*. In *B. S. Johnson Omnibus*, 3–180. London: Picador.

———. 1969 [1999]. *The Unfortunates*. London: Picador.

Margolin, Uri. 2003. "Cognitive Science, the Thinking Mind, and Literary Narrative." In *Narrative Theory and the Cognitive Sciences*, ed. David Herman, 271–94. Stanford: CSLI.

Miall, David. 2006. *Literary Reading: Empirical and Theoretical Studies*. New York: Peter Lang.

Palmer, Alan. 2004. *Fictional Minds*. Lincoln: University of Nebraska Press.

———. 2009. "Attributions of Madness in Ian McEwan's *Enduring Love*." *Style* 43 (3): 291–308.

Richardson, Alan. 1999. "Cognitive Science and the Future of Literary Studies." *Philosophy and Literature* 23 (1): 157–73.

———. 2004. "Studies in Literature and Cognition: A Field Map." In *The Work of Fiction: Cognition, Culture, and Complexity*, ed. Alan Richardson and Ellen Spolsky, 1–29. Burlington: Ashgate.

Richardson, Alan, and Francis Steen. 2002. "Literature and the Cognitive Revolution: An Introduction" *Poetics Today* 23 (1): 1–8.

Ryan, Marie-Laure. 2010. "Narratology and Cognitive Science: A Problematic Relation" *Style* 44 (4): 469–95.

Schleiermacher, Friedrich. 1998. *Hermeneutics and Criticism. And Other Writings*. Cambridge: Cambridge University Press.

Spolsky, Ellen. 1993. *Gaps in Nature: Literary Interpretation and the Modular Mind*. New York: State University of New York Press.

———. 2002. "Darwin and Derrida: Cognitive Literary Theory as a Species of Post-Structuralism." *Poetics Today* 23 (1): 43–62.

———. 2005. "Gapping." In *Routledge Encyclopedia of Narrative Theory*, ed. David Herman, Manfred Jahn, and Marie-Laure Ryan, 193–94. London: Routledge.

Sternberg, Meir. 1978. *Expositional Modes and Temporal Ordering in Fiction*. Bloomington: Indiana University Press.

———. 2003. "Universals of Narrative and Their Cognitivist Fortunes (I)." *Poetics Today* 24 (2): 297–395.

Stockwell, Peter. 2002. *Cognitive Poetics: An Introduction*. London: Routledge.

Turner, Mark. 1996. *The Literary Mind: The Origins of Thought and Language*. Oxford: Oxford University Press.

Zunshine, Lisa. 2006. *Why We Read Fiction: Theory of Mind and the Novel*. Columbus: Ohio State University Press.

———. 2010. "Introduction: What Is Cognitive Cultural Studies." In *Introduction to Cognitive Cultural Studies*, ed. Lisa Zunshine, 1–33. Baltimore: John Hopkins University Press.

PART 1 Minding the Reader

1 Minding the Text
Memory for Literary Narrative

MARISA BORTOLUSSI AND PETER DIXON

Introduction

Reading fiction can be an immensely pleasurable act. The popular expression "curl up with a good book" conjures up a somewhat romantic vision of a relaxed reader, temporarily detached from or oblivious to the surrounding environment and completely engrossed in the act of reading. Leisurely and pleasurable as reading may be, the mind that engages with the literary text is far from calm and still. On the contrary, the mind of the reader is a hub of activity involving a wide range of dynamic and complex mental processes, starting from word recognition, sentence parsing, semantic comprehension, building up to generic and other associations, inferences regarding character intentions, interpretations about authorial intentions and overall meanings, and so on.

Arguably the most important, but perhaps least understood, reading-related processes is memory. For example, the inferences we draw about characters or themes depend upon what we can retain in memory of the details strewn throughout the text. The same is true of our appreciation for or evaluation of a text's style. Given the enormous amount of information provided in a novel, or even short story, about characters, setting, time, style, and plot, it would seem highly unrealistic to suppose that even the best of readers could remember everything. But just what do we know about readers' memory for text? Surprisingly, very little. In what follows, we briefly summarize the extant research on this topic. Subsequently, we identify the important issues that remain to be addressed. Finally, we report a preliminary empirical investigation of one aspect of memory for literary style.

What We Know of Memory for Text: Literary Studies

A few studies in stylistics (Emmott 1997; Werth 1999) hypothesize about abstract memory structures, but they do not take the actual workings of the readers' online or post-processing into account. Apart from these, the issue of readers' actual memory for literary texts has received no systematic scholarly attention by literary critics and theoreticians, suggesting that for them, memory is a non-issue. This relative silence seems to suggest that literary studies are predicated on the assumption that readers have good memory for textual details. Nowhere in the lengthy and detailed descriptions of text and reading processes is this capacity ever considered seriously, regardless of theoretical orientation; it is simply taken for granted that readers are naturally equipped with a memory capacity that corresponds to the demands of the text; in other words, memory is thought of as a sponge—the longer and more detailed the text, the more it expands and holds.

This implicit perspective is all the more surprising given that the topic of memory and its representations is currently so popular. Studies on autobiographical memory and memory for historical events, both collective and personal, abound. The focus of these studies is the content and function of what is remembered. For example, how is the Civil War remembered in the American postwar period (Melosh 1988; Sachsman et al. 2007)? How do the Japanese remember the American occupation of Japan (Molasky 2001)? How are the Sandinistas remembered in post-revolutionary Nicaragua (Tatar 2009)? Or, how is the "I" of the past remembered by the "I" of the present in autobiographies, either fictional or nonfictional (Fivush and Hadan 2003)? One conclusion that emerges from this literature is that memory is reconstruction. Common words used to describe the causes or process of reconstruction include "selectivity," "embellishment," and "distortion." Interestingly, the insight that memory involves reconstruction has not carried over to studies of text processing, although there is no reason to assume that memory for text is necessarily better than memory for historical or autobiographical events.

What We Know of Memory for Text: Psychology

Within the field of psychology there is a wealth of research on human memory in general, and considerable research on memory for discourse specifically. As background to the latter, it is worth considering the major findings on the functioning of memory in general.

The main conclusion on which all psychologists concur is that memory is not a video camera that records an event and preserves it in a static form in the brain, where it can be played back at a later time. On the contrary, it is now acknowledged that all experience leaves merely a trace and that the act of recalling the event necessarily entails reconstruction. A classic demonstration of reconstruction in memory was conducted by Carmichael et al. (1932). In this experiment, subjects were told a label, such as "eyeglasses," "dumbbell," "ship's wheel," or "sun," which was followed immediately by a simple drawing corresponding to the word. Different subjects saw the same picture paired with different words. For example, "eyeglasses" and "dumbbells" were both followed by a drawing of two circles connected by a line. During later recall, they were then asked to draw the picture they had seen. Among the drawings that failed to reproduce a close approximation of the original drawing, 74 percent resembled the spoken label. What this demonstrates is that subjects did not have a picture-like memory for the drawing they had seen, but rather that they reconstructed what they saw on the basis of a fragmentary memory trace as well as whatever other information was available. In this case, the associated verbal label provided additional information about the picture and influenced how it was drawn.

One of the most influential figures in memory research is Elizabeth Loftus, whose seminal work on eyewitness memory has earned her many invitations to explain to members of the legal profession in American courts of law how memory functions. In a seminal study conducted more than four decades ago, she and her collaborators tested witnesses' recollection of details regarding a car accident (Loftus et al. 1978). In this experiment, subjects were shown a series of slides depicting a car accident involving a pedestrian and were instructed to pretend to be eyewitnesses. For half of the subjects, one of the pictures was of a red Datsun at a stop sign, and for the other half, there was a corresponding picture of the same Datsun at a yield sign. After seeing all slides, they were asked to answer twenty questions. Among these was a question with a presupposition that either matched or did not match the previous picture, that is, "Did a car pass the red Datsun while it stopped at the stop sign?" or "Did a car pass the red Datsun while it stopped at the yield sign?" Later, subjects were shown pairs of pictures and asked to select the one they had seen. Among these was a pair with the red Datsun, one at a stop sign and one at a yield sign. Accuracy was 71 percent when the supposition in the preceding question matched the picture that was actually viewed but dropped to 41 percent when the supposition was misleading. As with the Carmichael experiment, this result demonstrates that memory is susceptible to suggestion. Far from replaying a fixed recording of an event, memory reconstructs the fragmentary, piecemeal trace of the event, incorporating whatever additional information is available (see also the chapters of Auyoung and Caracciolo in this volume).

Memory for Discourse

There is no reason to assume that recalling text is immune to the limitations of memory that have been summarized so far. Just as past experience leaves but a trace in our minds, so too does a text after being read. In particular, recalling a text requires reconstruction. This conclusion is borne out by the research conducted by cognitive psychologists on memory for ordinary (nonliterary) discourse. According to this research, three levels of representation are constructed during reading. These levels of representation are depicted in figure 1.1. The first is the surface structure. The surface structure contains information about syntactic phrase structure as well as the choice and order of words in the text. Although the surface structure depends on the parsing of sentences into words of different types, it does not reflect the meaning of the sentence. The second is referred to as the "text base," and it represents the semantic content of the text. Sets of co-referential propositions are often used to describe that content. Importantly, the elements of the text base are concepts in semantic memory and not a representation of the words of the text per se. Finally, the third is the "situation model," which represents the state of affairs alluded to by the text; the literary analogue of the situation model would be the storyworld and its denizens. The situation model is sometimes depicted as a spatial or visual representation of the entities described by the text, along with their relationships. Often, knowledge and inferences are used to construct a situation model even if that information is not explicitly mentioned in the text. The memory implications for each of these will be discussed in turn.

Surface Structure

In an often-cited study, Jarvella (1971) found that verbatim memory for spoken discourse declined markedly at sentence and clause boundaries. In this study, subjects listened to pairs of sentences and were periodical-

Text

The woman sat at the window.

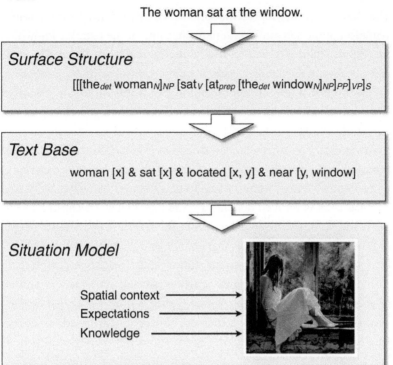

Surface Structure

[[[the$_{det}$ woman$_N$]$_{NP}$ [sat$_V$ [at$_{prep}$ [the$_{det}$ window$_N$]$_{NP}$]$_{PP}$]$_{VP}$]$_S$

Text Base

woman [x] & sat [x] & located [x, y] & near [y, window]

Situation Model

Spatial context ⟶
Expectations ⟶
Knowledge ⟶

Fig. 1.1. Three levels of representation of text. Created by the authors.

ly interrupted and asked to recall a portion of the previous item. When the phrase to be recalled was in the current sentence, recall was substantially better than when the same words were from a preceding sentence, even when the serial position was precisely controlled. Goldman et al. (1980) found a similar result with children's reading: verbatim recall was substantially better when the items to be recalled were from the sentence currently being read rather than the preceding sentence, even when the number of intervening words was the same. Such results are commonly interpreted as suggesting that surface structure is maintained while a sentence is being processed (presumably to support syntactic processing and interpretation) but is lost relatively quickly after the sentence has been understood and the information added to the text base.

Text Base

The second memory representation formed by readers of text is a representation of the semantic content or meaning of the text. We know that this representation is distinct from a representation of the words of the text because, for example, reading time increases with the number of propositions in a text, even if the number of words is the same (Kintsch and Keenan 1973). Researchers have found that although memory for this aspect of the text lasts longer than memory for surface structure, it is far from veridical even after a modest delay. For example, Kintsch et al. (1990) reported measurements of memory that corresponded to accuracies of 64 percent after forty minutes and 60 percent after two days. Moreover, because what is recalled depends on the representation constructed by the reader and not the actual words of the text, it is possible for people to think they recall sentences that are not actually in the text but plausibly could have been. For example, Bower et al. (1979) asked subjects to read descriptions of stereotyped activities (such as eating in a restaurant or going to a dentist) and found that typical actions were often recalled even if they did not appear in the text. Thus, memory based on the text base also involves reconstruction and is subject to the same distortions and biases that have been documented for memory in general.

Situation Model

The third level of memory representation depicts the state of affairs projected by the text. The situation model contains information about the entities (i.e., people, places, and things) described by the text and the relationships among those entities. Often, in constructing a situation model, readers will make inferences concerning the appearance, arrangement, and other properties of those entities even if such information is not explicitly indicated in the text. A variety of research indicates that a situation model is constructed in addition to the text base. For example, readers can make inferences concerning spatial relationships described by the text that would be slow or difficult using simply the information in a propositional text base (e.g., Bransford et al. 1972). Similarly, under some circumstances, readers seem to track the spatial location of the protagonist in the storyworld (Morrow et al. 1987). Research has found that readers have better memory for the situation model than for the surface structure or text base. Indeed, after a day or more, readers are likely to be able to recall only information in the situation model (e.g., Kintsch et al. 1990).

Critically, situation models are affected by the reader's expectations and knowledge. A classic experiment that shed light on the role of reader knowledge in text processing and recall was Bartlett's (1932) study of memory for narrative. After reading a folktale from an unfamiliar cultural background, subjects were asked to recall the story. Bartlett found that recall was generally poor and that subjects tended to drop certain events and add others. His explanation was that elements of the text were distorted to match the reader's cultural expectations and schemas. In other words, when the text does not match the reader's schematic knowledge, the material is either not remembered or normalized to make it more congruent with their expectations. More than four decades later, Kintsch and Greene (1978) replicated this pattern of results using different materials and more modern methodology. Both of the experiments demonstrate the central role of reconstruction in the recall of narrative.

Bransford and Johnson (1972) discovered that readers also rely on and bring world knowledge to bear on the comprehension of text. In a key experiment, they gave their subjects a short text in which a well-known task was described. An excerpt from the passage is as follows: "The procedure is actually quite simple. First you arrange things into different groups depending on their makeup. Of course one pile may be sufficient depending on how much there is to do. . . . It is better to do too few things at once than too many . . . complications from doing too many can easily arise. After the procedure . . . one arranges the materials into different groups again. Then they can be put into their appropriate places" (1972, 722). If we put ourselves in the place of the subjects of this experiment, we can readily understand that even though we may have a good comprehension of all the words in the passage, we are uncertain regarding what the passage is about, and, it turns out, memory for the text is poor. However, when subjects were told before reading that the topic was washing clothes, comprehension and memory were substantially improved. The important conclusion from this study is that readers attempt to construct a representation of the situation described by the text and that such a representation cannot, in general, be built out of just the information indicated by the words on the page. Rather, a situation model necessarily depends on the reader's knowledge of the world.

Memory for Literature

With the exception of the experiments that have used folktales as experimental materials, research on memory for discourse generally has used relatively short and simple prose passages, often created by the experimenters themselves. Thus, the extent to which the findings of these studies apply to memory for extended, real fictional literature is unclear. As a consequence, we know much less about memory for complex literary text and for extended narrative. Here, we describe three areas in which our knowledge is limited. In each case we suggest that the common intuitions or assumptions about the comprehension and memory for literary text is apparently at variance with what the research on discourse processing would seem to predict.

Surface-Structure Puzzle

As discussed earlier, psychologists have concluded that memory for the surface structure of a text is extremely short-lived. However, one of the hallmarks of good literary prose is its style, and what is interesting about literature is not just what is told but how it is told. Thus, it is plausible to suppose that, contrary to the general conclusion about memory for surface structure, some stylistic features are striking and therefore memorable. Thus, there are two possible resolutions to this apparent contradiction: aspects of style may be immune to the usual memory limitation for surface structure, and thus literary style is memorable; or stylistic features are as quickly forgotten as other aspects of the surface structure, such as word choice and order. In order to account for the importance of literary style in the latter case, we might assume that style leaves an impression, a trace, which is retained in some other form, even if the details of the text which led to that impression are lost.

An experiment conducted by Zwaan (1994) provides limited evidence in support of the hypothesis that style is immune to the rapid loss of surface structure. Two groups of subjects read the same short passage, but one was told that the text was a literary passage and the other that it was a news story. When tested for recall of the passage, the subjects who thought they had read a literary text showed better memory for the surface structure than those who thought they had read a news story. This might be construed as support for the special memorability of literary

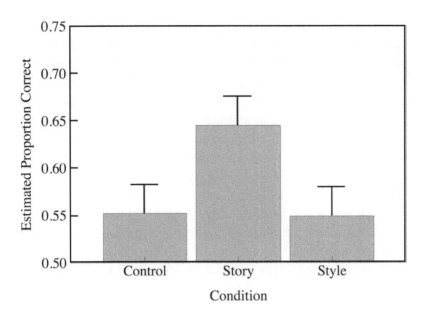

Fig. 1.2. Results of an investigation of memory for style. Created by the authors.

style. However, memory for surface structure was generally poor, even in the "literature" condition. In particular, the ability to distinguish actual sentences from paraphrases was measured using signal detection theory as a d' of .27; this value corresponds to an accuracy of only 55 percent correct. Moreover, the material was a brief experimental passage rather than an extended literary text, so the pattern of results may not generalize to more complex materials.

In an effort to shed some further light on the surface-structure puzzle, we conducted our own preliminary study. For our experiment we chose two stories by James Joyce, "Evelyn" and "After the Race." Words or phrases in the text that we deemed particularly interesting or evocative were presented either in the original form or in a more mundane or pedestrian paraphrase that preserved the meaning as much as possible. For example, "the harbour lay like a darkened mirror" was changed to "the harbour lay smooth and dark." As a control, we also changed what we deemed to be more ordinary word choices for other, equally mundane ones. For example, "Down far in the avenue she could hear a street organ playing" was changed to "Down far in the street she could hear a street organ playing."

Finally, we also changed other words in a way that changed the meaning of the story. For example, "Outside she heard a melancholy air of Italy" was replaced with "Outside she heard a lively air of Italy." Different subjects were given versions of the stories that had different selections of the original or modified sentences. After reading the story, subjects were shown a series of sentences and were asked to rate how confident they were that they had seen each sentence in the story they had just read. Using these responses, we were able to compare the memory for surface-structure style (i.e., the ability to distinguish original, evocative passages from paraphrases), memory for mundane surface structure, and memory for story content (i.e., the ability to distinguish the original from restatements that change the meaning). We refer to these as the style, control, and story conditions, respectively.

According to the results shown in figure 1.2, there was little memory for surface structure, either when the surface structure reflected mundane word choice or a more evocative literary style. In this figure, the confidence ratings were used to derive an estimate of subjects' ability to distinguish the original from a paraphrase in each of the three conditions. Thus, 0.5 represents chance performance and 1.0 would be perfect accuracy. In both the style and the control conditions, memory for the surface structure was near chance. Performance was substantially better (but still far from perfect) in the story condition, in which the changes affected the meaning of the text. This implies that subjects did have some memory for the material, even if they could not distinguish stylistic language use from paraphrases. In sum, the results of the study provide no evidence that evocative style as expressed in the surface structure is immune to the rapid forgetting demonstrated in other research in discourse processing. In this study, style was isolated in particular choices of words or phrases. However, van Peer (1986) used foregrounding more generally in order to identify stylistically evocative material and found similarly poor memory for surface features.

Distal-Coherence Puzzle

The evidence on memory for text does not seem to provide an adequate account of how complex literary text can be understood at a global level. As we saw from the summary of psychological studies of memory for discourse, memory for the situation model is better than memory for surface structure. However, the level of precision of situation model representations may not be high. Morrow and colleagues (e.g., Morrow et al. 1987) found that people can track the location of characters in a storyworld as the text describes their movements from place to place, but subjects in his experiments were required to memorize a map of the spatial layout prior to reading the text. The ability to do so under more natural reading conditions is much more limited (Wilson et al. 1993). Further, many readers may construct spatial representations of limited fidelity (Schneider and Dixon 2009). Graesser et al. (1999) demonstrated that under some circumstances readers can maintain a representation of who said what in a story, but this information was not uniformly accurate, ranging from .63 for third-person narrator to .72 for characters and .83 for a first-person narrator. This relatively weak memory for the situation model representations of the text creates a puzzle if an adequate understanding of an extended literary work requires integrating information from disparate parts of the text.

As articulated by Zunshine (2006, 60), "the ability to keep track of who thought what, and felt what, and when they thought of it, is crucial" for understanding complex narrative, but it is not clear that the reader's representation of the storyworld is typically adequate to support such a deep understanding. While it is certainly possible that most readers most of the time do not construct a detailed representation of the storyworld, this would seem to mean that they cannot arrive at a coherent understanding of the work that would support appropriate inferences about the theme and message that might have been intended. In turn, this would suggest that most readers cannot appreciate complex literary works. In our view, this is an unpalatable and unwarranted conclusion. Instead, it seems more reasonable to suppose that there are mechanisms that allow readers to construct a coherent and informed representation of complex, extended works. Such mechanisms may enable readers to overcome the apparent limitations of memory for text. Some theorists, for example, suppose that readers commonly draw "thematic" inferences in understanding text (e.g., Graesser et al. 1994), and perhaps such inferences may be more memorable than other details of the storyworld. However, the circumstances under which such inferences are drawn and the manner in which they may be used in understanding an extended text are not well understood.

Extended-Text Puzzle

Novels are rarely read in one sitting, for obvious reasons. Perhaps one of the least understood aspects of literary response is the effect of the lapse between reading sessions on memory and literary processing in general. Intuitively, we can assume that when readers resume their reading of a novel after some time lapse, they pick up where they left off, recalling the information they had encountered and perceiving the story as coherent. But how much do they actually recall? If memory for story is imperfect immediately after reading, how much is retained after a delay of hours, days, or weeks? Our analysis of memory for text is that readers will largely reconstruct what had been previously read. Reconstruction can entail various sorts of distortions: the interference of autobiographical episodes, idiosyncratic inferences, evaluations, and knowledge structures that the reader may have stored in the same memory representation. Another possibility is that during the time that elapses between readings, the reader changes, as a result, perhaps, of emotional events that may have occurred and new insights about life, some possibly generated by the reading and others not. In other words, the reader is constantly changing, and these changes may affect the way the story is recalled. Thus, it seems likely that the story the reader remembers differs in small and large ways from the story he or she had read.

The puzzle, then, is that, by and large, we are not aware of any discrepancy between the previously read (and recalled) story and the material that is currently being read. One possibility is that readers have low standards of coherence (cf. van den Broek et al. 1995) and that it is of little consequence if there are apparent contradictions between the current text and the recalled text. Alternatively, readers may be adept at revising misremembered events so as to match the current material. Still another possibility is that novels are generally written with the reader's limitations in mind, so that they provide the necessary reminders and memory cues to allow the story to be readily understood even in the face of fallible memory. In any case, this is a fertile problem for empirical studies of literary reception and response, because temporal gaps are inevitably part of reading an extended work. An issue related to the extended-text puzzle is the role of reader variables, such as literary training and expertise. Do better trained or more frequent readers retain more textual information?

And if so, what kind of information do different kinds of readers recall? Given that readers must engage in reconstruction, does literary training help objective recollection? Or does extensive training actually increase distortion? These remain unanswered questions.

Conclusions

We provide our students with stylistic and narratological tools of textual analysis, presumably because those tools will help them analyze and appreciate the important, meaningful features of the text. We then assess this appreciation through exercises and examination practices which presume that readers are able to recall the text under consideration. However, the research on memory for text and literary discourse that we have discussed has shown that the text readers remember is not a verbatim recording of the text they read but instead is a fallible and distorted rendition based on readers' reconstructions. This might seem to suggest that the pedagogical methods used for teaching literature are out of touch with readers' memorial reality and therefore inappropriate. However, we do not believe that such a conclusion is warranted. Even though expertise in textual analysis will never allow readers to reproduce a photographic copy of the text in memory, we would argue that the ability to recognize features of literary discourse allows readers to process and comprehend the text more deeply, promoting better recall, as well as providing some of the relevant knowledge structures to support accurate reconstruction. In other words, knowledge and expertise produce better memory, hence better representations, better reconstructions, and, ultimately, better appreciation. Perhaps the most critical role of literary training is to improve memory.

From a pedagogical perspective, instructors of literature must respect the fact that memory for text always involves reconstruction. As we have developed throughout this chapter, such reconstruction is a normal and expected part of mental processing and is not necessarily an indication that a literary work is ephemeral or unappreciated. Rather, it implies that readers have processed the text in relation to their own lives and knowledge. Far from being undesirable, this may be precisely what literature should accomplish. After all, the beauty and power of good literature is that it has the ability to engender memorable representations, that it allows readers to absorb and integrate the text, to apply it to their lives, to derive meaning from it, to make it theirs. As a consequence, a reader's representation is not merely a reflection of the objective text but instead a new product that depends as much on the reader as the work itself. Subject and object merge to create a new, meaningful product—the reader's mental model of the literary text.

References

Bartlett, Frederic C. 1932. *Remembering: A Study in Experimental and Social Psychology*. Cambridge: Cambridge University Press.

Bower, Gordon H., John B. Black, and Terrence J. Turner. 1979. "Scripts in Memory for Text." *Cognitive Psychology* 11:177-220.

Bransford, John D., J. Richard Barclay, and Jeffery J. Franks. 1972. "Sentence Memory: A Constructive versus Interpretive Approach." *Cognitive Psychology* 3:193-209.

Bransford, John D., and Marcia K. Johnson. 1972. "Contextual Prerequisites for Understanding: Some Investigations of Comprehension and Recall." *Journal of Verbal Learning and Verbal Behavior* 11:717-26.

Carmichael, L., H. P. Hogan, and A. A. Walter. 1932. "An Experimental Study of the Effect of Language on the Reproduction of Visually Perceived Form." *Journal of Experimental Psychology* 15:73-86.

Emmott, Catherine. 1997. *Narrative Comprehension: A Discourse Perspective*. Oxford: Oxford University Press.

Fivush, Robyn, and Catherine A. Hadan. 2003. *Autobiographical Memory and the Construction of a Narrative Self: Developmental and Cultural Perspectives*. Mahwah NJ: Erlbaum.

Goldman, Susan R., Thomas W. Hogaboam, Laura C. Bell, and Charles A. Perfetti. 1980. "Short Term Retention of Discourse during Reading." *Journal of Educational Psychology* 72:647-55.

Graesser, Arthur, Cheryl Bowers, Brent Olde, and Victoria Pomeroy. 1999. "Who Said What? Source Memory for Narrator and Character Agents in Literary Short Stories." *Journal of Educational Psychology* 91:284-300.

Graesser, Arthur C., Murray Singer, and Tom Trabasso. 1994. "Constructing Inferences during Narrative Text Comprehension." *Psychological Review* 101:371-95.

Jarvella, Robert J. 1971. "Syntactic Processing of Connected Speech." *Journal of Verbal Learning and Verbal Behavior* 10:409-16.

Kintsch, Walter, and Edith Greene. 1978. "The Role of Culture-Specific Schemata in the Comprehension and Recall of Stories." *Discourse Processes* 1:1-13.

Kintsch, Walter, and Janice Keenan. 1973. "Reading Rate and Retention as a Function of the Number of Propositions in the Base Structure of Sentences." *Cognitive Psychology* 5:257–74.

Kintsch, Walter, David Welsch, Franz Schmalhofer, and Susan Zimny. 1990. "Sentence Memory: A Theoretical Analysis." *Journal of Memory and Language* 29:133–59.

Loftus, Elizabeth F., David G. Miller, and Helen J. Burns. 1978. "Semantic Integration of Verbal Information into a Visual Memory." *Human Learning and Memory* 4:19–31.

Melosh, Barbara. 1988. "Historical Memory in Fiction: The Civil Rights Movement in Three Novels." *Radical History Review* 40:64–76.

Molasky, Michael S. 2001. *The American Occupation of Japan and Okinawa: Literature and Memory*. London: Routledge.

Morrow, Daniel G., Steven L. Greenspan, and Gordon H. Bower, 1987. "Accessibility and Situation Models in Narrative Comprehension." *Journal of Memory and Language* 26:165–87.

Sachsman, David B., S. Kittrell Rushing, and Roy Morris Jr., eds. 2007. *Memory and Myth: The Civil War in Fiction and Film from Uncle Tom's Cabin to Cold Mountain*. West Lafayette IN: Purdue University Press.

Schneider, Darryl W., and Peter Dixon. 2009. "Visuo-Spatial Cues for Reinstating Mental Models in Working Memory during Interrupted Reading." *Canadian Journal of Experimental Psychology* 63:161–72.

Tatar, Bradley. 2009. "State Formation and Social Memory in Sandinista Politics." *Latin American Perspectives* 36:158–77.

van den Broek, Paul, Kirstan Risden, and Elizabeth Husebye-Hartmann. 1995. "The Role of Readers' Standards of Coherence in the Generation of Inferences during Reading." In R. F. Lorch and E. J. O'Brien, eds., *Sources of Coherence in Reading*, pp. 353–73. Hillsdale NJ: Erlbaum.

van Peer, Willie. 1986. *Stylistics and Psychology: Investigations of Foregrounding*. London: Croom Helm.

Werth, Paul. 1999. *Text Worlds: Representing Conceptual Space in Discourse*. New York: Longman.

Wilson, Stephanie Gray, Mike Rinck, Timothy P. McNamara, Gordon H. Bower, and Daniel G. Morrow. 1993. "Mental Models and Narrative Comprehension: Some Qualifications." *Journal of Memory and Language* 32:141–54.

Zunshine, Lisa. 2006. *Why We Read Fiction*. Columbus: Ohio State University Press.

Zwaan, Rolf. 1994. "Effect of Genre Expectations on Text Comprehension." *Journal of Experimental Psychology: Learning, Memory and Cognition* 20:920–33.

2   Rhetorical Control of Readers' Attention

Psychological and Stylistic Perspectives on Foreground and Background in Narrative

CATHERINE EMMOTT, ANTHONY J. SANFORD,
AND MARC ALEXANDER

Introduction

Recent developments in psychology provide a new way of understanding the nature of readers' attention. In contrast to earlier theories,[1] psychologists now believe that attention to a text is variable. The term "depth of processing" describes how much detail readers notice, and a substantial amount of research shows that this depends on the types of linguistic features used by a writer (e.g., Ferreira et al. 2002; A. J. Sanford 2002; A. J. Sanford and Sturt 2002; A. J. Sanford and Graesser 2006). In certain respects, the idea of variable attention is not new, because scholars in stylistics and literary studies already draw on the notion of foregrounding (Mukařovský 1964). Nevertheless, the work in psychology is of considerable significance because it has led to a wide program of empirical research that provides objective evidence for the effect of particular stylistic items on readers. Also, psychologists have focused on low levels of attention as well as high levels, prompting us to look here at rhetorical control of background detail in narratives as well as foregrounded information.

In this article, we will first consider the psychological idea of depth of processing, tracing the idea from its origins in vision research and looking at classic work on "semantic illusions," experiments which show that depth of processing can sometimes be "shallow." We will then look at a new methodology developed to investigate depth of processing, the "text change detection experiment" (A. J. Sanford 2002; Sturt et al. 2004). We will show examples of some of the features examined that are of significance for narratologists and summarize a broad range of relevant research results from the last ten years. We will also consider some classic work in psychology, A. J. Sanford and Garrod's (1981) Scenario Mapping and Focus Model, which examines variable attention for major and minor characters in a story. We will show how in a recent experiment we have related this to the degree of interest readers show in different characters in stories, using another psychological method, the "continuation method" (Emmott et al. 2008). Then we will draw on these empirical findings to examine the relevance of this work to the stylistic analysis of foreground and background in mystery and detective writing, where authors may manipulate the attention of readers. Although the focus of our case study is specifically on mystery and detective writing, our observations have general applicability to the handling of attention in many different types of stories.

The empirical methodologies described in this article are from cognitive psychology and are scientific in nature. The materials used are relatively short and are carefully controlled, to allow researchers to focus on specific linguistic features, without distracting variables. This is radically different from the type of methodology used by many researchers in the area termed the "empirical study of literature" (e.g., van Peer 1986), where literary texts may be studied in full, but where it can be difficult to see the effect of any particular linguistic feature (see our discussion of such work in A. J. Sanford and Emmott 2012). We combine our scientific analysis with stylistic observations of narrative texts. This is partly to suggest, in the first place, the range of linguistic features that need to be studied empirically. Our stylistic observations have taken empirical work in cognitive psychology beyond the types of linguistic features normally examined by psychologists. Also, after the experiments are completed, we utilize the empirical findings to make assumptions about how mystery and detective writers might be drawing on particular stylistic features to manipulate readers by controlling foreground and background detail. This stylistic analysis of specific texts is more impressionistic, since it takes us beyond the types of materials used in the psychological experiments. The stylistic analysis is, nevertheless, rooted as far as possible in current psychological knowledge.

Attention and Depth of Processing

Psychologists have shown that readers may be relatively inattentive to what they read, not fully absorbing all the detail available to them in a text. Psychologists use the term "depth of processing" for this phenomenon, arguing that processing is often "shallow" (e.g., Ferreira et al. 2002; A. J. Sanford 2002; A. J. Sanford and Sturt 2002; A. J. Sanford and Graesser 2006). The idea that not all information is absorbed may be somewhat disturbing to literary researchers, since it suggests that some aspects of literary texts may be redundant to particular readers on particular occasions. However, Zwaan (1993) provides empirical evidence to indicate that readers may have a "cognitive control system" that makes them more attentive when they believe a text to be literary rather than nonliterary (even if it is actually the same text). Also, literary texts make use of foregrounding devices, with which writers may selectively capture and direct readers' attention. Conversely, some writers, such as detective fiction writers, may manipulatively take advantage of readers' inattentiveness. Information may be "buried" in the background so that a reader fails fully to notice details or take in all the implications of the information.

The study of attention has been pioneered in vision research in psychology (e.g., Rensink et al. 1997; Simons and Levin 1997; Simons 2000). In change detection tests, experimental participants are presented with two similar pictures in succession and asked to "spot the difference." Surprisingly, quite substantial changes can commonly be missed if the participant is not attending to the feature that is changed. This phenomenon is termed "change blindness" by these researchers. The test here is not of memory but for whether the perceiver has attended to the feature in the first place, since the amount of detail that can be focused on is limited.

Features that are most likely to be in the focus of visual attention include:

- Items in the physical foreground rather than items in the physical background
- Items in the center of an image rather than items in the periphery
- Items that are salient because of their size, color, unusualness, and so forth
- Items that do not have any competition from other salient details acting as distractors

Attention for linguistic features in texts also varies according to the focus of the reader. We will look at this in relation to some classic experiments first, then move on to more recent work. These classic experiments are termed "semantic illusions" or, after a famous material used in the experiment, "the Moses illusion" (Erickson and Mattson 1981; Bredart and Modolo 1988). The following type of question is asked:

(1) How many animals of each kind did Moses take on the ark?

Many participants in the experiment attempt to answer the question by speculating about the number, failing to notice that the question contains erroneous information (Noah, not Moses, took the animals on the ark), referred to as a "semantic anomaly."

Anomalies become more noticeable if there is a lack of situational fit (Barton and Sanford 1993). Hence, based on previous empirical evidence, we would expect the following anomaly to be more noticeable, since a nonbiblical individual is mentioned.

(2) How many animals of each kind did Obama take on the ark?

It is interesting that writers' rhetorical strategies can also control the degree of attention. Where the Moses information is embedded in a question, as in (1), it is treated as if it were "given information" and hence less likely to be challenged than a straightforward statement (e.g., "Moses took two of each kind of animal on the ark. True or false?"). Subordination also makes information less noticeable (Baker and Wagner 1987; Cooreman and Sanford 1996). Conversely, where information is placed in a cleft construction ("It was Moses"), as in the example below, it becomes more noticeable (Bredart and Modolo 1988).

(3) It was Moses who took two of each kind of animal on the ark.
True or false?

Overall, these experiments provide convincing evidence of how particular linguistic features can raise and lower attention.

Text Change Detection Experiments

The semantic illusion experiments provide classic illustrations of shallow processing, but it is difficult to use this testing method for a broad range of stylistic phenomena, since the materials are difficult to design and the participants (usually psychology undergraduates) can become wise to these kinds of tests. Hence, a new form of test, the text change detection experiment, has been developed in the last few years, by A. J. Sanford and colleagues (e.g., A. J. Sanford 2002; Sturt et al. 2004). Here the aim is not to fool participants, as in the Moses illusion, but to see to what extent participants notice possible changes when asked to do so. This type of test is parallel to the change detection tests in vision research discussed above.

The methodology for text change detection experiments is to give participants a short piece of text to read twice in close succession. Sometimes on the second showing there is a small change, sometimes not. Participants have to say whether they notice a change or not. The hypothesis is that participants may be more or less observant of changes depending on the type of linguistic/narrative structure in which they occur.

As part of the STACS (Stylistics, Text Analysis and Cognitive Science) Project, based at the University of Glasgow, we have used this method to examine a wide range of features that we have identified from narrative analysis. The example below (excluding the underlining) is typical of the type of material that we used to test sentence fragments, that is, linguistic phrases that are not full sentences but which are punctuated like sentences (Emmott et al. 2006). Here, "A brown envelope." is a sentence fragment. Sometimes on second showing it changes to "A white envelope." Participants are significantly more attentive when the change occurs in information appearing in a fragment, as in (4a), than when the key phrase appears embedded in a full sentence, as in (4b):

(4a) *Sentence fragment*
Peter had tried hard not to go over details of the interview in his mind. He tried not to rephrase his answers, tormenting himself with things he should have said. He tried hard especially not to listen out for the postman every morning, but at last there it was. A brown [white] envelope.

(4b) *No sentence fragment*
Peter had tried hard not to go over details of the interview in his mind. He tried not to rephrase his answers, tormenting himself with things he should have said. He tried hard especially not to listen out for the postman every morning, but at last there it was, a brown [white] envelope.

This type of test has now been conducted for a wide range of linguistic features, as shown below. Many results are as we predicted. In some cases, it is the first time that evidence for the foregrounding effect of some of these linguistic features has been produced, and in other cases (e.g., for cleft structures) the results provide further support for the earlier semantic illusion tests.

The empirical tests show that participants are more likely to notice changes when information is presented as follows:

- Using specific typographical features, for example, italics (A. J. S. Sanford et al. 2006)
- Using specific grammatical features, for example, clefting (Sturt et al. 2004; A. J. S. Sanford et al. 2009)
- Using certain types of lexical feature, for example, long words or low-frequency words (A. J. Sanford et al. 2006; Emmott et al. 2007)
- Using certain types of sentence formatting, for example, short sentences and sentence fragments (Emmott et al. 2006)
- Placing information in direct speech/thought, rather than indirect speech/thought (Bohan et al. 2008)
- Using second-person "You" narratives and first-person "I" narratives, rather than third-person narratives (Fukuda and Sanford 2008)

Conversely, complex structures such as subordinate clauses make participants less likely to notice detail (e.g., A. J. S. Sanford et al. 2005; Price 2008), as in the semantic illusion experiments.

Although most results were as we expected, some were surprising. In addition to testing sentence fragments, we placed the fragments in mini-paragraphs (very short paragraphs, such as those containing just a sentence fragment). The combination had an effect on readers' attention, as we predicted, but no more so than fragments alone. Possibly, this is what psychologists term a "ceiling effect," where there is a limit to the extent of the effect that can be found, at least with the simple materials used. We also tested narrative pre-announcements such as "Then something happened" (Emmott et al. 2007). We expected that a small change in wording that came in the sentence afterward would become more noticeable where the pre-announcement was used, in contrast with a control material where a pre-announcement was replaced with a neutral sentence such as "It had a thatched roof." So participants were asked to detect changes such as "A sports car drove [changed to "moved"] out in front of me." In fact, the result was that pre-announcements had no significant effect on participants' attention to such subsequent small changes in wording. We also tested indicators of surprise (e.g., where there is mention of the character being surprised) and, counter-intuitively, participants noticed significantly fewer wording changes (A. J. Sanford et al. 2006). The results for pre-announcements and surprise statements are difficult to explain, but one possibility is that the text change detection method is simply not suitable for testing this type of content statement. The other experiments conducted were for testing linguistic features (typography, grammar, vocabulary, etc.) rather than content statements, with the linguistic features generally giving the results predicted. The pre-announcements and surprise statements might raise the interest in the key events of the story, perhaps making participants less likely to bother about small wording issues. If so, it might be possible to use other testing methods for these items, such as the narrative continuation experiments discussed below. As yet, we do not have a full explanation for how content statements affect readers, but the results for a wide range of linguistic features provide a substantial body of robust evidence for many anticipated foregrounding effects.

Character Status and Narrative Continuations

Psychologists have also pointed to the difference in prominence given to different types of characters in a narrative text. A. J. Sanford and Garrod (1981; see also Anderson et al. 1983) distinguish between "scenario-dependent characters" and "principal characters." We have previously used these distinctions in the stylistic analysis of texts (Emmott 2003; Emmott and Alexander 2010; Emmott et al. 2010). Scenario-dependent characters are script-based, such as the classic example of the waiter in the restaurant (Schank and Abelson 1977). A. J. Sanford and Garrod's (1981) empirical work shows that they generally attract less attention than do "principal characters," who are better developed. It is, however, possible to raise attention levels by adding extra information to the description of scenario-dependent characters, such as specifying that the waiter is handsome (171–72). This is a point we will return to later in our discussion of mystery and detective fiction. A. J. Sanford and Garrod also show that attention can be raised if a character does something unexpected or is placed in an unexpected situation. Unexpected happenings make a series of events more "tellable" (Labov and Waletzky 1967). We demonstrated this in an experiment (Emmott et al. 2008) using the method of collecting continuations from participants who wrote in response to materials we provided. In each of the sample materials (5a) and (5b) below, the first section, labeled "Empirical material," was given to the participants (among other materials) by the experimenters, and the second section was the continuation written by a specific participant. In (5a) the assistant is a scenario-dependent character performing actions expected of such a character. In (5b) the assistant is still scenario-dependent but is behaving oddly. The continuations below were written by different participants.

(5a) *Empirical material*: Heather needed to buy stylish chairs for her new apartment. At the furniture store, she saw the assistant moving a sofa into the corner.
Participant's continuation: That looks quite nice she thought. Maybe I could get the sofa and one matching chair, instead of two chairs.

(5b) *Empirical material*: Heather needed to buy stylish chairs for her new apartment. At the furniture store, she saw the assistant lying under a table.
Participant's continuation: She approached wearily [warily?],[2] wondering what on earth the woman was doing under the table. As she got closer, Heather saw fear in the womans [*sic*] eyes, fear which Heather had never witnessed before.

Participants appear to focus their attention quite differently, depending on whether the scenario-dependent character is behaving oddly or not. For materials of type (5a), the vast majority of responses either ignore the scenario-dependent character completely (as in the continuation above) or continue with the character in a purely scenario-dependent role, performing anticipated actions. For materials of type (5b), the vast majority of responses include features such as extreme negative emotions, further information about the secondary character, and an attempt by the principal character to find out more. For type (5a), the scenario-dependent character often seems to blend into the background in the continuation, whereas for (5b) the scenario-dependent character often becomes a focal point of interest in the continuation.

This type of continuation experiment is a technique used by psychologists, but it seems particularly well suited to humanities work, since it provides some indication of the contents of readers' thoughts rather than judging mental processes by measuring readers' reaction times (which is what many psychological experiments do). Here, we may infer that the continuations provide information about what aspect of the scenario the participants are focusing their attention on as they read the provided material and hence what occupies their attention in the continuation that they subsequently write.

Rhetorical Control of Attention in Mystery and Detective Writing

Mystery and detective writing relies on the manipulation of readers' attention by writers. We will provide text examples below which suggest that writers are relying on four key processes to direct readers' attention for writers' ends: (1) burying information during the setting up of the puzzle, (2) the use of distractors to direct readers' attention toward a false trail, (3) the use of foregrounding devices at the point where key plot information is revealed as part of the solution, and (4) the use of false reconstructions at the denouement that treat information as if it were shared knowledge when it has in fact never been presented.

Burying Information

We have seen that the empirical work in psychology provides evidence that readers give less attention to details in subordinate clauses. In the following example from *Sparkling Cyanide*, Agatha Christie buries the initial reference to the character who will eventually be revealed as the murderer, so as not to draw attention to him as a possible suspect (see Emmott and Alexander 2010 for a detailed discussion of the full text). She presents the first reference to this character, introduced as "a son," in multiple embedding, as described below. The lack of a name (when other characters are named) suggests in itself that the character is of little importance.

> (6) In the meantime, the first thing to settle was [Iris's] place of residence. Mr. George Barton had shown himself anxious for her to continue living with him and had suggested that her father's sister, Mrs. Drake, who was in impoverished circumstances owing to the financial claims of <u>a son (the black sheep of the Marle family)</u>,

should make her home with them and chaperon Iris in society. Did Iris approve of this plan? (Christie 1955, 12)

In terms of grammatical embedding, the reference to the son occurs buried in a sentence structure that includes three subordinate structures (the that-clause after "suggested," the relative clause beginning with "who," and the clause beginning with "owing to"). In addition, there is discourse embedding to detract attention from this referent. The son is mentioned as part of an explanation of the circumstances of another character, Mrs. Drake, who is herself mentioned in relation to the main character, Iris. Iris is the central character not only in this paragraph but also in the chapter as a whole, which has her name as the title.

Christie also performs this type of burying act in presenting descriptive information. In the example below, from one of her short stories, it is the information that the characters are "not unalike" that will eventually become central to explaining events, since the two women are in fact related, hence providing a motive for the crime.

(7) The contrast between the two women struck me at once, the more so as in actual features and colouring they were not unalike—but oh, the difference! (Christie 1999, 34)

At this stage Christie needs to give low prominence to this information so that the reader does not guess the solution, while still mentioning it so that it can be later drawn on. Hence, this information is placed in a subordinate explanatory clause ("as . . .") and the opposite information, the contrast, is placed in the main part of the sentence (technically the matrix clause) at the start and also appended at the end. The information is also played down by using a double negative form "not unalike" rather than the positive form "alike." In addition, the contrast is given special status by showing its effect on the character (what "struck" the character and the exclamation at the end), which may serve to divert the attention of readers.

Distractors

Distractors attract readers' attention toward the wrong items. In detective fiction, the distractors are the red herrings. In example (7), above, we saw that Agatha Christie uses foregrounding to highlight a distractor (the contrast between the women) while the puzzle is being set up.

In *Sparkling Cyanide*, Christie quite explicitly provides the wrong information to misdirect readers. In example (8) she uses the direct speech of one of her characters to do this. The character speculates about possible suspects, including the observation "one of those people round the table, one of our friends," which is presumably foregrounded by the repetition. Nevertheless, the character's assumption is faulty because there are two murderers, not one, and because the main murderer was not one of the group of friends sat at the table.

(8) "*If* Rosemary was killed, <u>one of those people round the table, one of our friends</u>, must have done it." (Christie 1955, 83–84; Christie's italics)

In (9), below, there is an explicit evaluative statement that is wrong, even though it is made by one of the detectives. Although the girl gives evidence in good faith, she does, in fact, fail to notice the crime being committed.

(9) "That girl's <u>the right kind of witness</u>. Sees things and remembers them accurately. If there had been anything to see, she'd have seen it." (Christie 1955, 116–17)

In (10), below, the focalizing detective is again wrong, since the information given is, in fact, a red herring.

(10) The girl looked placid and unaware of any significance in what she had said. <u>But it *was* significant</u>. (Christie 1955, 132; Christie's italics)

Examples (9) and (10) potentially misdirect the reader, not just by giving erroneous information but also by sometimes putting these ideas into the speech or thoughts of characters whom we assume to be reliable (Booth 1991, 169 ff.; see also Zunshine 2006, 76 ff.), such as the detectives. We have previously termed this "reliability vouching" (Emmott and Alexander 2010), since a supposedly reliable individual vouches for the reliability of a suspect or witness. In reality, detectives can make mistakes, particularly when they are still at the stage of trying to solve a crime.

Foregrounding Devices for Revealing Information

Our empirical research has shown that devices such as sentence fragments combined with mini-paragraphs raise attention levels in readers (albeit no more so than fragments alone), as do italics. In the example below, these features, together with repetition, foreground a vital plot-central piece of information. So the language guides us toward the conclusion that the information is significant, simultaneously mimicking the character's realization process.

> (11) And then [. . .] [she] saw the name she hadn't even realised she'd been looking for, the unusual name that rose right up from the paper and traveled through her bones with a charge.
> *Muire Boland.*
> Flight attendant.
> Kathryn spoke the name aloud.
> *Muire Boland.*
> She was pretty sure it was a woman's name. (Shreve 1999, 182; Shreve's italics)

Attention can also be focused on specific characters by providing extra information. We have seen that empirical evidence shows that scenario-dependent characters can be brought into greater prominence by adding extra description (A. J. Sanford and Garrod 1981). Roald Dahl does this for the maid in example (12) below.

> (12) Then this happened: the maid, the tiny, erect figure of the maid in her white-and-black uniform, was standing beside Richard Pratt, holding something out in her hand [. . .] The maid was an elderly woman—nearer seventy than sixty—a faithful family retainer of many years' standing. (Dahl 1979, 20)

For most of the story the maid has been purely scenario-dependent and of no apparent significance. However, at this late point, she is about to make a surprising plot-central announcement. The extra information is likely not only to raise the readers' attention for her but may also, perhaps, by specifying that she is "a faithful family retainer," increase the sense of her reliability. Note that this example is fronted by a pre-announcement. This looks intuitively like a foregrounding device to us, but, as we discussed earlier, our empirical work does not yet provide any evidence for its being effective.

False Reconstructions

Alexander (2006, 2008, 2009) has pointed to the importance of the rhetorical construction of a detective's explanatory speech as the solution to a mystery is revealed. Rhetoric can make a solution seem plausible, even where a writer is misleading us. The denouement of a detective story often presents readers with a large amount of information at once, and it is possible to slip in details that sound as if they are being recapped but which have not in fact ever been mentioned to the reader. In the case of these false reconstructions, a sleight of hand is involved and the writer relies on the reader not noticing that this information has not been presented before or not recalling that it has been initially presented in a quite different light. In one Agatha Christie story, "The Tuesday Night Club," a maid is presented throughout the story in a scenario-dependent role, so a reader might be less likely to focus on her than on the central characters (see Alexander 2008 for a detailed discussion of this text). At the end of the story, Miss Marple's explanation suggests that the solution was obvious all along due to the fact that the girl was "a pretty young girl."

> (13) "I can't think how on earth you managed to hit upon the truth. I should never have thought of <u>the little maid in the kitchen</u> being connected with the case."
>
> "No, dear," said Miss Marple, "but you don't know as much of life as I do. A man of that Jones's type—coarse and jovial. As soon as I heard there was <u>a pretty young girl in the house</u> I felt sure that he would not have left her alone." (Christie 1997, 16)

In fact, we have never been told that the girl was pretty. The information is presented as a presupposition within a subordinate clause, which may make it less likely to be challenged. The above text also subtly changes the context by switching the location from "the kitchen," where the maid could function in a purely professional way, to "the house," which is more ambiguous.

The preceding example relies not only on downgrading information by utilizing the low prominence of scenario-dependent characters but may also play on the length of the story. We know that memory for texts is limited (Bartlett 1932; see also Bortolussi and Dixon in this volume), so a writer might hope that a reader does not remember the original omission of specific details.

In the novel *Sad Cypress*, there is a similar sleight of hand over a much longer stretch of text. Agatha Christie presents a character, Nurse Hopkins, who, by the end of the story, has been identified as a likely poisoner.

At the denouement it is revealed that she has probably murdered by poisoning both her victim and herself from the same pot of tea, then has secretly given herself a powerful antidote to purge the poison from her own system, hence making it seem impossible that the tea could be the cause. To make the reader believe in this solution over all other possible solutions, Christie needs to make this explanation credible. At the trial, the description of Nurse Hopkins provides support for this solution, since her appearance at the time of the murder is supposedly that of someone who has just been sick.

> (14) "Remember, too, that the accused has stated on oath that Nurse Hopkins, when she joined her in the pantry, <u>was looking ill</u>, and <u>her face was of a greenish colour</u>—comprehensible enough if she had just been <u>violently sick</u>." (Christie 1963, 179)

Nevertheless, if we look at the initial presentation of these events, much earlier in the book, the description is quite different and the context suggests a very different explanation. Example (15) occurs on the day of the murder, and, at this point in the novel, Christie does not want us to suspect Nurse Hopkins.

> (15) Nurse Hopkins was in the pantry. She was <u>wiping her face with a handkerchief</u>. She looked up sharply as Elinor entered. She said:
> "<u>My word, it's hot in here!</u>"
> Elinor answered mechanically:
> "<u>Yes, the pantry faces south.</u>"
> Nurse Hopkins relieved her of the tray.
> "You let me wash up, Miss Carlisle [Elinor]. You're not looking quite the thing." (Christie 1963, 80)

Here, Nurse Hopkins wipes her face and is presumably sweating, but there is a ready explanation due to the heat of the day and the south-facing pantry. Indeed, the character who is said to be "not looking quite the thing" is not Nurse Hopkins but the woman she is talking to, Miss Carlisle. There is no mention of Nurse Hopkins herself being ill or of her face being a greenish color. This episode is also placed strategically before the victim's body is discovered, so there is no reason for suspicion of anyone at this stage.

Rather than simply changing from one description to another, the text provides an intermediate description that has properties of both. The trial lawyer provides the instruction in court in example (14) to "Remember" what "the accused has stated on oath," so the reference is to the previous courtroom report in example (16) below rather than to the original incident which the reader has actually witnessed in example (15).

> (16) "What was her manner at the time?"
>   "I think <u>she was feeling the heat</u>. She was <u>perspiring</u> and <u>her face was a queer colour</u>." (Christie 1963, 171)

In this example the heat is mentioned, a fact that is true of the original incident in example (15) but dropped in the final explanation in example (14). Also, the detail about the "queer colour" of the Nurse's face is added in example (16), although not the fact that it is greenish, which appears in the final version, example (14). These inconsistencies in presentation seem to be highly manipulative, in order to control the reader's inferences at different stages in the story.

Conclusion

Psychological research has made considerable progress in explaining how readers' attention can be controlled by linguistic devices. We now have empirical evidence for which linguistic devices can be used for burying information and which can be used for foregrounding purposes. This empirical evidence can be used by literary researchers and stylisticians to take their analyses beyond speculation about the effect of these items on readers. Overall, the above discussion of mystery and detective fiction shows that writers seem to be intuitively making use of some of the devices that empirical work has shown to raise and lower attention. The linguistic features direct the reader in order to bury information during the setup of the puzzle and foreground it as the solution is revealed. It is because of their cognitive limitations that readers can be manipulated in this way, but ultimately the puzzle and the surprise ending can provide readers of these genres with considerable pleasure.[3]

Acknowledgments

The authors are grateful to the Arts and Humanities Research Council for funding for Emmott and A. J. Sanford's STACS Project (Stylistics, Text Analysis and Cognitive Science: Interdisciplinary Perspectives on the Nature of Reading) and for Alexander's M.Phil. thesis.

Notes

1. For example, Just and Carpenter (1980) argued that readers interpret words in sentences to the greatest degree possible.
2. The participant clearly wrote "wearily," but this appears to be a spelling error for "warily," which would make more sense in the context.
3. See Brewer and Lichtenstein (1982) for empirical work on the affective impact of these aspects of narratives.

References

Alexander, Marc. 2006. *Cognitive-Linguistic Manipulation and Persuasion in Agatha Christie*. M.Phil. thesis, University of Glasgow.

———. 2008. "The Lobster and the Maid: Scenario-Dependence and Reader Manipulation in Agatha Christie." Online Proceedings of the *Annual Conference of the Poetics and Linguistics Association* (PALA). http://www.pala.ac.uk/resources/proceedings/2008/alexander2008.pdf.

———. 2009. "Rhetorical Structure and Reader Manipulation in Agatha Christie's *Murder on the Orient Express*." *Miscelánea: A Journal of English and American Studies* 39:13–27.

Anderson, Ann, Simon C. Garrod, and Anthony J. Sanford. 1983. "The Accessibility of Pronominal Antecedents as a Function of Episode Shifts." *Quarterly Journal of Experimental Psychology* 35:427–40.

Baker, Linda, and Jody L. Wagner. 1987. "Evaluating Information for Truthfulness: The Effects of Logical Subordination." *Memory and Cognition* 15:247–55.

Bartlett, Frederick C. 1932. *Remembering: A Study in Experimental and Social Psychology*. Cambridge: Cambridge University Press.

Barton, Stephen B., and Anthony J. Sanford. 1993. "A Case-Study of Anomaly Detection: Shallow Semantic Processing and Cohesion Establishment." *Memory and Cognition* 21:477–87.

Bohan, Jason, Anthony J. Sanford, Sally Cochrane, and Alison J. Sanford. 2008. "Direct and Indirect Speech Modulates Depth of Processing." Poster presented at the 14th Annual Conference on Architectures and Mechanisms of Language Processing, September 2008, University of Cambridge, Cambridge.

Booth, Wayne. 1991 [1961]. *The Rhetoric of Fiction*. Harmondsworth: Penguin.

Bredart, Serge, and Karin Modolo. 1988. "Moses Strikes Again: Focalization Effects on a Semantic Illusion." *Acta Psychologica* 67:135–44.

Brewer, William F., and Edward H. Lichtenstein. 1982. "Stories are to Entertain: A Structural-Affect Theory of Stories." *Journal of Pragmatics* (6): 473–86.

Christie, Agatha. 1955 [1945]. *Sparkling Cyanide*. London: Pan.

———. 1963 [1933]. *Sad Cypress*. Glasgow: Fontana.

———. 1997 [1927]. "The Tuesday Night Club." In *Miss Marple: The Complete Short Stories*, 3–16. London: HarperCollins.

———. 1999 [1923]. "The King of Clubs." In *Hercule Poirot: The Complete Short Stories*, 28–40. London: HarperCollins.

Cooreman, A., and Anthony J. Sanford. 1996. "Focus and syntactic subordination in discourse" [online]. Human Communication Research Centre, Universities of Edinburgh and Glasgow. http://citeseer.ist.psu.edu/331528.html.

Dahl, Roald. 1979. "Taste." In *Tales of the Unexpected*. Harmondsworth: Penguin.

Emmott, Catherine. 2003. "Reading for Pleasure: A Cognitive Poetic Analysis of 'Twists in the Tale' and other Plot Reversals in Narrative Texts." In *Cognitive Poetics in Practice*, ed. Joanna Gavins and Gerard Steen, 145–60. London: Routledge.

Emmott, Catherine, and Marc Alexander. 2010. "Detective Fiction, Plot Construction and Reader Manipulation: Rhetorical Control and Cognitive Misdirection in Agatha Christie's *Sparkling Cyanide*." In *Language and Style. In Honour of Mick Short*, ed. Dan McIntyre and Beatrix Busse, 328–46. London: Palgrave MacMillan.

Emmott, Catherine, Anthony J. Sanford, and Marc Alexander. 2010. "Scenarios, Characters' Roles and Plot Status: Readers' Assumptions and Writers' Manipulations of Assumptions in Narrative Texts." In *Characters in Fictional Worlds: Understanding Imaginary Beings in Literature, Film and Other Media*, ed. Jens Eder, Fotis Jannidis, and Ralf Schneider, 377–99. Berlin: Walter de Gruyter.

Emmott, Catherine, Anthony J. Sanford, and Eugene J. Dawydiak. 2007. "Stylistics Meets Cognitive Science: Style in Fiction from an Interdisciplinary Perspective." *Style* 41 (2): 204–26.

Emmott, Catherine, Anthony J. Sanford, and Lorna I. Morrow. 2006. "Capturing the Attention of Readers? Stylistic and Psychological Perspectives on the Use and Effect of Text Fragmentation in Narratives." *Journal of Literary Semantics* 35 (1): 1–30.

Emmott, Catherine, Anthony J. Sanford, and Fiona Smith. 2008. "Then Somebody Appeared: Scenarios, Character Under-specification and Narrative Interest." Paper presented at the IGEL Conference, July 2008, University of Memphis, Memphis TN.

Erickson, Thomas D., and Mark E. Mattson. 1981. "From Words to Meaning: A Semantic Illusion." *Journal of Verbal Learning and Verbal Behavior* 20:540–51.

Ferreira, Fernanda, Vittoria Ferraro, and Karl G. D. Bailey. 2002. "Good-Enough Representations in Language Comprehension." *Current Directions in Psychological Science* 11:11–15.

Fukuda, Yuki, and Anthony J. Sanford. 2008. "The Effect of Personalization on Shallow Processing." Paper presented at the Society for Text and Discourse Conference, July 2008, University of Memphis, Memphis TN.

Just, Marcel A., and Patricia A. Carpenter. 1980. "A Theory of Reading: From Eye Fixations to Comprehension." *Psychological Review* 87:329–54.

Labov, William, and Joshua Waletzky. 1967. "Narrative Analysis: Oral Versions of Personal Experience." In *Essays on the Verbal and Visual Arts: Proceedings of the 1966 Annual Spring Meeting of the American Ethnological Society*, ed. June Helm, 12–44. Seattle: American Ethnological Society.

Mukařovský, Jan. 1964. "Standard Language and Poetic Language." In *A Prague School Reader on Esthetics, Literary Structure, and Style*, trans. Paul L. Garvin, 17–30. Washington DC: Georgetown University Press.

Price, Jessica M. 2008. "The Use of Focus Cues in Healthy Ageing." PhD thesis, University of Glasgow.

Rensink, Ronald A., Kevin O'Regan, and James T. Clark. 1997. "To See or Not to See: The Need for Attention to Perceive Changes in Scenes." *Psychological Science* 8 (5): 368–73.

Sanford, Alison J. S., Jessica Price, and Anthony J. Sanford. 2009. "Enhancement and Suppression Effects Resulting from Information Structuring in Sentences." *Memory and Cognition* 37:880–88.

Sanford, Alison J. S., Anthony J. Sanford, Ruth Filik, and Jo Molle. 2005. "Depth of Lexical-Semantic Processing and Sentential Load." *Journal of Memory and Language* 53:378–96.

Sanford, Alison J. S., Anthony J. Sanford, Jo Molle, and Catherine Emmott. 2006. "Shallow Processing and Attention Capture in Written and Spoken Discourse." *Discourse Processes* 42 (2): 109–30.

Sanford, Anthony J. 2002. "Context, Attention and Depth of Processing during Interpretation." *Mind and Language* 17:188–206.

Sanford, Anthony J., Eugene J. Dawydiak, and Catherine Emmott. 2006. "External and Internal Sources of Attention Control: Findings from Change Detection." Poster presented at the Society for Text and Discourse Conference, July 2006, University of Minnesota.

Sanford, Anthony J., and Catherine Emmott. 2012. *Mind, Brain and Narrative*. Cambridge: Cambridge University Press.

Sanford, Anthony J., and Simon C. Garrod. 1981. *Understanding Written Language: Explorations in Comprehension beyond the Sentence*. Chichester: Wiley.

Sanford, Anthony J., and Arthur Graesser. 2006. "Shallow Processing and Underspecification." *Discourse Processes* 42:99–108.

Sanford, Anthony J., and Patrick Sturt. 2002. "Depth of Processing in Language Comprehension: Not Noticing the Evidence." *Trends in Cognitive Sciences* 6:382–86.

Schank, R. C., and Abelson, R. P. 1977. *Scripts, Plans, Goals and Understanding: An Enquiry into Human Knowledge Structures.* Hillsdale NJ: Lawrence Erlbaum.

Shreve, Anita. 1999. *The Pilot's Wife.* London: Abacus.

Simons, Daniel J. 2000. "Attentional Capture and Inattentional Blindness." *Trends in Cognitive Sciences* 4:147–55.

Simons, Daniel J., and Daniel T. Levin. 1997. "Change Blindness." *Trends in Cognitive Sciences* 1:261–67.

Sturt, Patrick, Anthony J. Sanford, Andrew Stewart, and Eugene J. Dawydiak. 2004. "Linguistic Focus and Good-Enough Representations: An Application of the Change-Detection Paradigm." *Psychonomic Review and Bulletin* 11:882–88.

van Peer, Willie. 1986. *Stylistics and Psychology: Investigations of Foregrounding.* London: Croom Helm.

Zunshine, Lisa. 2006. *Why We Read Fiction: Theory of Mind and the Novel.* Columbus: Ohio State University Press.

Zwaan, Rolf A. 1993. *Aspects of Literary Comprehension.* Amsterdam: John Benjamins.

3 Partial Cues and Narrative Understanding in *Anna Karenina*

ELAINE AUYOUNG

Even in a novel as intricate and expansive as *Anna Karenina*, at any given moment in the text the reader encounters only a limited selection of information about a referred-to object, person, or scene. This observation recalls Roman Ingarden's remark that each "object, person, event, etc., portrayed in the literary work of art contains a great number of places of indeterminacy, especially the descriptions of what happens to people and things" (Ingarden 1973, 50). Ingarden defines "a place of indeterminacy" as any site in a given verbal representation that underdetermines the attributes of the object or situation being described. He goes on to claim that while readers may at times have no way to determine the nature of many of these unspecified attributes, they more often "involuntarily fill many of them out with determinacies which are not justified by the text" and thus "concretize" the referred-to objects and scenarios so that "they seem to be fully determined" (52–53).

Wolfgang Iser, however, takes issue with Ingarden's suggestion that a reader's "concretization" of referred-to fictional objects results in a degree of determinacy that is akin to an actual perceptual experience (Iser 1978, 176). According to Iser, mental imagery "accompanies" the act of reading, but the mental representation of fictional objects is distinguished by its "optical poverty," which becomes evident when "one sees the film version of a novel one has read" (136–39). Paradoxically, Iser reflects, it is precisely the "openness" of the reader's process of "ideation" that makes him or her resent the comparative determinacy and "optical enrichment" provided by the film version. Iser moreover concludes that all that can be said about Ingarden's "places of indeterminacy" is that they "may *stimulate*, but not . . . *demand* completion from our existing store of knowledge."

Iser himself is often credited with describing the act of reading as a process of "filling in the gaps left by the text." He explicitly defines what he means by "blanks" in the narrative, however, as something different "in kind and function" from Ingarden's "places of indeterminacy" (Iser 1978, 284–85). For him, they are the "unseen joints" or points of structural discontinuity between separate segments of the text, such as those between two consecutive chapters or when a narrative suddenly cuts to a different plotline or point of view. By leaving the "connections between perspectives in the text" open and unspecified, these points of discontinuity prompt the reader to coordinate these perspectives (169). The vocabulary of discourse comprehension provides a striking way to distinguish between Iser's and Ingarden's notions of "filling in." Iser's account of having to determine the unstated relation between a newly presented segment of narrative and a segment that has preceded it is known as a "bridging" or "backward" inference, while Ingarden's account of the reader's act of inferring properties of a fictional object that the text leaves unspecified is known as an "elaborative" or "forward" inference.

In this chapter I seek to provide a more in-depth consideration of the specific epistemic and aesthetic situation of encountering a partial set of representational cues, with the ultimate goal of explicating the effect of minimal cues in *Anna Karenina*. In particular, I will focus on the way in which a few verbal cues—a word, a sentence, or a phrase—can be sufficient to suggest something more at the same time that this *something* remains withheld. My approach to this phenomenon is not to regard it as a situation unique to the act of reading but rather to consider it in context of our readiness to contend with partial representational cues in everyday, nonliterary experience.

Mental Models

Before turning to the analogy between encountering limited verbal representation and encountering other forms of limited cues, however, I first want to clarify some aspects of the reader's process of comprehending narrative discourse. While the work of Ingarden and Iser has been instrumental in directing critical attention to the act of reading within literary studies, cognitive psychology "takes the role of the reader for granted" and offers an alternative, somewhat more standardized vocabulary for describing the reading process (Emmott 1997, viii). Psychologists in the field of discourse comprehension tend to presume that readers rely on the text as a set of cues for constructing mental representations of referred-to content (see Graesser et al. 1997). The act of forming these mental representations, however, is distinct from the act of extensively elaborating or "filling in" what a text leaves unspecified.

In order to get a better understanding of this process, we can begin by acknowledging that a novel reader's encounter with a fixed, finite body of literary representation presents a particular situation of trying to know about something based on a narrative report. To rely on a secondhand report, however, is not unique to literary experience but rather an extremely common epistemic situation. Because many aspects of the world extend beyond our reach in time and space, we are not in a position to observe them firsthand and instead depend on the testimony of others in order to know anything about them (Johnson-Laird 1983, 246). Readers form the idea of referred-to fictional persons, places, and events in the same way that they form an idea of referred-to actual persons, places, and events. John Searle has similarly argued that novelists do not employ a "separate class of illocutionary acts" that is distinct from the standard illocutionary acts of statements, assertions, descriptions, and explanations employed in nonfictional discourse (1975, 324).

If readers comprehend fictional narratives in the same way that they comprehend nonfictional ones, this raises the question of what actually gets comprehended. In the field of discourse processing, psychologists tend to adopt van Dijk and Kintsch's distinctions among three levels of representing a text in memory: the surface code, the text base, and the referential situation model (Kintsch and van Dijk 1983; cf. Bortolussi and Dixon in this volume).[1] The surface code consists of the exact wording and syntax of a given text, but it fades extremely rapidly in the reader's memory. The text base consists of the explicit propositions expressed in the text, but it does not preserve the exact wording and syntax of the surface code.[2] Although the text base is retained in memory for a little longer than the surface code, both of these levels of representation are grouped under the category of "shallow comprehension."

Finally, there is the situation model, which, unlike the surface code and the text base, is considered a level of "deep comprehension." The situation model constitutes not a mental representation of the text itself but a representation of the state of affairs referred to by the text, and corresponds to Philip Johnson-Laird's notion of a mental model.[3] This chapter uses the terms *situation model* and *mental model* interchangeably to refer to the reader's mental representation of the concepts and objects to which a text refers (Tapiero 2007, 7). Regardless of whether the referred-to object is real or imaginary, readers routinely form mental representations about referred-to persons, places, and events. The construction of a mental representation accounts for the fact that readers tend to forget the exact formal properties of the verbal representation, but remember the gist of its content (Rickheit and Sichelschmidt 1999, 13).

Situation models are so valuable for our understanding of literary experience because they make it possible to think of comprehending a text in terms of mentally representing the situation it describes. Elaine Scarry provides an especially helpful way to conceive of the precise nature of this process in *Dreaming by the Book*, which offers an extensive demonstration of how the words of a novel or poem serve as a set of authorial "instructions" that prompt readers to construct mental images of fictional objects, persons, and scenes (2001, 31–39). To use the vocabulary of discourse psychologists, readers rely on the surface code as a set of cues or instructions for building the situation model (Graesser et al. 1997, 169). This process involves the activation of associated background knowledge, which includes general knowledge structures, particular episodic memories, and even mental representations derived from previous encounters with other fictional and nonfictional texts (Graesser et al. 1994, 374). In one experiment, readers were presented with a brief description of *an electrician taking apart a light fixture*. Readers slowed down when they were then presented with a sentence referring to the electrician as "she," presumably because this conflicted with situation models in which the electrician was inferred to be male (Cain et al. 1996). Incidentally, the fact that verbal instructions activate familiar associations is also implied by the editorial practice of providing annotations to a literary text. Annotations to *Anna Karenina* might indicate to modern readers what a nineteenth-century Russian reader or even Tolstoy himself might have understood by a particular word or reference. In effect, annotations provide the background knowledge that could have been available to earlier readers as they constructed their mental models. Actively elaborating the background knowledge against which textual cues are understood in fact characterizes the work of much historically based literary scholarship. For example, in *The Ideas in Things: Fugitive Meaning in the Victorian Novel*, Elaine Freedgood (2006) constructs the unacknowledged histories tethered to the "mahogany furniture" referred to in *Jane Eyre* and to the "calico curtains" referred to in *Mary Barton*.

Here it is important to note that, while Iser's references to the "optical poverty" of the reader's mental representations imply that these representations are visual in nature, cognitive psychologists have recognized that mental imagery is "not just visual" but can exploit multiple modalities (Christen et al. 2002, 269). There is in fact no current consensus on the precise formal properties of mental models. They are simply considered to be structurally analogous to the state of affairs referred to by the text (Rickheit and Sichelschmidt 1999, 14–15; Tapiero 2007, 34). I would contend that it is the construction of situation models that accounts for the reader's commonly reported phenomenal experience of creatively "filling in" something that the text itself does not provide, since the reader comes away from the text with mental representations that resemble something *other* than words on a page. It is important to note, however, that these mental representations for the most part remain fragmentary and underdetermined.

In the same way that the exact composition of situation models remains a matter of debate, so does the extent to which readers make inferences during the reading process. One thing that is clear, however, is that in response to the fragmentary instructions that a text provides, readers generally do *not* pause to "concretize" or elaborate unspecified properties of the storyworld (Graesser et al. 1994, 383–85; Tapiero 2007, 119–20). By supplementing literary-critical reflections on the experience of reading with psychological accounts of discourse comprehension, we can now recognize that, in response to a limited set of verbal cues, readers construct "spotty" or fragmentary mental representations of the referred-to scene or object. In the remaining sections of this chapter I will focus on the particular epistemic and aesthetic situation of contending with partially determined mental representations. As Bertrand Russell observes, all human knowledge is "uncertain, inexact, and partial" (1948, 507). We are constantly faced with the cognitive challenge of having to form beliefs about objects, persons, and situations that are represented to us only in limited ways. In this light, we can gain insight into the literary response to partially determined mental models by taking into account our ordinary, nonliterary responses to partially determined perceptual experiences.

Getting Away with Partial Perception

A number of critics have already recognized the analogy between the cognition of verbal cues and the cognition of perceptual cues (Iser 1978, 107; Scarry 2001, 31; Johnson-Laird 1983, 397). For example, Wolfgang Iser describes a text as a stimulus that activates "the individual reader's faculties of perceiving and processing," while Elaine Scarry proposes that the encounter with "imaginary-objects-specified-by-instruction" is analogous to the encounter with perceptual objects. Finally, Lisa Zunshine argues that fiction "capitalizes on and stimulates Theory of Mind mechanisms that had evolved to deal with real people" (2004, 131). Mind reading, or the ability to recognize and to make inferences about other people's mental states based on their observable outward behavior, itself presents a major instance of our everyday habit of contending with a limited number of available cues. Zunshine proposes that fictional narratives "cheat" our mind-reading mechanisms into operating as if they are in the presence of the cues they were developed to process. Even when a text "has left us with the absolute minimum of necessary cues," our readiness to recognize other minds at work allows novelists to get away with a surprising degree of "undertelling" (Zunshine 2006, 23–24). Tolstoy himself is distinguished for relying on the "language of gesture," in which one "glance, one wrinkle, one quiver of a muscle in the face, may express the unutterable" (Merejkowski 1902, 178).

As significant as mind reading is to literary experience, recognizing more than meets the eye is not a skill that is specific to the encounter with other minds. It is a major strategy for contending with the limits that attend many occasions of perception. The minds of real and imaginary persons are just one of the many kinds of obscured objects that we attempt to identify based on a partial set of cues. There are two practical reasons why the ability to recognize something more than meets the eye is an important skill in everyday experience. The first reason is that, at any given moment, it is typical rather than exceptional to have limited perceptual and epistemic access to objects in our environment. Ellen Spolsky says that contending with gaps in our understanding of the world "is the daily business of all human minds" (1993, 2). With respect to visual object recognition alone, a constant challenge for perceivers is the fact that objects are so frequently occluded by other opaque objects. The perceptual system must contend with objects that are missing some of their parts or presented as simple line drawings instead of richly colored images. Despite these limitations, we almost always manage to identify quickly and accurately what partial images represent. As Jerome Bruner observes, a "speck on the horizon surmounted by a plume of smoke is identified as a ship, so too a towering transatlantic liner at its dock, so too a few schematic lines in a drawing" (1973, 219; also see Palmer 1999, 297).

One influential theory of visual object recognition proposes that the visual system parses complex objects into a configuration of simpler, separate shapes. In one experiment, cognitive psychologists tested the identification of objects represented only by a partial set of features (Biederman 1987; Biederman 1995). They began with complete line drawings of objects such as a penguin or an airplane, each composed of nine total components. When subjects were given a subset of just two or three components, the partial image was sufficient to prompt rapid identification of most objects. When three or four components were provided, object recognition became almost 90 percent accurate. Here it is important to note that recognition takes place in the *absence* of the object's additional components. When presented with a partial image, perceivers do not "fill in" missing features *until* the image can be identified. Rather, they must first recognize what the partial image represents in order to know which additional features might be appropriate to supply.

The successful identification of images composed of a partial set of components reveals our ordinary capacity to do without full representation. In some cases, a single, relatively small component may be "highly diagnostic" of the whole object and therefore sufficient to render the object identifiable (Biederman 1987, 129). This particular phenomenon presents a cognitive context for what literary critics have described as a "telling" detail. The fact that objects can sometimes be identified based on a single representative component points up the role of synecdoche in everyday experience, along with the notion that literary devices reflect and reinforce ordinary cognitive mechanisms (see, e.g., Johnson and Lakoff 1980). Our ability to identify objects based on a subset of components is valuable not only because we so often have only partial access to objects in our environment, but also because being able to make educated guesses about what limited cues imply offers an advantageous degree of epistemic efficiency. In other words, the necessity of making do with incomplete representation has translated into a cognitive capacity to *get away* with only partial perception, which is the second major benefit of being able to recognize more than meets the eye.

The mind's ordinary aliveness to what limited perceptual cues imply provides a suggestive model for understanding the reader's encounter with a limited set of representational cues. In fact, Catherine Emmott describes the practice of relying on general knowledge to make basic, "highly probable" inferences during the act of reading in terms of occasions in visual perception when "although we may not see all of an object which is hidden by another object, we still assume it to be there in its entirety" (1997, 26, 28). Now that we have considered the reader's construction of fragmentary mental representations as well as our more general readiness to respond to a limited set of perceptual cues, we can turn to a series of examples from *Anna Karenina* that foreground the encounter with a limited set of representational cues. Before examining the reader's encounter with Tolstoy's fragmentary representation of fictional objects, however, I will first present two occasions when Tolstoy's fictional persons demonstrate the capacity to recognize what minimal cues imply.

Minimal Cues for Tolstoy's Characters

On her son's birthday, Anna Karenina pays a secret visit to him; as she approaches his room, the narrator says, "Anna heard the sounds of a child yawning; she recognized her son by the sound of the yawn and pictured him vividly before her" (Tolstoy 1992, 629). Here the single, acoustically minimal cue of a yawn is more than sufficient for a mother to identify her son. This act of recognition in turn instantly prompts Anna to retrieve a vivid mental representation of Serezha based on her memory of his appearance. The associative manner in which Anna's mind moves from the sound of yawning to a mental image of Serezha happens to dramatize the metonymic path of attention that is a signature structure of prose fiction. To recall Roman Jakobson's classic account, fictional narratives follow a "path of contiguous relationships," moving from one component of the fictional world to another (Halle and Jakobson 1956, 91–92). The movement of Anna's attention from the sound of a yawn to the mental image of Serezha models, on a very small scale, one reason why prose fiction seems to follow a "path of contiguous relationships." The associative structure of narrative representation reflects the mind's ordinary readiness to move from one metonymic cue to another, contiguously related aspect of a larger implied pattern.

This metonymic structure underlies a very different kind of moment in the novel, which is the exchange of an inside joke between Levin and Oblonsky. Levin asks,

"Are you selling the forest to Ryabinin?"
"Yes. Do you know him?"
"Of course I know him. I have had dealings with him, positively and finally."
Oblonsky laughed. "Positively and finally" were the dealer's favourite words. (1992, 191)

Just as Serezha's yawn is a sound that prompts Anna to recognize her not-yet-visible son, here the words "positively and finally" are sufficient to prompt Oblonsky's recognition of Ryabinin's implied person. This ventriloquized fragment of Ryabinin's voice is a cue that not only promises the existence of a speaking person with physical extension but also implies a pattern of speech that extends across time. There are two more small stories enfolded in Levin's oblique reference to Ryabinin: the independent implied narratives of how Levin and Oblonsky each come to recognize Ryabinin's pattern of saying "positively and finally" over the course of their separate encounters with him.

Minimal Cues for Tolstoy's Readers

At the same time that fictional persons in *Anna Karenina* demonstrate a capacity to recognize what minimal cues imply, Tolstoy's representational strategies in turn engage the *reader's* readiness to recognize something more based on a few components. As we turn to consider this dynamic more closely, it at first seems counterintuitive to speak of representational economy in a novel regarded as such a masterpiece of high realism. What I want to acknowledge and bring to light, however, is that as comprehensive as *Anna Karenina* seems to be in its scope and detail, Tolstoy achieves this degree of comprehensiveness in part by taking advantage of how effective a partial selection of cues can be.

For example, when Kitty Scherbatsky and her mother ascend the stairs to a ballroom, Tolstoy provides a brief verbal sketch of one of the men they pass along the way: "An officer, buttoning his glove, stood aside at the doorway to make room for them, and smoothing his moustache looked with evident pleasure at the rosy Kitty" (1992, 90). For the purposes of the narrative, this officer is one of a handful of superfluous men Tolstoy invents to dramatize the impression Kitty makes at the ball, and the officer fulfills his duty within a single sentence. If we consider the mental model that can be constructed from the selection of cues presented in this sentence, however, we can see Tolstoy's economy of representation at work.

The officer's person is represented by two gestures: buttoning his glove and smoothing his mustache. When constructing a mental representation of this situation, one might conceive of fingertips first on the button of a glove and then on the sides of a mustache. What exactly lies in between these two separate points in space remains indeterminate. We already know that readers do not ordinarily pause to imagine, for example, a waistcoat or a collar or shiny shoes. Instead, the two components alone are sufficient to prompt recognition of the fact of the officer's bodily extension, not so much in the form of a fully fleshed-out mental image but in the form of a readily formed belief. The officer performs two additional gestures: he stands aside "to make room" for the two women, and he looks at Kitty "with evident pleasure." While these two details give us scant information with respect to *his* face and body, they register his response to the physical presence of *other* persons and thus alert us to the operation of his conscious mind. The officer's significance to the novel begins and ends with a single sentence, but the components Tolstoy provides are sufficient to prompt recognition of something more—the promise of the officer's implied physical and mental extension.

We find a similar example when Anna is trying to read on the train and the narrator reports that Anna's maid, Annushka, "was already dozing, the red bag on her lap, clutched by her broad hands, in gloves, of which one was torn" (1992, 118). Here the components for constructing a mental representation of the described situation include a dozing woman, a red bag clutched in her lap, and gloved hands. Although the components provided by this sentence focus on the space where the hands, the bag, and the lap come together, they are sufficient to elicit a sense of something more. One can recognize the objects as part of a larger implied scene that has not only spatial extension but temporal extension as well (the fact that one of the gloves is torn implies the existence of some unspecified cause from an earlier moment in time). Of course, the precise nature of what lies beyond the object of narrative attention remains unknown, but the mind readily grants the existence of a larger, implied state of affairs that has the property of *being knowable*. Put another way, while we remain unable to elaborate the referred-to scene in any extensive way, we nevertheless immediately recognize the scene as one that *can* be elaborated.

Recognizing the promise of a larger, implied scene corresponds to John Dewey's observation that, regardless of whether our "scope of vision be vast or minute, we experience it as a part of a larger and inclusive whole" (1934, 201). However broadly we might expand our perceptual field, "it is still felt as not the whole; the margins shade into that indefinite expanse beyond which imagination calls the universe." In other words, we are accustomed to believing that more lies beyond the scope of our knowledge and perception. Dewey observes that this belief—this "sense of something that lies beyond"—is "implicit in ordinary experiences" but that the effect is "rendered intense within the frame of a painting or poem."

The mind's readiness to recognize that something more "lies beyond" helps to account for the effectiveness of telling details like a torn glove or even a maid dozing on a train. In fact, our cognitive responsiveness to what limited cues imply offers an alternative way to understand what Roland Barthes famously identifies as the "reality effect." Within the framework of structuralism, realistic details merely reinforce the pretense of reporting about an actual, referred-to world. Barthes dismisses what he calls the "referential illusion" (1989, 148). For him, words like *button* or *red bag* are arbitrary and irrelevant, nothing but devices that declare, "I am realism" (Wood 2008, 82). The trouble with trying to pull the rug out from under the word *rug*, however, is the readiness with which the concept of a rug comes to mind.

If we take the text to be a set of instructions for readers to construct a mental representation of the referred-to state of affairs (cf. Caracciolo's view on the text, in this volume), we have another way to describe the reality effect. A reference to the button on an officer's glove is not merely an arbitrary, artificial reminder that the narrative aspires to resemble a realistic account. Instead, the idea of buttoning a glove really *can* be sufficient to prompt readers to infer that such a gesture takes place within a larger pattern of reality. In this light, Barthes's critique about the arbitrariness of realistic details almost seems like a reaction against the remarkable ease with which minimal cues *can* seem to imply the existence of something more. Whereas his account of the reality effect dismisses the "referential illusion," a cognitive approach to reading comprehension restores the centrality of reference to the effectiveness of metonymic cues.

Thus far I have drawn upon cognitive accounts of reading comprehension and object recognition to describe the mechanism by which a limited selection of cues in *Anna Karenina* can be sufficient to prompt the reader's recognition of something more. I turn now to an account of how this same mechanism leads to the reader's recognition of representational limits, which in turn gives rise to the "tension" between explicit cues and "hidden" objects that Wolfgang Iser (1978, 177–78) mentions in *The Act of Reading*. Consider this account of Vronsky's first sight of Anna Karenina when they meet at the train station:

> When he looked round she too turned her head. Her bright grey eyes which seemed dark because of their black lashes rested for a moment on his face as if recognizing him, and then turned to the passing crowd evidently in search of some one. In that short look Vronsky had time to notice the subdued animation that enlivened her face and seemed to flutter between her bright eyes and scarcely perceptible smile which curved her rosy lips. It was as if an excess of vitality so filled her whole being that it betrayed itself against her will, now in her smile, now in the light of her eyes. (1992, 72)

This passage provides some components for constructing a mental representation of Vronsky's brief glimpse of Anna's face: bright eyes with dark lashes, a slight smile with rosy lips. Both here and later in the novel, the narrator notes the vitality that appears "now in her smile, now in her eyes" (Tolstoy 1992, 84; see Smith 1995, 133–34). The rapid, repeated shifts in attention from Anna's smile to her eyes enact the animation that Tolstoy attempts to describe. Still, this gives us only two features from which to construct a mental representation of a face that Vronsky actually perceives.

While the passage is more than sufficient to register the vitality expressed in Anna's face, it nonetheless seems insufficient as a representation of the perceptual experience it describes. As Iser observes, the act of reading obviously does not involve a "face-to-face situation" (1978, 166); nor does its content "pass before the reader's eyes like a film" (282). A mental representation constructed from verbal instructions is simply not the same kind of thing as an actual sensory percept. Mental objects cannot be expected to have the solidity and determinacy of the material world for the tautological reason that they are mental objects. Their indeterminacy only becomes a concern when our conceptions of fictional objects are measured against the comparative completeness of real objects (Ronen 1988, 498). Why, then, do readers persist in making this comparison? Why point out that a narrator's testimonial account of Anna's eyes and smile provides only a partial idea of the face that Vronsky is said to perceive firsthand? Why point out, as William Gass does, that characters "in fiction are mostly empty canvas," that some have "passed through their stories without noses, or heads to hold them," and "others have lacked bodies altogether" (1958, 45)? Why reflect, as Catherine Gallagher does, that no matter how many times we reread the finite sentences that comprise *Anna Karenina*, "there will never be more to learn about, say, the childhoods of the heroine and her brother" (2006, 357)?

These observations are symptoms of the paradoxical way in which mimetic representation alternately seems astonishingly effective and irreducibly incomplete. To elaborate this phenomenon, consider the fact that an artist starts from nothing—a blank page, a bare canvas, a block of marble—and begins to construct the semblance of *something*. While this *something* may consist of no more than a few cues, we have seen that it can still be tremendously effective at prompting the recognition of more: a person, a mind, an extended life, an enterable world. Elaine Scarry reminds us that, although mental objects "may sometimes be inferior to naturally occurring objects, they will always be superior to naturally occurring objectlessness" (1985, 166). What is remarkable about the reader's encounter with fictional representation is that a yawn or a torn glove or the words "positively and finally" can be sufficient to suggest an implied person in place of nothing. At the same time, it is precisely the effectiveness of these cues that brings us up against the limits of representation. While a few cues can be sufficient to give us the idea of an object, they remain insufficient to present us with the object itself.

Cognitive psychology offers an elegant way to account for the mechanism by which representational cues can seem both sufficient and insufficient. Psychologists commonly refer to a perceptual process based on given cues as a *stimulus-driven* or *bottom-up* process. In a bottom-up approach, one or two components constitute a stimulus from which a viewer comes to recognize the representation of a woman's face. Alternatively, the viewer might regard the given cues with the concepts of a particular woman's face in mind. This is referred to as a *concept-driven* or *top-down* process. The viewer who is guided by a knowledge-based concept of what the cues are *supposed* to represent might search for additional features closely associated with a human face and, in doing so, come to find that a number of components remain unspecified. Tolstoy's repeated references to Anna's eyes and smile are sufficient to suggest the kind of perceptual experience Vronsky has when he catches a glimpse of her face, but they are insufficient as a replication of that experience. It is when we take a concept-driven approach to the passage, guided by the knowledge of what perceiving a face is really like, that we are struck by the underdetermined nature of Tolstoy's verbal instructions.[4] Ironically, the limits of literary representation become apparent as a result of the reader's readiness to recognize what the text seems to suggest.

Tolstoy himself dramatizes a reader's frustration with representational limits in *Anna Karenina* when Anna attempts to read on the train:

> Anna read and understood, but it was unpleasant to read, that is to say, to follow the reflection of other people's lives. She was too eager to live herself. When she read how the heroine of the novel nursed a sick man, she wanted to move about the sick-room with noiseless footsteps; when she read of a member of Parliament making a speech, she wished to make that speech; when she read how Lady Mary rode to hounds, teased her sister-in-law, and astonished everybody by her boldness—she wanted to do it herself. But there was nothing to be done, so she forced herself to read, while her little hand toyed with the smooth paper-knife. (1992, 118)

Anna's dissatisfaction with having "to follow the reflection of other people's lives" points up the sustained orientation toward mental representation that characterizes the condition of reading. While Anna forces herself to construct mental representations of nursing a sick man or making a parliamentary speech according to the instructions provided by the text, she is impatient for firsthand knowledge of what her book describes. Roman Ingarden speaks of "a kind of unsatisfied hunger which appears when and only when we have already been excited by a quality but have not yet succeeded in beholding it in direct intuition" (1973, 191). For Anna

Karenina, literary experience promises the possibility of knowing, feeling, and encountering something more, but this is a promise that the text itself cannot fulfill.

Minimal Cues, Themes, and Style

I want to conclude this consideration of reading *Anna Karenina* by situating the mind's aliveness to limited cues within a broader critical context. In literary history, the situation of recognizing something based on a few pieces of evidence is already a major thematic and stylistic concern. Thematically, one of the most enduring topics of literature has been the problem of delayed, mistaken, or otherwise failed recognition. From Oedipus to Othello and from Emma Woodhouse to Briony Tallis, literature imagines overconfident protagonists who form beliefs about a larger state of affairs without bothering to consider more than a few cues. Not surprisingly, this tendency has been regarded not in terms of cognitive economy but in terms of blindness and epistemic error. Again and again, fictional narratives unfold to reveal that a few cues are *insufficient* for knowing what something is really like.

On a stylistic register, we find the same concern expressed in Viktor Shklovsky's classic account of defamiliarization, which he champions as a way to resist "algebrization," or the "over-automatization" of perception (1965, 12). When the perception of familiar objects becomes habitual, it no longer becomes necessary to "see them in their entirety." The fact that objects can be identified by a single metonymic feature translates into abbreviated forms of representation and attention. Phrases can be left "unfinished and words half expressed." While the cognitive capacity to know without needing to look permits an "economy of mental effort," Shklovsky construes this as a breakdown of perception itself: "The object is in front of us and we know about it, but we do not see it."

In his call for artistic techniques that prolong the process of perception, Shklovsky singles out Tolstoy's consistent use of defamiliarization. It is especially ironic, then, that one also finds in *Anna Karenina* recurrent, idealized occasions of abbreviated or "algebraic" perception, in which one fictional person manages to understand another even when provided with only a minimum of cues. For Tolstoy, the payoff of perceptual economy is the possibility for almost wordless understanding and mutual recognition without needing to spell everything out. When one person readily comprehends another, phrases really *can* be left "unfinished and words half expressed"; there really is no need to hear them "in their entirety."

For example, when Anna must leave her son after only a brief visit, the narrator reports that she "did not know what to say and could not speak. But Serezha understood all she wanted to tell him. He understood that she was unhappy and that she loved him. He had even understood what the nurse had said in a whisper. He had caught the words 'always before nine o'clock,' and he understood that they referred to his father and that his mother and father must not meet" (1992, 633). From the fragment of a whispered sentence and from the expression on his mother's face, Serezha recognizes more than can be directly represented to him.

Perhaps the most remarkable and the most literal instance of recognizing what abbreviated symbols imply, however, is Levin's unforgettable second proposal to Kitty. The given components of this scene consist of Kitty, Levin, a card table covered in green cloth, and a piece of chalk. Levin writes a series of initial letters on the table: "W, y, a: I, c, n, b; d, y, m, t, o, n?" (1992, 469). After some reflection, Kitty says, "I have understood." The letters stand for, "When you answered: it can not be; did you mean then or never?" She proceeds to write, "T, I, c, n, a, o," which Levin understands as, "Then I could not answer otherwise." At the end of the proposal, Kitty writes another series of initial letters, and the narrator says of Levin: "He could not find the words she meant at all; but in her beautiful eyes, radiant with joy, he saw all that he wanted to know."

This impossible feat of almost wordless communion at first seems to suggest a fantasy of virtually telepathic understanding between lovers. What underlies this miraculous performance of reading between the letters is not a moment of telepathic communication, however, but the implication that both Kitty and Levin have been dwelling on and wishing for the same possibility (see Morson 2007, 77). It is their shared mental representation of hope and regret that allows them to decode the quasi-algebraic string of initials. Later in the novel, this idealized meeting of minds goes on to characterize their marriage: the narrator reports that Levin knew that "his wife would understand what he meant from a mere hint, and she did understand him" (1992, 660). Through Levin and Kitty, Tolstoy presents a fantasy of representational and perceptual economy. They are able to understand each other without needing to exchange more than a mere hint. A cognitive account of this phenomenon might enlist the vocabulary of efficiency and inference making, of probability and prediction, or of theory of mind. What Tolstoy's representation of Levin and Kitty brings to light, however, is that their ability to understand each other "from a mere hint" rests not only upon epistemic skill but also upon an exercise of faith. In fact, everyday acts of inference involve a reliance on faith. To make an inference about what is not completely represented based on what *is* represented is a probabilistic affair characterized by an irreducible "lack of ascertainability" (Iser 1978, 166). To do without more than a mere hint is to sustain a belief in what is not fully expressed. It is to acknowledge what is left unrepresented and to refrain from needing to ascertain it.

Literary history impresses upon us the fact that, given our readiness to recognize what something is based on, just one or two features can lead to mistaken recognition, failed perception, and false belief. Shklovsky reminds us of what is lost when we no longer need to see objects in their entirety. Yet, we have examined many instances when the mind's aliveness to what minimal cues might imply is what makes it *possible* to recognize something that has been represented *only* in a limited way. When full representation or attention is not a practical possibility, we rely on the fact that one or two cues can be sufficient for belief in the existence of someone or something that might otherwise go unacknowledged. It is perhaps for this reason that recognizing more than meets the eye affords so much aesthetic pleasure, and that Levin marvels at Kitty's ability to understand him by means of no more than a hint. Incomplete images and words half expressed may not prolong the process of perception itself, but they engage the cognitive mechanism by which actual and artistic representation can seem to hold the promise of something more.

Notes

1. For examples, see Graesser et al. (1994) and Tapiero (2007).
2. There is some disagreement about the existence and role of a separate text base. It is possible that the text presents direct cues or instructions for constructing the situation model, without involving the representation of an intermediate text base of propositions.
3. Kintsch and van Dijk (1983) introduce the term "situation models" in *Strategies of Discourse Comprehension*, which appeared in the same year as Philip Johnson-Laird's *Mental Models*. Marcel Just and Patricia Carpenter

use the term "referential representation" to refer to the same kind of mental representation in *The Psychology of Reading and Language Comprehension* (Carpenter and Just 1987, 8).

4. The shift between a bottom-up, stimulus-driven approach to a top-down, concept-driven approach also accounts for the way readers effortlessly begin to think and talk about fictional persons as if they were actual people. Lisa Zunshine identifies this as a "cognitive catch-22": while a few textual cues can be sufficient for readers to invest fictional persons with minds of their own, these minds then become capable of "an inexhaustible repertoire" of mental states stretching beyond the scope of the text (Zunshine 2006, 20).

References

Barthes, Roland. 1989. "The Reality Effect." In *The Rustle of Language*, trans. Richard Howard, 141–48. Berkeley: University of California Press.

Biederman, Irving. 1987. "Recognition-by-Components: A Theory of Human Image Understanding." *Psychological Review* 94:115–47.

———. 1995. "Visual Object Recognition." In *An Invitation to Cognitive Science*, ed. Stephen M. Kosslyn and Daniel N. Osherson, 2:121–66. Cambridge: MIT Press.

Bruner, Jerome. 1973. *Beyond the Information Given: Studies in the Psychology of Knowing*. New York: Norton.

Cain, Kate, Manuel Carreiras, Alan Garnham, and Jane Oakhill. 1996. "The Use of Stereotypical Gender Information in Constructing a Mental Model: Evidence from English and Spanish." *Quarterly Journal of Experimental Psychology* 49:639–63.

Carpenter, Patricia, and Marcel Just. 1987. *The Psychology of Reading and Language Comprehension*. Boston: Allyn and Bacon.

Christen, Yves, Albert M. Galaburda, and Stephen M. Kosslyn. 2002. *The Languages of the Brain*. Cambridge: Harvard University Press.

Dewey, John. 1934. *Art as Experience*. New York: Penguin.

Emmott, Catherine. 1997. *Narrative Comprehension: A Discourse Perspective*. Oxford: Clarendon Press.

Freedgood, Elaine. 2006. *The Ideas in Things: Fugitive Meaning in the Victorian Novel*. Chicago: Chicago University Press.

Gallagher, Catherine. 2006. "The Rise of Fictionality." In *The Novel*, ed. Franco Moretti, 2:336–63. Princeton NJ: Princeton University Press.

Gass, William. 1958. *Fiction and the Figures of Life*. New York: Vintage.

Graesser, Arthur C., Keith K. Millis, and Rolf A. Zwaan. 1997. "Discourse Comprehension." *Annual Review of Psychology* 48:163–89.

Graesser, Arthur C., Murray Singer, and Tom Trabasso. 1994. "Constructing Inferences During Narrative Text Comprehension." *Psychological Review* 3:371–95.

Halle, Morris, and Roman Jakobson. 1956. *Fundamentals of Language*. The Hague: Mouton.

Ingarden, Roman. 1973. *The Cognition of the Literary Work of Art*. Trans. Ruth Ann Crowley and Kenneth R. Olson. Evanston IL: Northwestern University Press.

Iser, Wolfgang. 1978. *The Act of Reading: A Theory of Aesthetic Response*. Baltimore: Johns Hopkins University Press.

Johnson, Mark, and George Lakoff. 1980. *Metaphors We Live By*. Chicago: University of Chicago Press.

Johnson-Laird, Philip. 1983. *Mental Models: Towards a Cognitive Science of Language, Inference, and Consciousness*. Cambridge: Harvard University Press.

Kintsch, Walter, and Teun A. van Dijk. 1983. *Strategies of Discourse Comprehension*. New York: Academic Press.

Merejkowski, Dimitri. 1902. *Tolstoi as Man and Artist*. New York: Putnam.

Morson, Gary Soul. 2007. *"Anna Karenina" in Our Time: Seeing More Wisely*. New Haven: Yale University Press.

Palmer, Stephen. 1999. *Vision Science: Photons to Phenomenology*. Cambridge: MIT Press.

Rickheit, Gert, and Lorenz Sichelschmidt. 1999. "Mental Models: Some Answers, Some Questions, Some Suggestions." In *Mental Models in Discourse Processing and Reasoning*, ed. Gert Rickheit and Christopher Habel, 9–40. Amsterdam: Elsevier.

Ronen, Ruth. 1988. "Completing the Incompleteness of Fictional Entities." *Poetics Today* 9:497–514.

Russell, Bertrand. 1948. *Human Knowledge: Its Scope and Limits*. New York: Simon and Schuster.

Scarry, Elaine. 1985. *The Body in Pain: The Making and Unmaking of the World*. Oxford: Oxford University Press.

———. 2001. *Dreaming by the Book*. Princeton NJ: Princeton University Press.

Searle, John. 1975. "The Logical Status of Fictional Discourse." *New Literary History* 6:319–32.

Shklovsky, Viktor. 1965. "Art as Technique." In *Russian Formalist Criticism: Four Essays*, trans. Lee T. Lemon and Marion J. Reis, 3–24. Lincoln: University of Nebraska Press.

Smith, Mack. 1995. *Literary Realism and the Ekphrastic Tradition*. University Park: Pennsylvania State University Press.

Spolsky, Ellen. 1993. *Gaps in Nature: Literary Interpretation and the Modular Mind*. Albany: State University of New York.

Tapiero, Isabelle. 2007. *Situation Models and Levels of Coherence: Toward a Definition of Comprehension*. Mahwah NJ: Erlbaum.

Tolstoy, Leo. 1992. *Anna Karenina*. Trans. Louise and Aylmer Maude. New York: Knopf.

Wood, James. 2008. *How Fiction Works*. New York: Picador.

Zunshine, Lisa. 2004. "Richardson's *Clarissa* and a Theory of Mind." In *The Work of Fiction: Cognition, Culture, and Complexity*, ed. Alan Richardson and Ellen Spolsky, 127–46. Aldershot: Ashgate Press.

———. 2006. *Why We Read Fiction: Theory of Mind and the Novel*. Columbus: Ohio State University Press.

PART 2 : Experiencing Minds

4 Blind Reading

Toward an Enactivist Theory
of the Reader's Imagination

MARCO CARACCIOLO

Introduction

In front of a class of about three hundred students, Professor Franz K. Stanzel invited the listeners to imagine a man running across a square. He then asked if the man wore a coat and a hat, but no one knew how to answer. The students had imagined the man without deciding whether the man had a coat and a hat or not.[1] At least, this story confirms the widespread view that mental images are indeterminate—a view espoused by, among others, Wolfgang Iser (1978, 137–39). This chapter attempts to explain why the students thought that the man may have worn a coat and a hat only after Stanzel's question, and why they did not fill in the gap beforehand. More generally, I will put forward an enactivist account of the imagination, which I will define as the active exploration of a nonactual environment. Although I will have to examine the workings of the imagination across the board, my focus will be, of course, on the reader's imaginative engagement with narrative texts.

This chapter has two parts. In the first, I advance the main theses of the enactivist approach to perception and experience. Moreover, embracing Alvin Goldman's (2006a; 2006b, 149–51) concept of "enactment imagination," I argue that the imagination works by simulating (or enacting) a hypothetical perceptual experience, and that this accounts for its experiential quality. In the second part, I develop an enactivist model of the reader's imagination, suggesting that narrative texts are sets of instructions for the enactment of a storyworld. I also question the view that fictional consciousnesses are *represented* in narrative texts, adding some remarks concerning the relationship between narrative and qualia (defined as the intrinsic, ineffable qualities of our experience). The analogy that steers me through this argument is that, in their imaginative engagement with narratives, readers are like blind people tapping their way around with a cane. Every tap of the cane corresponds to the reader's being invited to imagine a non-actual object. Catherine Emmott uses a similar analogy in her *Narrative Comprehension* (1997): having worked for several years with blind people, Emmott has compared the reader's monitoring of fictional contexts with the way a blind person keeps track of a conversation between a group of sighted people. Like a blind person, she explains, "the reader receives only intermittent signals of the presence of the characters from the text and must therefore monitor the fictional context mentally" (1997, 118).

Despite using roughly the same analogy, my account differs from Emmott's in two respects. On the one hand, Emmott's approach is (broadly speaking) psycholinguistic, whereas I draw on a tradition of research within the philosophy of perception, enactivism. On the other hand, I use the "blind reading" metaphor to stress not the cognitive, information-processing aspect of reading but rather the quasi-experiential "feel" of the reader's imaginings. This is why I insist on the similarity between perceptual and imaginative experiences. To make a case for this (and in line with my central metaphor), I offer some readings of passages from José Saramago's *Blindness* (1999) throughout the chapter. In this novel, the government of an unknown country tries to combat an epidemic of "white blindness" (a mysterious blindness that makes people see white) by quarantining the sufferers in a mental asylum. Because of the way it problematizes the characters' perceptual experiences, this novel is especially suitable for highlighting the similarity between perception and imagination, and thus the experientiality of the reader's engagement with narratives.

At this point, and without further ado, I would like to spell out what is at stake in my investigation into the reader's imagination. In her *Towards a "Natural" Narratology*, Monika Fludernik has insisted on the experientiality of narrative texts, which she defines as the "quasi-mimetic evocation of 'real-life experience'" (1996, 12; see also Fludernik 2003). In her exposition, however, Fludernik seems to merge experientiality with the way characters' experiences are represented by narrative texts. Consider this key passage: "(narrative) experientiality always implies—and sometimes emphatically foregrounds—the protagonist's consciousness. Narrativity can emerge from the experiential portrayal of dynamic event sequences which are already configured emotively and evaluatively, but it can also consist in the experiential depiction of human consciousness *tout court*" (1996, 30). Of course, both "portrayal" and "depiction" are synonymous with "representation," and *what* is represented is the character's (in this case, the protagonist's) consciousness, or events mediated by that consciousness.[2] Fludernik's bundling together experientiality with the representation of the characters' experiences is certainly understandable if we consider that (1) there is a deep connection between experience and consciousness, inasmuch as "to have subjective experience" is synonymous with "to be conscious" (see, e.g., Chalmers 1996, 6); and that (2) the representation of characters' consciousnesses has played and still plays a key role in narratology (see, e.g., Cohn 1978; Banfield 1982; Fludernik 1993; Palmer 2004). And yet, it makes little sense to talk about the experientiality of narrative texts if we do not factor in the *reader's* experience. It may sound obvious, but the depiction of "what it is like" to be a certain character, to borrow Thomas Nagel's (1974) famous phrase, is not autonomous: paraphrasing Fludernik's words, narrative experientiality always implies the *reader's* consciousness. In my view, narrative texts can be considered instruction manuals (or, as Herman [2009, 209] writes, "blueprints") for the simulation of fictional consciousnesses.

This point requires two qualifications. First of all, it is important to pin down the relationship between the "instruction manual" metaphor and another metaphor I will use in these pages, that of texts "inviting" readers to imaginatively enact something. The metaphor of stories as instruction manuals (blueprints, scripts, or musical scores) should be reasonably straightforward, since these "things" are texts, after all. By contrast, it may be wondered how a text (be it narrative or not) could *invite* someone to do something. The easy answer is that this is just a metaphor, and that, in a way, instruction manuals (blueprints, scripts, or musical scores) could also be seen as inviting their users to perform some actions in a certain way. Being like instruction manuals, narrative texts "invite" their readers to entertain certain imaginings (and not others) because there is only a limited number of ways of complying with the textual instructions. A more complete answer would have to fall back on an intentionalist theory of narrative similar to Herman's (2008), in order to claim that—ultimately—it is the author, through the text, that *invites* the reader to attend to some features of a non-actual world. This move would probably make the "invitation" metaphor less metaphorical. But this is, of course, beyond the scope of this chapter.

Moreover, and this is the second clarification I would like to make, we should get the meaning of "simulation" straight, particularly since this word is at the center of a heated philosophical debate.[3] I'm referring to the simulation theory versus theory theory debate, which centers on how we come to understand other people's minds. In my use of the term, "simulating" means enacting a mental state, trying to produce it in the absence of the appropriate stimulus (Goldman 2006b, 149–51). In this chapter, I will focus almost exclusively on simulated perception, in order to make a parallel between the enactivist account of perception and the reader's imagination (a complementary approach is provided by Kuzmičová in this volume). It is important to stress that we do not simulate the experience of every character, and this is why Kieran's (2003) objection to the simulation theory of fiction misses the mark (Goldman 2006b, 288–89). We simulate only those characters to whose consciousnesses we are given direct access. But since these consciousnesses are simulated or enacted by readers, the experiences involved are, after all, the reader's own. Without bringing into play the reader, it would not be easy to understand why stories provide "an environment in which versions of what it was like to experience situations and events can be juxtaposed [and] comparatively evaluated" (Herman 2009, 151). But this is possible precisely because these situations and events are experienced by readers.

I believe that my approach has one definite advantage over Fludernik's: since I foreground the reader's subjective experience, and the reader's consciousness, I steer clear of Fludernik's claim (which I regard as fundamentally problematic) that narrative is constituted by the representation of either a narrator's (in Fludernik's "telling" frame) or a character's (in her "experiencing" frame) consciousness. Linking too tightly together narrative and the *representation* of a character's experience has the inevitable consequence that when there are no represented consciousnesses, one has to posit the projection of the reader's own consciousness into the storyworld, as in Fludernik's "viewing" frame—"the most marginal of basic-level frames" (Fludernik 2003, 247). It would be beside the point here to articulate the argument against Fludernik's figuralization (the "empathic projection" [1996, 198] of the reader's consciousness into the gap left by the absence of fictional consciousnesses). To make a long story short, it is theoretically more economical to loosen the tie between narration and the representation of characters' consciousnesses in order to give pride of place to the reader's consciousness.

On my account, engaging with narrative texts involves directing one's consciousness toward non-actual entities through the intentional mode of the imagination. This view is consistent with intentionalist accounts of the mind, such as those provided by Searle (1983) and Crane (2001; 2003). Most of the time, as Fludernik correctly points out, the perceptual experiences that texts invite us to simulate are presented as actually occurring within the storyworld. But this is by no means a necessary requirement. Indeed, I would argue that the absence of fictional consciousnesses (in Fludernik's "viewing" frame) lays bare the workings of the reader's own consciousness: metaphorical talk about the reader's projection into the storyworld points to the intentional structure of consciousness, its being directed at objects. In Herman's words, "more than just representing minds, stories emulate through their temporal and perspectival configuration the what it's like dimension of conscious awareness itself" (2009, 157). But, and this is the thrust of my argument, this emulation (or simulation), far from being *represented* in narrative texts, is made possible by the reader's imaginative engagement with them.

Before starting, I would like to make the following proviso: the reader I have just referred to is an ideal reader, largely based on theories about the interaction between readers and texts. Although there is no decisive empirical evidence for the account of the reader's imagination that I will propose here, it is consistent with psycholinguistic research on the role that embodied simulations play in language understanding.[4] Moreover, my theoretical model rests on a view of experience, and of perception in particular—enactivism—that I deem to be fairly solid, even from an empirical viewpoint. There have been other attempts (notably, by Nigel Thomas [1999; 2010]) to provide an enactivist account of the imagination. I will try to refine this account, tackling the problems specifically posed by the interaction between readers and narrative texts.

The Enactivist Theory of Experience

Let us return for a moment to Stanzel's informal experiment. In a way, it could seem that the students, who had been asked to imagine a man running across a square, had not *noticed* whether the man they imagined wore a coat and a hat. By contrast, it is widely assumed that when we see (as opposed to imagine) a man running across a square, we cannot help noticing whether he wears a coat and a hat. On this account, perception yields a continuous and highly detailed image of the world, where there is nothing similar to Iser's "gaps" or "blanks." However, I believe that this traditional view of perception has been convincingly proved wrong by the proponents of the enactive theory, such as Alva Noë, Kevin O'Regan, and Eric Myin. Consider an already classic experiment by Daniel Simons and Christopher Chabris (1999), in which the subjects were asked to watch a video recording of some people playing basketball, and to count the number of passes made by each team. In a version of the experiment, someone disguised as a gorilla walks through the scene—but half of the subjects (when asked if they noticed anything unusual in the video) did not report seeing it. This phenomenon (known as inattentional blindness) shows that perception is much more attention-dependent than it was thought before (see the chapter of Emmott et al. on this topic): we do not always see everything that is in our visual field. The subjects of the experiment were too concentrated on counting the passes to spot the gorilla. Consequently, it is reasonable to suppose that we may see a man running across a square without noticing whether he wears a coat and a hat, just as Stanzel's students may have overlooked that detail in their imaginings.

In his *Action in Perception* (2004), Alva Noë uses inattentional blindness (and other, similar phenomena) to dispel the illusion that the perceived world is like a gap-free and highly detailed photograph (he calls it the "snapshot conception" of perception). In this section, after expanding on the enactivist theory of perception, I will turn to the enactivist view of experience as an embodied activity. This will enable me to bring into focus the structural analogy between perception and imagination, defining the imagination as the simulation of a hypothetical perceptual experience. In the final part, I will argue that the imagination cannot be identified with the production of mental images.

Let's start by introducing the enactive theory of perception (see O'Regan and Noë 2001; Noë 2004; O'Regan et al. 2005), which—as Stephen Torrance (2005) explains—is a spin-off from the larger enactivist project initiated by Varela, Thompson, and Rosch in their *The Embodied Mind* (1991). The main thrust of enactivism is that experience—far from being the computational process whereby an internal model of the world is constructed—

is an active exploration of the world. In Rodney Brooks's (1990) slogan, the world is "its own best model," so that we do not need to download it onto our brains. Consider the case of vision (I am following Noë's [2004] account here). It is well known that our retinal image is full of imperfections: apart from being upside-down, it has few cones at the edges (so that we are almost color blind at the borders of our visual field) and it contains no photoreceptors where the optic nerve passes through it (this is the so-called blind spot). Together with the experiments on inattentional blindness, these findings show that the "snapshot conception" of perception is illusory, as Elaine Auyoung confirms in the previous chapter, in the analysis of "partial perception." Where, then, does the sense that the perceived world is gap-free come from? Traditionally, computational theories of perception (such as the one advanced by David Marr in his celebrated *Vision* [1982]) insisted that we make up for the shortcomings of our retinal image by constructing an internal model of the world. By contrast, the enactivists hold that there is no need to posit the existence of these "mental representations" (as far as perception is concerned). We perceive the world as gap-free because we move our body, head, and eyes; subjectively, there are no gaps because, in whatever direction we look, the world is there.

Thus, retracing the footsteps of phenomenologists such as Edmund Husserl and Maurice Merleau-Ponty (see Gallagher 2009), the enactivists focus on the sensorimotor patterns that we trace while interacting with the environment.[5] For instance, Noë calls attention to the sensorimotor patterns typical of vision: the "visual field . . . is not the field available to the fixed gaze. The visual field, rather, is made available by *looking around*. . . . It is no part of our phenomenological commitments that we take ourselves to have all that detail at hand *in a single fixation*" (2004, 57). In fact, as O'Regan and Noë (2001, 1015) explain, virtual or potential movements play a role in maintaining the illusion of the continuity of the perceived world. To clarify this point, let us consider how blind people explore the environment with their cane. This illustration of how perception works, which has antecedents in both Maurice Merleau-Ponty and Gregory Bateson, is Noë's favorite. In order to do a reconnaissance of the space around them, blind people need to tap around with their cane. But even if they are not waving the cane, the world feels present to them all the same, because a simple movement would give them access to the spatial information they need.

This view of perception is closely connected with the assertion that experience cannot be separated from the environment with which the experiencer interacts; experience is not "in the head." Daniel Hutto has highlighted this point in his critique of what he calls the "object-based schema" (2000, chap. 4; 2006a; 2006b). According to Hutto, cognitive scientists should abandon their quest for the "neural correlates" of conscious experience, since experiences are not spatiotemporal objects—they are meaningful interactions between the subject and the environment. There is one passage from Hutto's essay that is worth quoting in full:

> The only way to understand "what-it-is-like" to have an experience is to actually undergo it or re-imagine undergoing it. Gaining insight into the phenomenal character of particular kinds of experience requires *practical* engagements, not theoretical insights. The kind of understanding "what-it-is-like" to have such and such an experience requires responding in a way that is enactive, on-line and embodied or, alternatively, in a way that is re-enactive, off-line and imaginative—and still embodied. It involves undergoing and/or imagining experiences both of acting and of being acted upon. (2006a, 52)

We will have to bear in mind these remarks, for they will play a very important role in the next section. However, I have to take issue with a possible interpretation of Hutto's claim. The imagination is not re-enactive in the sense that it is forced to reenact past experiences, as when one hits the replay button on an electronic device, for this would imply denying it an experiential dimension in its own right. The kind of imagination that I am interested in depends on knowledge or past experiences, but only insofar as it can use them as raw material for experiences that are, to some extent, unprecedented.

Consider this passage from Saramago's *Blindness*:

> It was a long room, like a ward in an old-fashioned hospital, with two rows of beds that had been painted grey, although the paint had been peeling off for quite some time. (1999, 71)

When I read these lines, my imagination draws on general knowledge (what a ward is) and past experiences (what peeling paint looks like), but it does not reenact a past experience, for the obvious reason that I have never been to this place. On the contrary, it seems to me that reading these lines is *almost* like experiencing this place for the first time. Following Goldman (2006a; 2006b), I would argue that the imagination required to experience this place is an "enactment imagination." "To enactively imagine seeing something, you must 'try' to undergo the seeing—or some aspects of the seeing—despite the fact that no appropriate visual stimulus is present," Goldman (2006b, 152) writes. Likewise, Evan Thompson has suggested that "to say that I imagine X is to say that I mentally re-present X as given to a neutralized perceptual experience of X.... [T]o visualize X is to mentally re-present X by subjectively simulating or emulating a neutralized perceptual experience of X" (2007, 154). In short, enactment imagination consists in the simulation of perception (and, on Goldman's account, of other mental states—but this need not concern us here). Of course, it is the similarity between perception and imagination (which is supported by extensive empirical evidence: see, e.g., Currie and Ravenscroft 2002, 78–84; Goldman 2006b, 151–60) that accounts for the quasi-experiential "feel" of imaginings, the fact that they strike us *almost* as experiences. But this similarity has its roots in the embodied nature of perception and enactment imagination alike.

Before moving on, I would like to prevent a possible misunderstanding of my claims about perception and imagination. Their similarity is grounded in the (active, embodied) structure of experience; it has little to do with their content: imagining is enacting seeing, not seeing a picture-like mental image. When I experience the room described by Saramago's passage, I experience it *as absent*; I don't inspect the picture-like mental image of a room. This amounts to saying that the pictorial conception of the imagination is, just like the view that we perceive the world by constructing an internal model, fundamentally flawed. Thompson makes a case for this by applying Husserl's distinction between presentation and re-presentation. He writes: "In a perceptual experience, the object is experienced as present in its 'bodily being,' and thus as directly accessible. In a re-presentational experience, on the other hand, the object is not experienced as present and accessible in this way, but rather as absent" (2007, 151). It is the object itself that is experienced, not its mental image. At best, it could be argued that mental images are the *means* through which I reach toward the intentional object. Hence, according to Thompson, mental images are "had" or "undergone," as a by-product of one's imaginings, but never inwardly seen (156). What really matters is the experiential character of our imaginings; as Thompson writes, in imagination "we do not experience mental pictures, but instead visualize an object or scene by mentally enacting or entertaining a possible perceptual experience of that object or scene" (138). And, according to the enactivist work I have just reviewed, experience is an activity; it is an embodied exploration of the world.

Imagination as the Enactment of a Non-Actual World

In what follows I will draw on the insights of the enactivists to cast light on the workings of the reader's imagination. To begin with, I will examine how storyworlds are enacted (or imaginatively explored) and look into the problem of the indeterminacy of our imaginings. I will argue that the dynamics of our imaginative engagement with narrative texts are, to a great extent, experiential, because of the way they involve the reader's virtual movements. I will then consider the typical scenario in which the reader's access to the storyworld is mediated by the consciousness of a fictional character, contending that fictional consciousnesses should not be regarded as textual objects but rather as, in themselves, enacted by the reader. Finally, I will touch on the relationship between narrative and qualia, highlighting the role that metaphorical language seems to play in conveying the ineffable qualities of experience.

I have already argued that the imagination is the intentional mode through which one directs one's consciousness toward non-actual objects. It should be acknowledged, however, that the imaginings associated with narrative texts have two distinctive features. This is why I now turn from the imagination as such to the specific kind of imaginings that are triggered in the act of reading. On the one hand, being a way of complying with the instructions given by the text, these imaginings are not entirely free. In this respect, narrative texts are similar to Stanzel's invitation to imagine a man running across a square: they guide our imagination by limiting the number of acceptable responses, just like scripts or musical scores. In her *Dreaming by the Book*, Elaine Scarry has made a case for this, suggesting that stories try to mimic the "givenness" of perception by temporarily suspending the voluntary character of the imagination (2001, 31–39). Indeed, it is as if every sentence were preceded by an instruction to imagine. On the other hand, the readers of narrative texts do not produce isolated, unrelated imaginings but a sequence of more or less continuous ones—where "continuous," of course, refers to the spatiotemporal coherence of the existents and events toward which the reader's consciousness is directed. This intuition underlies the "fictional worlds" metaphor (see Eco 1979; Pavel 1986; Ryan 1991; Doležel 1998). Thus, keeping in mind the metaphorical nature of this phrasing, I would argue that the imagination is the intentional mode through which readers direct their consciousness toward non-actual worlds.

This formulation makes the problem of the indeterminacy of our imaginings even more pressing. We have seen that perception is an active, embodied exploration of the world. Our sensory organs are not like built-in cameras: they do not shoot a series of photographs that our brain rearranges in an internal, seamless image of the world. There is no need to do that, as we get all the information we need by way of bodily movements. In order to ground my theory of the reader's imagination in the enactivist account of experience, I will have to make the case that, in their imaginative engagement with narrative texts, readers do not need to construct a picture-like mental image. Of course, they do use internal models, such as "fictional contexts" (Emmott 1997, chap. 4) and "situation models" (see, e.g., Zwaan and Radvansky 1998), to keep track of the states of affairs described by the text. However, in my view these sketchy and non-pictorial models are constructed through a process that simulates perception, since it is not only cognitive but also *experiential*. Accordingly, while following the instructions of the text, readers enact the storyworld by relying on the virtuality of their movements, and usually without noticing the "gaps" in the presentation of narrative existents, such as characters and, centrally, spaces.[6] In the next sections, I will try to show that the reader's engagement with narrative texts, despite being mediated by language, simulates the online, embodied responding that characterizes our basic interaction with the real world, and that this explains the experiential dimension of the imagination.

Imaginatively Enacting Narrative Space

I would like to start by examining another passage from Saramago's *Blindness*. The scene is set inside the asylum, where all the internees (who suffer from a mysterious form of blindness) are asleep. As a consequence, the readers are left by themselves; in the storyworld, there is no act of perception to which their imaginings can anchor. Thus, these lines are especially suitable for showing that the experientiality of the text can be detached from the experiences of fictional characters in Fludernik's "telling" frame (corresponding to Gérard Genette's [1980] "zero focalization" and to Stanzel's [1984] "authorial narrative situation").

> Some [of the internees] had covered their heads with a blanket, as if anxious that a pitch-black darkness, a real one, might extinguish once and for all the dim suns that their eyes had become. The three lamps suspended from the high ceiling, out of arm's reach, cast a dull, yellowish light over the beds, a light incapable of even creating shadows. (1999, 70–71)

This short passage does give readers an idea of what it is like to experience a space such as this. In other words, this space has a distinct phenomenal character—an experiential feel that cannot easily be reduced to the linguistic meaning of the text. As the phrase "out of arm's reach" implies, this spatial description is tailored to the body and sensory systems of a human being, so that, even if we could train a machine to understand the linguistic meaning of the text, it probably would not be able to make sense of it. It would miss the experiential feel, and fail to see why this is a spatial description as opposed, for instance, to a list. And yet, we are hard pressed to form a picture-like mental image of the space described, since the objects seem to float about in a sea of indetermination.

Any attempt at making a sketch of this space would reveal the vagueness of the description: we would have to decide, among other things, how many of the internees have covered their heads with a blanket, what is the shape of the lamps, and more in general the spatial arrangement of the dormitory. This filling-in process can be very lengthy and, it seems to me, we do not have the time for it while reading: we get the experiential feel well before having had the time to form a spatially coherent mental image. It is at this point that the "snapshot conception" of the imagination breaks down. But then, we may ask, where does the experiential dimension of this description come from? In my view, it has its roots in the structural resemblance between the reader's imaginative engagement with this passage and perception (conceived of as an active exploration of the world). Let us return for a moment to the image of the blind person making his or her way through an environment with the help of a cane. To those who see, the world of the blind seems a vast expanse of indeterminacy—and yet, if we think about it, there is no "gap" in the world of blind people that they cannot fill in by moving their body, arms, and cane. This means that, subjectively, these gaps are only marginally relevant—what really matters is that the tip of the blind person's cane makes repeated contacts with the world. So to speak, the blind person's world is "enacted" or "brought forth" through a pattern of meaningful interactions, as Varela, Thompson, and Rosch would write (see, e.g., 1991, 156). The "gaps" that remain lie outside the scope of the meaningful, just as there was no point for Stanzel's students to decide if the man wore a coat and a hat or not—hence, they did not notice any gap at all in their imaginings until Stanzel asked the question. (Remember the experiment on inattentional blindness.)

My claim is that the reader's consciousness works like the blind person's cane: while being directed toward the storyworld (through the intentional mode of the imagination), it comes into contact first with the internees, then with the blankets that cover some of the heads, then again with the three lamps, and finally with the light projected onto the beds. From the reader's subjective viewpoint, there are no gaps between these intentional objects, for they are the only ones that the text presents as meaningful. Like the blind person's cane, or the beam of a flashlight in a dark room, the reader's consciousness explores the storyworld—except that it is not completely free, since it is guided by the description. We assume that what is left outside the text is just not interesting enough to repay attention. Moreover, it can be hypothesized that the series of contacts between the reader's consciousness and the intentional objects simulates the bodily movements that accompany perception: Saramago's description invites readers to imagine visually scanning the dormitory by drawing their attention to the heads of the internees, to the blankets that cover some of the heads, then (with an upward movement) to the lamps that hang from the ceiling. Finally, with a downward movement, following the light that falls from the lamps, the reader's attention comes to rest on the beds. Readers of this passage are thus likely to run an embodied simulation of this circular motion, enacting the movements that would be required to perceive a similar scene. This hypothesis is consistent with the findings of Richardson et al. (2003) and Bergen et al. (2007). Keeping in mind Noë's claim that the sense of the presence of the world depends on the virtuality of our movements (the fact that we *could* move, even if we do not actually do so), we may add that the (illusion of the) presence of the storyworld goes hand in hand with the reader's virtual (simulated, enacted) movements.

More generally, my point is that the reader's embodiment and the simulation of bodily movements are highly instrumental in enacting the storyworld. On the one hand, there is ample empirical evidence for the role that embodiment and kinesthetic activity play in language understanding.[7] On the other, the link between language understanding and embodiment is provided by what I call, with Goldman, "enactment imagination." In his in-depth survey of the literature on embodiment, Raymond Gibbs comments on the relationship between imagery and embodiment by writing that, as "a simulator, mental imagery provides a kinesthetic feel that is not simply the output of some abstract computational machine, but provides something of the full-bodied experiences that have textures and a felt sense of three-dimensional depth" (2005, 136). All in all, it is the close connection among perception, enactment (simulative) imagination, and language understanding that accounts for the experientiality of reading. As I have argued in this section, readers enact narrative space by simulating a hypothetical perceptual experience, even in the absence of fictional characters to which they could attribute that experience. "Gaps" do not play a significant role in the enactment of narrative space, unlike the reader's virtual movements, which appear to contribute to the experientiality of reading.

Imaginatively Enacting Fictional Consciousnesses

What happens, however, when the text invites the reader to simulate the perceptual experience of a fictional character, as in Fludernik's (1996) represented experientiality? In this section I will argue that this kind of imaginative engagement is not fundamentally different from the one I have examined in the foregoing paragraphs. Consider another passage from Saramago's *Blindness*. A few lines after the description of the dormitory, one of the characters (a professional car thief) attempts to crawl out of bed despite his severely injured leg:

> Very slowly, resting on his elbows, the thief raised his body into a sitting position. He had no feeling in his leg, nothing except the pain, the rest had ceased to belong to him. His knee was quite stiff. He rolled his body over on to the side of his healthy leg, which he

allowed to hang out of the bed, then with both hands under his thigh, he tried to move his injured leg in the same direction. . . . Resting on his hands, he gradually dragged his body across the mattress in the direction of the aisle. (1999, 71)

This passage is centered on the character's proprioception—that is, on his "non-observational . . . awareness of [his] body in action" (Gallagher and Zahavi 2008, 143)—and on his bodily sensations (such as pain). As we will see in the next section, pain is the quintessential example of the private character of experience. It follows that the second and third sentences of this description are almost automatically processed by readers as internally focalized. Thus, in accordance with Jahn's (1997) primacy rule, readers are likely to retain the frame of internal focalization and interpret the whole passage as internally focalized. Now, a number of empirical studies (Tversky 1996; 2009; and see Coplan 2004, 142–43, for a comprehensive survey of this literature) have shown that, when confronted with internally focalized passages, readers tend to adopt the perspective of the reflector-character. This is a valid interpretation of the experimental findings, but it requires qualification. In my view, the problem with this formulation is that it tends to reify the character's perspective, presenting it as an object that preexists the reader's interaction with the text. On the contrary, I would argue that the character's perspective is simulated, or rather enacted, by the reader, while reading. For the same reason, I doubt that passages such as this can be said to *represent*, in the strong sense, the character's experience: as a matter of fact, there is no experience other than the reader's at stake here. Indeed, readers enact the character's consciousness just as they enacted narrative space in the passage I have analyzed before—by following the textual instructions and by simulating a hypothetical perceptual experience. In Herman's words, this passage acts as a "blueprint" (2009, 209) for the construction of the character's perspective, experience, and consciousness. It is no more the representation of a fictional consciousness than the instruction manual for a Lego toy can be said to be the representation of its end product, except that there is *no* end product here. In fact, we should not fall into the trap of viewing the character's perspective, experience, and consciousness as stand-alone objects: they *are* the shape taken by the reader's imaginative engagement with the text, and this engagement is (in conformity with the enactivist view of experience) exploratory and embodied. They are processes, or activities, that readers enact through their imagination. In Hutto's words, "it is better to regard consciousness, not as what is experienced, but as *how* things are experienced" (2000, 135; emphasis added). A fictional consciousness is a way of experiencing (non-actual) things that is impressed on the reader's consciousness by a narrative text.

Thus, I would argue that the excruciating quality of the description of the thief's movements (which goes on, meticulously, for almost six pages, till he is shot down by a guard) depends on the fact that the reader is no mere spectator. Understanding this passage requires running embodied simulations of the actions described,[8] and these simulations are hardwired in the reader's own body—only in a second moment do we attribute these experiences to a fictional character, in accordance with the textual instructions. In other words, on my hypothesis, the effectiveness of Saramago's passage is intimately connected with the involvement of the reader's own body (through the mediation of mental simulations). This is why I would argue that the reader's engagement with narratives, despite being linguistically mediated, can simulate the directness of basic perceptual acts.

Of course, I do not deny that it is of some practical utility to talk about the reflector-character's perspective, experience, and consciousness as if they were items we could relate to. I am not arguing against the common use of these terms. I am just suggesting that there is a sense in which this use (related to what Hutto has called the "object-based schema," as discussed above) overlooks an important aspect of our imaginary engagement with narrative texts: the character's perspective, experience, and consciousness are not given anywhere in the text; they are not objects. Fludernik's represented experientiality rides piggyback on the *reader's* experience, and from this perspective the internally focalized passage just quoted does not appear substantially different from the description of the dormitory (characterized by the absence of fictional consciousnesses).

Imaginatively Enacting Qualia

How do narratives enable us to simulate the intrinsic or ineffable qualities of an experience? This is the question I will try to answer in this section, in which I explore the relationship between narrative and qualia. Herman has already devoted an excellent chapter of his *Basic Elements of Narrative* (2009, chap. 6) to this problem, but I would like to follow up on that discussion by drawing attention to the role metaphorical language plays in enabling the reader to simulate the ineffable qualities of an experience. Again, my focus will be on the reader's experientiality and on how readers run embodied simulations of experiences they subsequently attribute to characters.

It is beyond the scope of this chapter to provide detailed coverage of the philosophical debate on qualia, which Daniel Dennett has characterized as "a tormented snarl of increasingly convoluted and bizarre thought experiments" (1991, 369). The problem with qualia is that this term has been used in at least three distinct senses. Following Michael Tye's (2009) reconstruction, a mental state has qualia, in the broadest sense, when it has a phenomenal character, when there is something it is like for you to be in that mental state. In this sense, it is hard to deny that there are qualia, since "to have qualia" is almost interchangeable with "to have subjective experience" and "to be conscious." In another, stronger sense, qualia are intrinsic, non-intentional qualities of our experience. A case in point is that of bodily sensations (such as pain), which are sometimes said to possess a qualitative character without being intentional states. The existence of qualia, in this sense, is controversial—Crane (2001, 78–83), for instance, denies it. Finally, some philosophers (see, e.g., Dennett 1991, 373) highlight the link between qualia and the ineffability of experience. Herman's chapter deals with qualia in the broadest sense, whereas I will focus on ineffability in order to complement the theory of the reader's experientiality I have put forward in the foregoing pages.

In Frank Jackson's (1982) famous thought experiment, a character named Mary grows up in a black-and-white room, with her body painted black and white, watching black-and-white television. Nevertheless, she becomes the world's leading authority on color vision. She comes to know everything there is to know about the physics of colors and about the physiology and psychology of color vision. Does she come to know something new when she finally sees red? The answer to this question has been hotly disputed, but this need not concern us here, since Jackson's thought experiment has been generally used as an argument against physicalism (the doctrine that mental states are identical with physical states of the brain, i.e., states that come under the jurisdiction of physics). However, its "intuitive starting point wasn't just that *physics* lessons couldn't help the inexperienced to know what it is like. It was that *lessons* couldn't help" (Lewis 1999, 281; emphasis in the original). In other words, as Hutto puts it, the experience of redness cannot "be stated and fully captured propositionally" (2006a, 62). In a way, then, Jackson's thought experiment shows that experiences are ineffable: no matter how hard you try, it is impossible to describe the experience of seeing red to someone who has never seen red. This is, of course, undeniable. And yet, I believe that narratives (and especially literary narratives) have a special tool for showing readers how to enact a given experience: I am thinking about metaphorical language, and in particular about metaphors that emphasize the active nature of experience. Through these metaphors, the reader is invited to imagine experiences "both of acting and of being acted upon" (Hutto 2006a, 52) and to associate them with the target experience, thus being provided not with the experience itself but with a good approximation to it. If experience has an active character, it is by metaphorically associating the experience to be described with an activity that we can give an idea of what it is like to have that experience.

Because of its private (and, according to some, non-intentional) nature, bodily pain is the quintessential example of the ineffability of experience. Scarry, for example, has made a case for the non-representability of pain in *The Body in Pain* (1985). Now, consider a variant on Jackson's thought experiment in which there is someone who, suffering from a rare condition called "congenital insensitivity to pain," does not know what it is like to be in pain. For whatever reason, she has never seen anyone in pain either. This person would lack the qualia of pain, in all the three senses discussed above. Let us suppose that this person is asked to read the following passage from Saramago's *Blindness*, in which the thief, after getting out of bed, feels an intense pain in his leg:

> The pain came back instantly, as if someone were sawing, drilling, and hammering the wound. (1999, 71–73)

In order to describe the phenomenal character of this pain, the text invites the reader to imagine someone inflicting damage on the already injured limb. In the simile the felt quality of the pain is rendered through the activities (sawing, drilling, hammering) that would *cause* a similar pain. It is easy for the reader to imaginatively perform these actions (which are shared, external happenings) and at the same time to relate the pain they would cause to the character's internal state, as suggested by the simile. However, in a sense, it is the sequence of actions itself, and not only the pain these actions would cause, that ends up being associated with the thief's pain. Thus, pain is externalized as *damage caused to the body*. Interestingly, this ties in with one of the intentionalist approaches to pain on the market, Tye's theory that pains are "*sensory* representations of tissue damage" (1997, 333; emphasis in the original). On this view, then, someone who read these lines without having ever *felt* pain would probably come to know something about pain: she would not be able to imaginatively enact pain, but she would be able to imaginatively enact bodily damage, and would associate the two states (one of which is internal, the other external). Further, it can be speculated that the fierceness of the damage inflicted on the human body would inform the subject of our thought experiment about the subjective quality of pain. Of course, this would be a far cry from undergoing the experience of pain, but it would be a reasonable approximation of it.

Leaving aside my thought experiment, the point I would like to make here is that readers form a more precise idea of what it was like for the character to feel this pain by imaginatively enacting the content of the simile. In fact, as I have tried to explain above, it is the reader who enacts this pain before attributing it to the character: the thief's consciousness, experience, pain are a posteriori constructions based on the reader's own simulative activity. Moreover, through a metaphorical mapping, the text invites the reader to associate the qualia of the character's pain with external, embodied activities, confirming the enactivist view that experience is, centrally, an active engagement with the world (or, in this case, with one's body), not a mental object of sorts. However, a fuller investigation of the relationship between qualia (or ineffable qualities of experience) and metaphorical language will have to wait for another occasion.[9]

Conclusion

The purpose of this chapter was to apply the insights of enactivism to the reader's imaginative engagement with narratives. I have drawn on the enactivist view of experience as an active and embodied exploration of an environment to point out why the reader's imaginative engagement with narratives can be said to be experiential. Like a script or a musical score, a story is a set of instructions for the enactment of a storyworld (cf. Auyoung's discussion of Tolstoy's text in this volume), and it is its enactment, not the story per se, that possesses an experiential quality. Hence, in my view, the experientiality of narratives should be defined primarily in terms of the experiences undergone by the readers while complying with the instructions of the text, and only secondarily (or a posteriori) as the representation of the characters' experiences (see Fludernik 1996).

In the first part of this chapter, I prepared the groundwork for my claims about the reader's experientiality by tracing a brief outline of the enactivist theory of experience and perception. More specifically, I argued that the kind of imagination I am interested in (I call it, following Goldman [2006a; 2006b]), "enactment imagination") consists in the enactment or simulation of a perceptual experience, in the absence of the intentional object. In the second part I advanced the fundamental claims of my chapter, taking as examples some passages from Saramago's *Blindness*. The choice of Saramago's novel has been influenced by an analogy that I have used throughout the chapter: that between the way a blind person explores the environment with his or her cane and the reader's imaginative engagement with narratives. In both cases, I argued, the world (perceived or imagined) is enacted through a pattern of meaningful interactions. Indeed, this applies both to readers' enactment of narrative space and to their enactment of fictional consciousnesses—two activities that involve embodied simulations. On the one hand, the reader's simulated movements could play a role in the enactment of narrative space. On the other, the consciousness (experience, perspective) of a fictional character is the shape the reader's own consciousness takes on while complying with the instructions of the text. Finally, I proposed that narrative texts use metaphors to convey the qualia (or ineffable qualities) of specific experiences.

I believe that the enactivist approach to cognition has considerable potential for the study of the interaction between readers and narratives. The active, embodied nature of the reader's imaginings deserves further investigation, both from the speculative and the empirical standpoint, and enactivism provides a comprehensive framework for taking up this challenge.

Notes

1. This anecdote was told by Monika Fludernik at the 2010 conference of the International Association of Literary Semantics in Genoa.
2. For an even more explicit acknowledgment of the link between experien-

tiality and representation, see Fludernik (1996): "If the model which I am proposing goes beyond Stanzel's dichotomy, it is in the sense of reversing the emphasis in the teller-vs.-reflector mode dichotomy, by grounding narrativity in the representation of experientiality" (28).

3. See Stitch and Nichols (1997) for a thorough critique of the concept of "simulation."

4. Pecher and Zwaan (2005) and Kaschak et al. (2009) offer a survey of this literature. See also the various studies quoted below.

5. I avoid speaking of "sensorimotor knowledge" here, since this concept—popularized by O'Regan and Noë—has been, I believe, rightly criticized by Hutto (see, e.g., 2005).

6. Of course, I am not talking about Meir Sternberg's (1993) "gaps" in the telling of past events here, for which a kind of filling-in is, obviously, needed.

7. On this point see, e.g., Zwaan (2004) and Zwaan and Taylor (2006). For a useful review of the literature on the embodiment of language comprehension, see Fischer and Zwaan (2008).

8. Zwaan et al. (2004) suggest that language understanding involves dynamic mental simulations.

9. See Caracciolo (2013).

References

Banfield, Ann. 1982. *Unspeakable Sentences: Narration and Representation in the Language of Fiction*. Boston: Routledge and Kegan Paul.

Bergen, Benjamin K., Shane Lindsay, Teenie Matlock, and Srini Narayanan. 2007. "Spatial and Linguistic Aspects of Visual Imagery in Sentence Comprehension." *Cognitive Science* 31:733–64.

Brooks, Rodney A. 1990. "Elephants Don't Play Chess." *Robotics and Autonomous Systems* 6:3–15.

Caracciolo, Marco. 2013. "Phenomenological Metaphors in Readers' Engagement with Characters: The Case of Ian McEwan's *Saturday*." *Language and Literature* 22 (2): 1–17.

Chalmers, David J. 1996. *The Conscious Mind: In Search of a Fundamental Theory*. New York: Oxford University Press.

Cohn, Dorrit. 1978. *Transparent Minds: Narrative Modes for Presenting Consciousness in Fiction*. Princeton NJ: Princeton University Press.

Coplan, Amy. 2004. "Empathic Engagement with Narrative Fictions." *Journal of Aesthetics and Art Criticism* 62 (2): 141–52.

Crane, Tim. 2001. *Elements of Mind: An Introduction to the Philosophy of Mind*. Oxford: Oxford University Press.

———. 2003. "The Intentional Structure of Consciousness." In *Consciousness: New Philosophical Perspectives*, ed. Aleksander Jokic and Quentin Smith, 33–56. Oxford: Oxford University Press.

Currie, Gregory, and Gregory Ravenscroft. 2002. *Recreative Minds*. Oxford: Oxford University Press.

Dennett, Daniel. 1991. *Consciousness Explained*. New York, Boston and London: Back Bay Books.

Doležel, Lubomír. 1998. *Heterocosmica: Fiction and Possible Worlds*. Baltimore: Johns Hopkins University Press.

Eco, Umberto. 1979. *The Role of the Reader: Explorations in the Semiotics of Texts*. Bloomington: Indiana University Press.

Emmott, Catherine. 1997. *Narrative Comprehension: A Discourse Perspective*. Oxford: Clarendon Press.

Fischer, Martin H., and Rolf A. Zwaan. 2008. "Embodied Language: A Review of the Role of the Motor System in Language Comprehension." *Quarterly Journal of Experimental Psychology* 61 (6): 825–50.

Fludernik, Monika. 1993. *The Fictions of Language and the Languages of Fiction: The Linguistic Representation of Speech and Consciousness*. London: Routledge.

———. 1996. *Towards a "Natural" Narratology*. London: Routledge.

———. 2003. "Natural Narratology and Cognitive Parameters." In *Narrative Theory and the Cognitive Sciences*, ed. David Herman, 243–67. Stanford: CSLI Publications.

Gallagher, Shaun. 2009. "Philosophical Antecedents of Situated Cognition." In *The Cambridge Handbook of Situated Cognition*, 35–51. Cambridge: Cambridge University Press.

Gallagher, Shaun, and Dan Zahavi. 2008. *The Phenomenological Mind: An Introduction to Philosophy of Mind and Cognitive Science*. Abingdon: Routledge.

Genette, Gérard. 1980. *Narrative Discourse: An Essay in Method*. Trans. J. E. Lewin. Ithaca: Cornell University Press.

Gibbs, Raymond W. 2005. *Embodiment and Cognitive Science*. Cambridge: Cambridge University Press.

Goldman, Alvin I. 2006a. "Imagination and Simulation in Audience Responses to Fiction." In *The Architecture of the Imagination: New Essays on Pretence, Possibility, and Fiction*, ed. Shaun Nichols, 41–56. Oxford: Oxford University Press.

———. 2006b. *Simulating Minds: The Philosophy, Psychology, and Neuroscience of Mindreading*. Oxford: Oxford University Press.

Herman, David. 2008. "Narrative Theory and the Intentional Stance." *Partial Answers* 6 (2): 233–60.

———. 2009. *Basic Elements of Narrative*. Chichester: Wiley-Blackwell.

Hutto, Daniel D. 2000. *Beyond Physicalism*. Amsterdam: John Benjamins.

———. 2005. "Knowing What? Radical Versus Conservative Enactivism." *Phenomenology and the Cognitive Sciences* 4:389–405.

———. 2006a. "Impossible Problems and Careful Expositions: Reply to Myin and De Nul." In *Radical Enactivism: Focus on the Philosophy of Daniel D. Hutto*, ed. Richard Menary, 45–64. Philadelphia: John Benjamins.

———. 2006b. "Against Passive Intellectualism: Reply to Crane." In *Radical Enactivism: Focus on the Philosophy of Daniel D. Hutto*, ed. Richard Menary, 121–49. Philadelphia: John Benjamins.

Iser, Wolfgang. 1978. *The Act of Reading: A Theory of Aesthetic Response*. Baltimore: Johns Hopkins University Press.

Jackson, Frank. 1982. "Epiphenomenal Qualia." *Philosophical Quarterly* 32:127–36.

Jahn, Manfred. 1997. "Frames, Preferences, and the Reading of Third Person Narratives." *Poetics Today* 18 (4): 441–68.

Kaschak, Michael P., John L. Jones, Jacqueline M-Coyle, and Andrea Sell. 2009. "Language and Body." In *Beyond Decoding: The Behavioral and Biological Foundations of Reading Comprehension*, ed. Richard K. Wagner, Christopher Schatschneider, and Caroline Phythian-Sence, 3–26. New York: Guilford.

Kieran, Matthew. 2003. "In Search of a Narrative." In *Imagination, Philosophy, and the Arts*, ed. Matthew Kieran and Dominic Lopes, 69–87. London: Routledge.

Lewis, David. 1999. "What Experience Teaches." In *Papers in Metaphysics and Epistemology*, 262–89. Cambridge: Cambridge University Press.

Marr, David. 1982. *Vision: A Computational Investigation into the Human Representation and Processing of Visual Information*. New York: Freeman.

Nagel, Thomas. 1974. "What Is It Like to Be a Bat?" *Philosophical Review* 83:435–50.

Noë, Alva. 2004. *Action in Perception*. Cambridge: MIT Press.

O'Regan, J. Kevin, Erik Myin, and Alva Noë. 2005. "Sensory Consciousness Explained (Better) in Terms of 'Corporality' and 'Alerting Capacity.'" *Phenomenology and the Cognitive Sciences* 4:369–87.

O'Regan, J. Kevin, and Alva Noë. 2001. "A Sensorimotor Account of Vision and Visual Consciousness." *Behavioral and Brain Sciences* 24 (5): 883–917.

Palmer, Alan. 2004. *Fictional Minds*. Lincoln: University of Nebraska Press.

Pavel, Thomas. 1986. *Fictional Worlds*. Cambridge: Harvard University Press.

Pecher, Diane, and Rolf A. Zwaan. 2005. *Grounding Cognition: The Role of Perception and Action in Memory, Language, and Thinking*. Cambridge: Cambridge University Press.

Richardson, Daniel C., Michael J. Spivey, Lawrence W. Barsalou, and Ken McRae. 2003. "Spatial Representations Activated During Real-time Comprehension of Verbs." *Cognitive Science* 27 (5): 767–80.

Ryan, Marie-Laure. 1991. *Possible Worlds, Artificial Intelligence and Narrative Theory*. Bloomington: Indiana University Press.

Saramago, José. 1999. *Blindness*. Trans. Giovanni Pontiero. Orlando: Harcourt.

Scarry, Elaine. 1985. *The Body in Pain: The Making and Unmaking of the World*. Oxford: Oxford University Press.

———. 2001. *Dreaming by the Book*. Princeton: Princeton University Press.

Searle, John. 1983. *Intentionality: An Essay in the Philosophy of Mind*. Cambridge: Cambridge University Press.

Simons, Daniel, and Christopher Chabris. 1999. "Gorillas in Our Midst: Sustained Inattentional Blindness for Dynamic Events." *Perception* 28 (9): 1059–74.

Stanzel, Franz Karl. 1984. *A Theory of Narrative*. Cambridge: Cambridge University Press.

Sternberg, Meir. 1993. *Expositional Modes and Temporal Ordering in Fiction*. Bloomington: Indiana University Press.

Stitch, Stephen, and Shaun Nichols. 1997. "Cognitive Penetrability, Rationality, and Restricted Simulation." *Mind and Language* 12 (3/4): 297–326.

Thomas, Nigel J. T. 1999. "Are Theories of Imagery Theories of Imagination? An Active Perception Approach to Conscious Mental Content." *Cognitive Science* 23 (2): 207–45.

———. 2010. "The Multidimensional Spectrum of Imagination: Images, Dreams, Hallucinations, and Active, Imaginative Perception." http://www.imagery-imagination.com/spectrum.htm.

Thompson, Evan. 2007. "Look Again: Phenomenology and Mental Imagery." *Phenomenology and the Cognitive Sciences* 6:137–70.

Torrance, Steve. 2005. "In Search of the Enactive." *Phenomenology and the Cognitive Sciences* 4:357–68.

Tversky, Barbara. 1996. "Spatial Perspectives in Descriptions." In *Language and Space*, ed. Paul Bloom, Mary A. Peterson, Lynn Nadel, and Merrill F. Garrett, 462–91. Cambridge: MIT Press.

———. 2009. "Spatial Cognition: Embodied and Situated." In *The Cambridge Handbook of Situated Cognition*, ed. Philip Robbins and Murat Aydede, 201–16. Cambridge: Cambridge University Press.

Tye, Michael. 1997. "A Representational Theory of Pains and Their Phenomenal Nature." In *The Nature of Consciousness*, ed. Ned Block, Owen Flanagan, and Güven Güzeldere, 329–40. Cambridge: MIT Press.

———. 2009. "Qualia." In *The Stanford Encyclopedia of Philosophy*, ed. Edward N. Zalta. http://plato.stanford.edu/archives/sum2009/entries/qualia/.1997.

Varela, Francisco J., Evan Thompson, and Eleanor Rosch. 1991. *The Embodied Mind: Cognitive Science and Human Experience*. Cambridge: MIT Press.

Zwaan, Rolf A. 2004. "The Immersed Experiencer: Towards an Embodied Theory of Language Comprehension." In *The Psychology of Learning and Motivation*, ed. Brian H. Ross, 35–63. San Diego: Elsevier Academic Press.

Zwaan, Rolf A., Carol J. Madden, Richard H. Yaxley, and Mark E. Aveyard. 2004. "Moving Words: Dynamic Representations in Language Comprehension." *Cognitive Science* 28 (4): 611–19.

Zwaan, Rolf A., and Gabriel A. Radvansky. 1998. "Situation Models in Language Comprehension and Memory." *Psychological Bulletin* 123 (2): 162–85.

Zwaan, Rolf A., and Lawrence J. Taylor. 2006. "Seeing, Acting, Understanding: Motor Resonance in Language Comprehension." *Journal of Experimental Psychology* 135 (1): 1–11.

5 The Words and Worlds of Literary Narrative

The Trade-off between Verbal Presence and Direct Presence in the Activity of Reading

ANEŽKA KUZMIČOVÁ

> We can have mental images without reading, or we can read without experiencing mental images, but imaginal activity as part of reading is common and a matter of degree.
>
> SADOSKI AND PAIVIO 2001, 53

This chapter deals with the embodied mind of the reader and the ways in which it spontaneously responds to the sensorimotor qualities elicited by literary narrative. The aim is to begin filling a gap in the scholarship on narrative reading. Although most scholars would agree that narratives make readers experience processes beyond conceptual thought, namely, various kinds of sensorimotor imagery, few have looked into how such vicarious perceptions are structured and prompted. While elaborating on and revising some of the scant suggestions about this topic, my chapter draws upon a variety of findings stemming mainly from outside the domain of literature, for example, from experimental psychology and neuroscience, evolutionary anthropology, philosophy of perception, and history.

The opening section disputes the notion, endorsed by much of narrative theory, that the reading of literary narrative is functionally analogous to an act of communication, where communication stands for the transfer of thought and conceptual information. The next section offers a basic typology of the sensorimotor effects of reading, which fall outside such a narrowly communication-based model of literary narrative. Possible psychophysiological, experiential, and text-linguistic underpinnings are discussed. A main typological distinction is drawn between those sensorimotor effects pertaining to the narrative *qua* verbal utterance (*ver-*

bal presence) and those sensorimotor effects pertaining to the imaginary physical world(s) of the story (*direct presence*). While verbal presence refers to the reader's vicarious perception of the voices of narrators and characters, direct presence refers to the emulated sensorimotor experience of the imaginary worlds that the narrators' and characters' utterances refer to. The third section further elaborates on how, or by which kinds of narrative content and structure, direct presence may be prompted. The final section addresses some of the observational and historical caveats that must be attached to any theoretical inquiry made into the sensorimotor effects of reading. As a preliminary for further research, a few ideas about the model's potential for empirical validation are put forward. A brief, tentative history of the sensorimotor benefits of literary narrative reading is then outlined.

The main hypotheses are the following: Contrary to common assumption, the reader's body participates in imagining the world(s) of the story to such a degree that bodily movement is frequently emulated from an enactive first-person perspective rather than visualized from the perspective of a passive beholder. As a consequence, references to bodily movement have a unique capacity to make the reader vicariously perceive the world(s) of the story. However, where the reader is prone to vicariously hearing the narrative as if read out loud, perception of the world(s) of the story is backgrounded due to the mutually exclusive relationship between verbal presence and direct presence. While the world(s) of the story seem to constitute the main object of reader imagery today, vicarious listening may have dominated reader imagery until around the turn of the twentieth century.

Phenomenal Presence of the World in Language: Some Prerequisites

The functions of natural language are many. I will open this section by isolating two of them, but I will further focus on only one—namely, the capacity to make absent phenomena present to the senses. I will argue that this function, albeit often overlooked, becomes vital whenever language is used and processed aesthetically.

Whether oral or written, language is generally assumed to communicate information, where information stands for snippets of higher-level conceptual knowledge. This view of language seems to inform the research methodologies of most narrative theorists, regardless of whether they come from a hermeneutic or narratological perspective. Hermeneutic approaches look into the concepts that are communicated—directly or indirectly. Narratological approaches look into the means of such communication—as employed by the narrator, character, implied author, and so forth. Although it is now common to define narrative in versatile categories such as Monika Fludernik's *experientiality* (Fludernik 1996), the main focus is still on reflective if not conceptual thought. Diverse theoretical works such as those of Lisa Zunshine (2006), David Herman (2009), and many others deal with how it is represented in and structured by narrative and how it is involved in the process of reading. The more or less undivided interest in the narrowly communicative aspects of language use is remarkable, because language does much more than convey conceptual information. It has a unique capacity to substitute for absent bodies (i.e., any sensible objects in physical space) and forces. It emulates preconceptual phenomena. The effects of this capacity on the mind of the comprehender will hereafter be referred to as *phenomenal presence*, or simply *presence*.

According to a recent theory proposed by evolutionary anthropologist Robin Dunbar (2003), emulating the presence of absent bodies and forces is literally what our linguistic skills evolved for. An advanced extension of inarticulate communal singing, language is believed to have developed due to a dramatic increase in the size of social groups. Once the mean social group size surpassed a certain number of individuals, the distant ancestors of humans were no longer capable of maintaining a proportionally advantageous number of allies by the bodily act of grooming alone. Producing articulate sounds instead, they acquired an ability to manage their social relations without having to physically attend to one individual at a time. Thus, in Dunbar's account, language, rather than having evolved from abstract, that is, highly conceptual, visual gestures (as suggested in previous research), came into being in order to replace the preconceptual bodily action of touching.

Although gradually overruled by more complex functions, such sensorimotor benefits have by no means vanished from language. For instance, when an expectant mother and father talk about how small their unborn baby is, they usually do not want to communicate information about the size of their offspring. Rather, their primary goal is to emulate in their minds the physical presence of the baby they are so eager to meet, with all the sensorimotor (and affective) processes it entails. This aspect of their discourse holds irrespective of how they converse, whether orally or in writing. However, should their intimate conversation take place in writing, for instance, in a computerized chat interface, their minds may at times (i.e., for fractions of a second) refocus on yet another form of presence—the presence of the partner's absent voice. My suggestion here is that, in the reading of literary narratives, the sensorimotor and, in a sense, primordial benefits of language have not only been exceptionally well preserved, but their workings actually precede the reader's mental construction of the storytelling scenario itself.

Phenomenal Presence in Theory: Verbal versus Direct

As hinted at by the above example of mundane linguistic behavior, phenomenal presence in reading is split into two elementary forms. One, hereafter to be called *verbal presence*, pertains to the written *word* as vicariously voiced in the mind of the reader by an imaginary speaker. The other, hereafter to be called *direct presence*, pertains to phenomena (bodies, forces) of the *world(s)* the imaginary speaker's words refer to—worlds emulated in the mind of the reader. The former kind of presence concerns chiefly the sense of hearing and has not been systematically treated within the realms of narrative theory, where the term *voice* is used as a metaphor, without phenomenal implications (see, e.g., Aczel 1998). The latter mode of presence, in the scant theoretical corpus hitherto produced on the topic, has been explicitly linked mainly to the senses of sight and hearing, with some cursory acknowledgment of the other exteroceptive senses (smell, touch, and taste).

The reader may alternate between the two forms of presence in the course of a reading session or read a single narrative passage twice, inclining first toward one and then toward the other. More often than not, the stylistic tuning of the text will make the decisions for the reader, prompting in each instant the most aesthetically rewarding strategy of processing. Whereas flashes of mute visual imagery with narratorial voice-over may occur in longer pauses between clauses, sentences, paragraphs, and so forth (i.e., offline), in the ongoing (online) process of reading as such there will probably be a significant degree of instantaneous trade-off between verbal and direct presence. That is, on the level of conscious or near-conscious experience, one of the forms will always remain backgrounded unless the reader possesses exceptional attentional skills.[1] Needless to say, any visualization of a narrative passage *qua* utterance, consisting of a visual image of the speaker rather than that of the contents of the speaker's utterance, remains unaffected by the attentional trade-off between verbal and direct presence. On the contrary, in the kind of mundane readerly/writerly situation mentioned in the previous section, verbal presence beyond audition is highly probable due to mutual familiarity. In the reading of literary narrative, dialogue and embedded narration may be especially well suited for prompting instances of such a multimodal variety of verbal presence, making the reader visualize the speaker and the situation in which the speaker's words are being uttered.

Subvocalization (i.e., the matching of sounds to signs in silent reading), which is constitutive of verbal presence, may occur irrespective of the inferred identity or ontological status of the imaginary voice—be it the author, an omniscient narrator, a marginal character, a free-floating consciousness, or an empty deictic center, whatever narratological concept is applicable. No textual markers of overt vocalization are necessary. Explicit signs of a passage representing verbalized thought as opposed to speech should not preclude verbal presence, since research suggests that some form of subvocalizing may be inherent to silent reading (for a review, see Abramson and Goldinger 1997). As for the psychophysiological substrates feeding into verbal presence, more specifically, similarities of format have been found between actual speech and its *acoustic representation* (also known as *auditory imagery*). For instance, behavioral experiments conducted by cognitive psychologists Marianne Abramson and Stephen D. Goldinger with readers of English have shown that the phonetic length of words substantively affects the time required for processing. These findings suggest that the acoustic foundations of silent reading literally consist of an *inner speech* of sorts, rather than of an abstract phonological code (see also Ehrich 2006).

Given that inner speech is proposed to be intrinsic (to some extent) to silent reading in general, verbal presence as used here refers in particular to those instances in which inner speech is driven toward the threshold of the reader's consciousness, especially if tinted by individual voicing that is different than the reader's own. Arguably, such instances occur more frequently in literary rather than nonliterary reading. Among possible facilitating conditions, the following seem most self-evident: direct discourse, compelling rhythm, and perceived realism of speech.

Unlike verbal presence, direct presence, or theoretical notions closely related to direct presence, have had some outspoken advocates throughout the history of modern narrative theory, such as Percy Lubbock, Marie-Laure Ryan, and Thor Grünbaum. Lubbock handles the matter of presence in what has remained the standard way: "The art of fiction does not begin until the novelist thinks of his story as a matter to be *shown*, to be so exhibited that it will tell itself" (1921, 62); "His object is to place the scene before us, so that we may take it in like a picture gradually unrolled or a drama enacted" (65).[2] The reader is assumed to vicariously observe the imaginary world of the story from the position of a passive and detached beholder. Lubbock does not provide much detail about which textual devices may prompt the effect or how it is psychophysiologically or experientially structured. By implication, the addressed sensorimotor modalities amount to sight and hearing.

As part of her treatise on narrative immersion,[3] Marie-Laure Ryan theorizes direct presence under the label of *spatiotemporal immersion* (2001, 130–39). In contrast to Lubbock, she rids spatiotemporal immersion of the sensorimotor detachment entailed by the age-old metaphor of theatrical spectatorship. Instead, she refers to ways of "transporting the reader onto the scene" (130). Ryan provides specific suggestions as to how spatiotemporal immersion may be cued by the text, although she does not offer an account of its psychophysiological or experiential foundations. What is symptomatic about the prompting mechanisms Ryan enumerates—namely, adverbial deictic shift, present tense, and second-person narration—is that they all consist of subtle devices of narrative construction. Meanwhile, the phenomenal substance proper of direct presence, that which is *given* in language rather than constructed, remains unexplored. As will soon become evident, I have chosen to proceed differently, giving theoretical priority to narrative content in a rather trivial sense.

In Ryan's study, the addressed sensorimotor modalities do not receive systematic treatment. However, Ryan's remarks on the matter, along with her choice of literary examples, suggest a sensorimotor array limited to the exteroceptive senses of sight, hearing, smell, touch, and taste. Despite her use of the transportation metaphor, any notion of direct presence extractable from her theory is basically reducible to a presence *of the imaginary world* alone in front of (or at best around) a mentally attached but nevertheless physically *passive* beholder. Here lies another difference between

Ryan's theory of spatiotemporal immersion, Lubbock's idea of "showing," and similar concepts hitherto proposed, on the one hand, and my theory of direct presence on the other. In my definition, direct presence is a fully reciprocal phenomenon—the reader becomes as physically present in the imaginary world as the imaginary world becomes physically present in front of and around the reader. The difference is not merely one of nomenclature. Rather, it stems from a broader redefinition of what the reader's mind is and how the sensorimotor benefits of language accrue to the reading process.

Direct Presence of the Reader in the World: Psychophysiological, Experiential, and Text-Linguistic Underpinnings

Those narrative theorists who in some way or another address direct presence have a propensity to illustrate their points using literary excerpts taken either from Gustave Flaubert's 1857 novel *Madame Bovary* (e.g., Lubbock, Ryan) or from Alain Robbe-Grillet's 1957 novel *Jealousy* (*La Jalousie*) (e.g., Ryan, Grünbaum)—two French novels famous for being steeped in sensorimotor detail. I will follow these theorists' choice of literary examples, using a passage from each of the texts in order to highlight the distinctiveness of my own approach.

(1) Flaubert
They had been sitting over the meal for two hours and a half. Artémise the serving-girl, listlessly dragging her carpet slippers over the flagstones, brought in the plates one at a time, failed to remember or understand anything she was told, and kept leaving the billiard-room door open so that the latch banged against the wall.

While he talked, *Léon had unconsciously placed his foot on the bar of Madame Bovary's chair.* She was wearing a little blue silk neckerchief which kept her goffered cambric collar as stiff as a ruff, and when she moved her head, the lower part of her face sank down into the linen or rose gracefully out of it. (Flaubert 1995, 97; emphasis added)

(2) Robbe-Grillet
In broad daylight, the contrast of the two shades of gray—that of the naked wood and that, somewhat lighter, of the remaining paint—

creates complicated figures with angular, almost serrated outlines. On the top of the handrail, there are only scattered, protruding islands formed by the last vestiges of paint. On the balusters, though, it is the unpainted areas, much smaller and generally located toward the middle of the uprights, which constitute the spots, here incised, where the fingers recognize the vertical grain of the wood. At the edge of the patches, new scales of the paint are easy *to chip off; it is enough to slip a fingernail beneath the projecting edge and pry it up by bending the first joint of the finger*; the resistance is scarcely perceptible. (Robbe-Grillet 1965, 48; emphasis added)

In a recent contribution to presence-related narratology, Thor Grünbaum (2007) argues that, due to the reader's tacit knowledge of their biomechanics, renditions of simple bodily actions—as in Flaubert's "Léon had unconsciously placed his foot . . ."—are visualized in reading with exceptional ease. Overall, Grünbaum's thesis is meant to dispute the imprecise yet common assumption that perceived phenomenal vividness is directly proportional to the degree of static visual detail provided in a description (see, e.g., Nünning 2007, 113). I agree with Grünbaum when it comes to the importance of bodily actions for direct presence. However, I suggest that the reader's knowledge of these actions is so deeply grounded in the reader's body that, rather than being visualized from the viewpoint of a passive third-person observer, the actions in question are emulated from an *enactive*, first-person perspective.

Direct Presence beyond Exteroception

I assume that the reader experiences, mostly—but not always—without noticing, the phenomenon of *motor resonance* (also known as *motor simulation*).[4] Motor resonance refers to the actual covert movement that has been unequivocally proven to occur when isolated literal (i.e., non-metaphorical, non-idiomatic) sentences referring to bodily movement are processed (Fischer and Zwaan 2008). Neuroimaging evidence produced by the research teams of Lisa Aziz-Zadeh (Aziz-Zadeh et al. 2006) and Ana Raposo (Raposo et al. 2009) implies that, when reading clauses such as Robbe-Grillet's "pry it up by bending the first joint of the finger," the motor and pre-motor areas of the reader's cortex become somatotopically activated, emulating finger movement specifically. As for behavioral evidence, when readers in experiments conducted by Rolf A. Zwaan and others were asked to perform a motor task in order to make their way through a sentence referring to bodily movement, their reading and motor performances interfered with one another (Zwaan et al. 2010; Taylor and Zwaan 2008; Taylor et al. 2008). Convergent results have been obtained from a first neuroimaging study, carried out by Nicole Speer and colleagues, in which the experimental stimuli consisted of longer narrative passages (Speer et al. 2009). Importantly, measurements of augmented physiological reactivity (so-called efferent leakage) in guided imagery experiments indicate that language has the capacity to stimulate more extended parts of the motor system than the cortex alone—including muscles and proprioceptive receptors. During action imagery, these experiments have shown increased muscle tension (Cuthbert et al. 1991).

The overarching theories of language to which the above findings have given support are referred to as "grounded," "embodied," or "perceptual," or alternatively as "theories of simulation/resonance" (cf. the enactivist model introduced by Caracciolo in this volume). They are increasingly acknowledged by cognitive scientists worldwide as part of the broader theoretical frameworks of *embodiment, grounded cognition,* and *situated cognition.* The labels are not interchangeable, but all of them signal an effort to falsify the enduring assumption that human mental activity is fully amodal. When applied to direct presence in literary narrative, these theories seem to suggest that readers, by means of their embodied minds, are physically present and engaged in the imaginary world of the story in ways extending beyond exteroception, with *the motor and proprioceptive modes* (the senses of limb and organ position, velocity, effort, acceleration, balance, etc.) just as exposed to vicarious stimulation as the exteroceptive senses.

Motor resonance is intrinsic to language processing in general. However, there are many reasons to assume—as in the case of inner speech and verbal presence—that, in the reading of literary narrative in particular, motor resonance is continuously driven toward the threshold of the reader's consciousness. Based on my own experience, I further suggest that it does not always remain pre-reflective. Literary narratives can elicit a level of sensorimotor activity that is not only amenable to guided self-report but also attracts the attention of the reader. Such instances of literary reading may even provide some of the strongest evidence in favor of a hypothesis currently advocated by physiologists-cum-philosophers such as Vittorio Gallese (2000) and Marc Jeannerod (2006). They contend that motor imagery and actual movement literally form one experiential continuum and that motor imagery is actual movement that merely lacks an overt execution phase.

Transitive Bodily Movement as a Prompter of Multimodal Direct Presence

Since resonance in language processing has also been identified for sensorimotor modalities other than movement (e.g., Zwaan 2004), my focus on the motor mode alone calls for an explanation: I believe that motor resonance is unique in its potential to make the reader feel physically present in the imaginary world. Hypothetically, the wider the range of sensorimotor modalities simultaneously active in the reader's mind while he or she engages with a literary narrative, the more compelling the image of the world(s) presented by that narrative will be. However, imagery does not seem to come to the mind in neatly synchronized multimodal packages. Particularly, the short-lived imagery elicited in the linear act of reading differs substantially from the structure of real-world experience, without the discrete sensorimotor modality tracks necessarily overlapping or fitting into any preconceived model of spatiotemporal order. Given these prerequisites, I suggest that, of all linguistic expressions addressing the senses, references to bodily movement have the best ability to offset the linearity of language. They impose on the reader's imagery a world-like order by way of emulating agency, which automatically entails a first-person perspective. A first-person perspective in turn entails instantaneous sensorimotor unity (encompassing *both* proprio- and exteroception), prompting the most phenomenally replete kind of direct presence achievable.

What lies behind this accentuation of the motor mode, apart from introspection, is a philosophically and scientifically informed view of movement, interaction, and agency as formative of and intrinsic to all actual perception. "The world makes itself available to the perceiver through physical movement and interaction," Alva Noë asserts (2006, 1). Noë is one of the philosophers who have recently made an effort to reconcile the two domains of knowledge in order to advocate the centrality of bodily movement in perception, cognition, experience, and subjectivity. Drawing upon behavioral evidence, Noë argues that vision in the sense of a conscious experience of the size, shape, voluminousness, and distance of an object is always based on the perceiver's previous eye and body movements related to that or a similar object. As for the scientific branch of this broad approach to mind-world interactions, both neuroimaging and behavioral evidence suggest that the mere process of visually attending to an object is partly based on covert preparation of a bodily action to be performed in connection with that object (Rizzolatti and Gallese 1988). Moreover, the processing of images and names of manipulable artifacts has been found to elicit covert motor activity corresponding to fixed patterns of interaction (so-called canonical affordances) with the artifacts in question (Martin 2007; Glover et al. 2004; Borghi 2005).

If the physical world we live in is not truly perceived and experienced unless interacted with via bodily movement, then the reader's sense of having physically entered a tangible world should somehow be connected to narrative renditions of bodily movement.[5] However, unlike Grünbaum, I am not suggesting that all simple bodily actions have an equal potential to tease the reader's sensorimotor imagery. There is a particular reason why the leaning of Léon's foot toward the bar of Madame Bovary's chair is underscored above, whereas the movements of Madame Bovary's head, mentioned just a few clauses later, are not. I suggest that the imaginary world is unlikely to feel tangible and present unless physical stimuli that can be interacted with are mentioned (or strongly implied), that is, unless the furnishing of the imaginary world is reached, grasped, manipulated, leaned against, and so forth. In other words, the most stimulating movements of all should be *transitive movements*. This applies particularly to transitive movements that are *object-directed*, as opposed to self-, person-, or animal-directed. Unlike images and names of man-made artifacts and other inanimate objects, images and names of animate beings have not been found to stimulate covert motor activity. The difference has been explained by the fact that animate beings usually afford a more flexible range of interactions, thus having no canonical affordances in a strong sense of the term (e.g., Borghi 2005, 29).

As indicated, scientists and philosophers alike currently view perception as an auxiliary of action. I suggest that, in the linear process of reading, the relation is often the reverse: the object-directed movement of a literary character—and its first-person, enactive emulation run by the embodied mind of the reader—can, especially under certain conditions to which I will now turn, prompt a vivid multimodal image of the imaginary world that the character's movement is being performed in and upon.

Multimodal Direct Presence: Further Facilitating Conditions

Despite sharing a comparable prominence of what is commonly called description (i.e., a verbal representation of spatial particulars and their phenomenal properties), Flaubert's *Madame Bovary* and Robbe-Grillet's *Jealousy* represent two fundamentally different narrative styles. Given the evidence cited above, the presence-promoting effect of transitive bodily movement should indeed operate, on spontaneous reading, across all kinds of narration, focalization, possible-world ontology, hermeneutic implication, or whatever distinctive features there are to be isolated by narrative theory. However, presence via the emulation of transitive bodily movements may be significantly enhanced by certain conditions and prerequisites (and inhibited by their opposites) pertaining to narrative content and structure. Relevant conditions and prerequisites include the following:

First, the more familiar the transitive bodily movement and object in question are to the reader and the more canonical and semantically sensible the movement is in relation to the object, the stronger the multimodal direct presence will be. Of the two literary excerpts quoted above, Flaubert may comply with this prerequisite to a higher degree than Robbe-Grillet.

Second, in order for the reference to transitive bodily movement to elicit multimodal direct presence, it should be comparably *dynamically veracious*. That is, the time the text passage takes to read should be commensurable with the duration of the movement as performed in the real world. Generally speaking, dynamic veracity may be more readily perceived as applying to punctual ("had unconsciously placed his foot") rather than iterative ("brought in the plates one at a time") verbal constructions. This condition is partially met in both literary excerpts (see also Zwaan 2008).

Third, in order for the reference to transitive bodily movement to elicit multimodal direct presence, the movement in question should be rendered as a *volitional* movement. Volitional movements entail particular attentional focus on the environment interacted with (Allport 1987), which is absent from reflexive or otherwise unintended movements. This condition is strictly met in Robbe-Grillet.

Fourth, in order for the reference to transitive bodily movement to induce multimodal direct presence, the bodily movement referred to and its sensory outcome must not be excessively conceptualized, that is, defamiliarized, in relation to real-world experience. Otherwise, the reader may refocus on the linguistic medium instead and switch to a form of verbal presence. A comparably unmarked proportion between, on the one hand, the exteroceptive aspects of the narrated event, and, on the other hand, its proprioceptive and motor aspects—which largely escape natural verbalization—must be sustained. This condition is met in various degrees in both literary excerpts.

Fifth, any detailed exteroceptive description of the object interacted with should ideally *precede* and not follow the reference to bodily movement, so that the movement itself can tie together the various sensorimotor modalities involved into a transitory unitary perspective. This condition is met in the Robbe-Grillet passage.

Sixth, in order for the reference to transitive bodily movement to have any of the instantaneous impact outlined above, it must appear as comparably *marked* in relation to the narrative passage immediately preceding it. In a narrative passage consisting mainly or even solely of references to bodily movement, the motor mode may become subject to phenomenal habituation (and, on the conceptual side, a means of pronounced aesthetic foregrounding), and its capacity to prompt multimodal direct presence may therefore decrease. The markedness condition is met to varying degrees in both literary excerpts.

Seventh, in order for the literary narrative as a whole to retain a *stable level* of direct presence, references to bodily movement must be evenly distributed throughout but moderately dosed. This condition is not met in either Flaubert's *Madame Bovary* or Robbe-Grillet's *Jealousy*. Both abound in detailed visual descriptions that press against the limits of conceptualization, while passages like those quoted above are relatively sparse. One example of a literary narrative complying with this condition is, to credit yet another French novel, Jean-Philippe Toussaint's 1988 text *Camera* (*L' Appareil-photo*). The text of *Camera* is continuously dynamized—and its reader and imaginary world made strongly present to each other—by means of explicit references to transitive bodily movement:

(3) Toussaint
As she was really cold, she got up, a coat covering her shoulders, and, *pushing aside [du bras = with her arm] a chintz curtain*, left to

look for another portable heater in a tiny dark storage room, where, in a shower no longer used, next to an azure anorak dangling on a hanger, were stacked several piles of papers. She had asked me to follow her to help her look and, while *I pensively flipped through some old registration applications* in the darkness, *she moved a poorly closed box* spilling over with orange parking cones and *found [attira vers nous = pulled toward us] a small propane tank for cooking* topped with a little radiator with a grilled front. (Toussaint 2008, 22; emphasis added)[6]

The effects listed in this and previous sections readily combine with the effects of other presence-promoting elements of narrative structure, such as those proposed by Ryan. For example, the presence-promoting potential of the above passage may increase if the following is added: "*Come* and help. She *shows* me where to hold it. So *here* I was, pulling a propane heater out of a box." The reader's multimodal imagery, stimulated as it is by the basic contents (the action of lifting an object of a certain weight, form, and size) alone, may then be further enhanced by particular elements of construction, namely, by an (admittedly awkward) admixture of adverbial deictic shift ("here"), present tense ("shows"), and second-person address ("come"). These presence-promoting devices, in turn, might lose some or most of their impact if they were employed to represent a content less familiar to the reader than a series of mundane bodily movements. To the extent that reading is an embodied activity, it is thus reasonable to strive for a theory of direct presence in which content is treated before construction. Indeed, as far as linguistic representations of phenomena (objects and forces) are concerned, the experimental evidence reviewed above seems to suggest that few sorts of words are as widely and deeply familiar to readers as are laconic references to transitive bodily movement.

Phenomenal Presence in Evidence:
Observational and Historical Issues

The neuroimaging and behavioral setups employed by researchers investigating inner speech or sensorimotor resonance are based on very limited sets of textual stimuli. Technical constraints do not allow the use of larger segments of complex literary discourse, not to speak of the paradigms' limitations when it comes to accounting for phenomenal presence *qua* experience, reflective or pre-reflective. However, experimental methods of the kind used in guided imagery tasks may be applicable in localizing direct presence, which may prove to entail a kind of efferent leakage (i.e., augmented physiological reactivity, such as increased muscle tension). As for the textual stimuli used to explore aspects of presence, researchers will need to factor in two problematic—and language-specific—contrasts: between explicit and inferred presence-promoting cues, on the one hand, and between encoded and emergent (i.e., untraceable to the actual wording of the text) sensorimotor imagery, on the other hand. Experiments mapping the distribution and intensity of verbal rather than direct presence may be even more difficult to design, since auditory imagery does not "leak." While it is possible to observe subvocalization via measurements of increased activity in the silent reader's vocal musculature, voices in the reader's mind cannot be directly recorded.

Whenever subjective experience is to be laid bare, introspection is indispensable. Hence, introspective self-report, whether in the form of spontaneous verbal protocol or questionnaire data, will be a necessary complement to any psychophysiological or behavioral setup. Some of the paradigms elaborated by empirical narrative studies provide solid methodological foundations to build on in designing such experiments. They also hew closer to veridical reading situations, as compared to the experiments of traditional cognitive psychology. For instance, the framework of psychonarratology proposed by Marisa Bortolussi and Peter Dixon (2003) allows us to trace meaningful variation in readers' responses to discrete textual cues. In Bortolussi and Dixon's experiments, competing versions of a narrative text are produced, and readers' accounts of their experience are then interpreted in relation to the feature that has been manipulated. But given the preconceptual character of phenomenal presence, it may be difficult to determine how much of the verbalized readerly experience really is elicited in the course of reading (online) and how much of it arises during the process of retrieval (offline) used to fill out the questionnaire. In any case, no paradigm will fully eliminate the risk of an experimenter demand effect, and any paradigm will end up defining correlations rather than causalities.

What may perhaps seem even more pressing from the viewpoint of theoretical narrative studies are the caveats made necessary by the possible historical variability of readers' responses across different epochs.

Neither cognitive science nor empirical studies of literary response can do anything about the fact that they are limited to samples of contemporary readership. If the psychophysiological substrates of reading have been found to vary synchronically across today's cultures (Saenger 2000, 1–6), then it is more than likely that they have also been changing diachronically within the broadly conceived Western modernity (say, post-Gutenberg European and American culture) that sets the norms and boundaries of most narrative theory. We cannot produce experimental evidence of how silent reading was structured on a psychophysiological level in the past. What we can do is speculate about how it was experienced by means of deduction from the antecedents of narrative theory such as ancient rhetoric, from historians' accounts of reading practices, and from the evolution of literary narrative as such. The three perspectives seem to converge.

In rhetoric, poetics, and other writings prefiguring narrative theory, as well as in historical scholarship dealing with the practices of reading, references to the preconceptual benefits of reading in general—and phenomenal presence in particular—are rare. Lubbock's figure of speech comparing the creative process to putting events before one's eyes dates back to pre-Aristotelian antiquity (Halliwell 2002, 20). However, a systematic account of how that process is meant to affect reception was not put forward. Rather, as far as explicit mentions of the discrete sensorimotor modalities are concerned, aural qualities enhancing verbal presence seem clearly to prevail, starting with Aristotle's (1995, 123) comments on how Homer evokes characters' voices and continuing throughout medieval and early modern accounts of reading, whether out loud or silently, as a largely aural experience (Ong 2002, 119). Although the quality of poetic *vividness* (*enargeia*), most famously addressed by Demetrius (1995, 473–79) and occasionally invoked in post-medieval rhetorical writing (see, e.g., Alexander 2010), was commonly understood to entail a readerly vision of sorts, it is unclear whether the term was ever used to denote direct presence in my sense, or even in the sense of Lubbock's showing (i.e., divorced from conceptual thought). Apart from one single reference to the visual, Demetrius himself seems to present vividness as a matter of vicarious hearing pertaining mainly to verbal presence and of the reader's affect and higher judgment. In sum, mentions of sensorimotor processes relevant for direct presence seem to be relatively sparse in older theoretical writings, and it is unlikely that they would be able to capture what the experience of direct presence is like today.

To turn to the history of reading practices, cultural theoretician Walter J. Ong (2002, 155–57) asserts that literary narrative did not emancipate itself from classical, orality-driven rhetoric until as late as the 1800s. In accordance with his assertion, contemporary historians of reading suggest that the engrossed reader of the sentimental era still engaged in narrative texts as if they were instances of codified oral (and, one may thus assume, largely aural) narration, while seeking imaginary friendship with the author or protagonist (see Wittmann 1999, 295–97). This sort of reading strategy seems largely to favor verbal presence over direct presence. Furthermore, when embodied reader response was theorized by aestheticians and physiological literary critics Edward Bain, Grant Allen, and others working in the latter half of the nineteenth century (see Dames 2007, 25–69), these authors did not define readerly embodiment (such as muscular tension or neural excitation) in ways that would account for the sensorimotor benefits entailed by direct presence. Rather, presence was assumed to result from rhythm of speech, speed of narration, and other characteristics of the narrative *qua* verbal utterance—yet another fact pointing up how verbal presence constituted the standard of sensorimotor readerly experience.

Finally, clues about readers' experiences of presence can be gleaned from the evolution of literary narrative itself. Since any generalizations regarding the history of (post-Gutenberg, Western) literary style would require rigorous corpus-based cross-linguistic analyses, the following observations relate to the limited yet widely influential canon of the French novel. In this connection, it is interesting to note that it was not until the nineteenth century that renditions of transitive bodily movement began to occur on a more regular basis. They seem to have made a sudden appearance as part of an overall shift of content, a movement away from the sublime and universal toward the particular, quotidian, and experiential. This shift, which can be traced back to the scenic craftsmanship of Flaubert, must have had consequences for readerly expectations regarding the two forms of phenomenal presence and the distribution of attention between them. More specifically, the shift toward the quotidian and the experiential may have relocated the readers' focus from verbal presence to direct presence. Moreover, there are many reasons to believe that this same shift had gradually yet irreversibly modified the practice of literary reading in general, including the reading of pre-1800 narrative, making it an ever more "directly" phenomenal and multimodally embodied activity.

On the level of narrative structure, the gradual exploitation of sensorimotor experience was paralleled by a phasing out of the omniscient narrator (who had still routinely addressed the "dear reader" at the beginning of the nineteenth century) and of other oral residues such as a linear, moral-driven plot. In other words, it was accompanied by a significant loss in overt prompters of verbal presence, and hence by a loss in similarity to communication narrowly defined. This was a matter of necessity rather than coincidence: in a successful rendering of sensorimotor experience proper, there is no point or conceptual knowledge to be communicated, solely the seemingly unmediated (at least for fractions of a second) phenomenal benefits entailed by direct presence. As long as oral language respects the rules of higher-level conceptual communication—the rules that are flouted by the parents-to-be mentioned in the beginning of this chapter—sensorimotor detail as provided for instance in the above excerpt from Toussaint's *Camera* is rarely heard.

Last but not least, the period in which such sensorimotor detail surfaced in the French novel roughly coincides with the moment in the history of reading when literary narratives, too, ceased to be commonly heard. Despite the fact that mentions of silent reading date back to the times of Saint Augustine and that silent reading was widespread in certain contexts by the end of the Middle Ages (Saenger 2000), reading aloud was presumably the mode in which literary narratives were received by a substantial part of the European public until as late as the nineteenth century (Lyons 1999, 342–44). Throughout the 1800s there is abundant evidence that authors explicitly envisioned their novels to be read aloud and that they even read their own prose aloud when writing. Around 1900, collective practices of reading aloud (in forms considered largely uncustomary only a few decades later) still occurred on a regular basis (Ong 2002, 146; 154). The subsequent abrupt disappearance of reading aloud may have further reinforced the shift in phenomenal sensitivity imposed on the reader's mind by the novelties of literary style. It may have made vicarious voicing less readily accessible.

Assuming that the hypothesis of an attentional trade-off between verbal and direct presence is correct, preliminary evidence thus suggests that direct presence is not only historically determined but also a fairly recent phenomenon. This is true at least for direct presence in its stronger forms, which make the reader feel physically present in the imaginary world of the story. In this case, the notion of presence, also known as "being there," is used as in interactive media studies (see, e.g., Schubert et al. 2001). Ironically, although the experience of direct presence coincides with the rise of modern narrative theory itself, both theoretical and empirical studies continue to disregard it, along with its more senior but equally disregarded verbal counterpart. This chapter is a first step toward recognizing—and analyzing—the role of these modes of phenomenal presence in the activity of reading.

Notes

1. It has also been suggested that the two processes are mutually constraining on cognitive levels prior to consciousness (see Fischer and Zwaan 2008, 837).
2. As is apparent from Lubbock's appeal to drama, the concept of *showing* crosscuts the distinction between direct presence and verbal presence (in its multimodal variety).
3. *Immersion*, an umbrella term encompassing—apart from what I define as presence—a variety of effects, such as suspense, affective arousal and other emotional responses, cognitive flow, or susceptibility to belief change, is sometimes used to denote direct presence. A similarly broad concept often conflated with direct presence is *transportation* (see, e.g., Gerrig 1998).
4. The arguments presented in the following three subsections are further elaborated elsewhere (Kuzmičová 2012).
5. Experimental studies have shown that spatial modeling in reading (i.e., the deliberate retrieval of spatial information from memory) is also facilitated when the reader expects a story character to move (Rapp et al. 2006). Spatial modeling should not be confused with direct presence.
6. My corrections appear in brackets and are based on the French original (Toussaint 1988, 25).

References

Abramson, Marianne, and Stephen D. Goldinger. 1997. "What the Reader's Eye Tells the Mind's Ear: Silent Reading Activates Inner Speech." *Perception and Psychophysics* 59 (7): 1059–68.
Aczel, Richard. 1998. "Hearing Voices in Narrative Texts." *New Literary History* 29 (3): 467–500.

Alexander, Gavin. 2010. "Seeing through Words in Theories of Poetry: Sidney, Puttenham, Lodge." In *A Companion to Tudor Literature*, ed. Kent Cartwright, 350–63. Chichester: Wiley-Blackwell.

Allport, Allan. 1987. "Selection for Action: Some Behavioral and Neurophysiological Considerations of Attention and Action." In *Perspectives on Perception and Action*, ed. Herbert Heuer and Andries F. Sanders, 395–419. Hillsdale: Erlbaum.

Aristotle. 1995. "Poetics." In *Aristotle: Poetics; Longinus: On the Sublime; Demetrius: On Style*, trans. Stephen Halliwell, W. H. Fyfe, and Doreen C. Innes, 1–141. Cambridge: Harvard University Press.

Aziz-Zadeh, Lisa, Stephen M. Wilson, Giacomo Rizzolatti, and Marco Iacoboni. 2006. "Congruent Embodied Representations for Visually Presented Actions and Linguistic Phrases Describing Actions." *Current Biology* 16 (18): 1818–23.

Borghi, Anna M. 2005. "Object Concepts and Action." In *Grounding Cognition: The Role of Perception and Action in Memory, Language and Thinking*, ed. Diane Pecher and Rolf A. Zwaan, 8–34. Cambridge: Cambridge University Press.

Bortolussi, Marisa, and Peter Dixon. 2003. *Psychonarratology: Foundations for the Empirical Study of Literary Response*. Cambridge: Cambridge University Press.

Cuthbert, Bruce N., Scott R. Vrana, and Margaret M. Bradley. 1991. "Imagery: Function and Physiology." *Advances in Psychophysiology: A Research Annual* 4:1–42.

Dames, Nicholas. 2007. *The Physiology of the Novel: Reading, Neural Science, and the Form of Victorian Fiction*. New York: Oxford University Press.

Demetrius. 1995. "On Style." In *Aristotle: Poetics; Longinus: On the Sublime; Demetrius: On Style*, trans. Stephen Halliwell, W. H. Fyfe, and Doreen C. Innes, 309–525. Cambridge: Harvard University Press.

Dunbar, Robin I. M. 2003. "The Social Brain: Mind, Language, and Society in Evolutionary Perspective." *Annual Review of Anthropology* 32 (1): 163–81.

Ehrich, John F. 2006. "Vygotskian Inner Speech and the Reading Process." *Australian Journal of Educational & Developmental Psychology* 6:12–25.

Fischer, Martin H., and Rolf A. Zwaan. 2008. "Embodied Language: A Review of the Role of the Motor System in Language Comprehension." *Quarterly Journal of Experimental Psychology* 61 (6): 825–50.

Flaubert, Gustave. 1995. *Madame Bovary*. Trans. Allan Russell. London: Penguin Popular Classics.

Fludernik, Monika. 1996. *Towards a "Natural" Narratology*. London: Routledge.

Gallese, Vittorio. 2000. "The Inner Sense of Action." *Journal of Consciousness Studies* 7 (10): 23–40.

Gerrig, Richard J. 1998. *Experiencing Narrative Worlds: On the Psychological Activities of Reading*. Boulder: Westview Press.

Glover, Scott, David A. Rosenbaum, Jeremy Graham, and Peter Dixon. 2004. "Grasping the Meaning of Words." *Experimental Brain Research* 154 (1): 103–8.

Grünbaum, Thor. 2007. "Action between Plot and Discourse." *Semiotica* 165 (1): 295–314.

Halliwell, Stephen. 2002. *The Aesthetics of Mimesis: Ancient Texts and Modern Problems*. Princeton: Princeton University Press.

Herman, David. 2009. *Basic Elements of Narrative*. Chichester: Wiley-Blackwell.

Jeannerod, Marc. 2006. *Motor Cognition: What Actions Tell the Self*. New York: Oxford University Press.

Kuzmičová, Anežka. 2012. "Presence in the Reading of Literary Narrative: A Case for Motor Enactment." *Semiotica* 189 (1/4): 23–48.

Lubbock, Percy. 1921. *The Craft of Fiction*. London: Jonathan Cape.

Lyons, Martyn. 1999. "New Readers in the Nineteenth Century: Women, Children, Workers." In *A History of Reading in the West*, ed. Guglielmo Cavallo and Roger Chartier, trans. Lydia G. Cochrane, 313–44. Cambridge: Polity Press.

Martin, Alex. 2007. "The Representation of Object Concepts in the Brain." *Annual Review of Psychology* 58:25–45.

Noë, Alva. 2006. *Action in Perception*. Cambridge: MIT Press.

Nünning, Ansgar. 2007. "Towards a Typology, Poetics and History of Description in Fiction." In *Description in Literature and Other Media*, ed. Werner Wolf and Walter Bernhart, 91–128. Amsterdam: Rodopi.

Ong, Walter J. 2002. *Orality and Literacy*. London: Routledge.

Raposo, Ana, Helen E. Moss, Emmanuel A. Stamatakis, and Lorraine K. Tyler. 2009. "Modulation of Motor and Premotor Cortices by Actions, Action Words and Action Sentences." *Neuropsychologia* 47 (2): 388–96.

Rapp, David N., Jessica L. Klug, and Holly A. Taylor. 2006. "Character Movement and the Representation of Space during Narrative Comprehension." *Memory and Cognition* 34 (6): 1206–20.

Rizzolatti, Giacomo, and Vittorio Gallese. 1988. "Mechanisms and Theories of Spatial Neglect." *Handbook of Neuropsychology* 1:223–46.

Robbe-Grillet, Alain. 1965. *Jealousy*. In *Two Novels by Robbe-Grillet*, trans. Richard Howard, 33–138. New York: Grove Press.

Ryan, Marie-Laure. 2001. *Narrative as Virtual Reality: Immersion and Interactivity in Literature and Electronic Media*. Baltimore: Johns Hopkins University Press.

Sadoski, Mark, and Allan Paivio. 2001. *Imagery and Text*. Mahwah: Erlbaum.

Saenger, Paul. 2000. *Space between Words: The Origins of Silent Reading*. Stanford: Stanford University Press.

Schubert, Thomas, Frank Biocca, and Holger Regenbrecht. 2001. "The Experience of Presence: Factor Analytic Insights." *Presence: Teleoperators and Virtual Environments* 10 (3): 266–81.

Speer, Nicole K., Jeremy R. Reynolds, Khena M. Swallow, and Jeffrey M. Zacks. 2009. "Reading Stories Activates Neural Representations of Visual and Motor Experiences." *Psychological Science* 20 (8): 989–99.

Taylor, Lawrence J., Shiri Lev-Ari, and Rolf A. Zwaan. 2008. "Inferences about Action Engage Action Systems." *Brain and Language* 107 (1): 62–7.

Taylor, Lawrence J., and Rolf A. Zwaan. 2008. "Motor Resonance and Linguistic Focus." *Quarterly Journal of Experimental Psychology* 61 (6): 896–904.

Toussaint, Jean-Philippe. 1988. *L'appareil-photo*. Paris: Minuit.

———. 2008. *Camera*. Trans. Matthew B. Smith. Champaign: Dalkey Archive Press.

Wittmann, Reinhard. 1999. "Was There a Reading Revolution at the End of the Eighteenth Century?" In *A History of Reading in the West*, ed. Guglielmo Cavallo and Roger Chartier, trans. Lydia G. Cochrane, 284–312. Cambridge: Polity Press.

Zunshine, Lisa. 2006. *Why We Read Fiction: Theory of Mind and the Novel*. Columbus: Ohio State University Press.

Zwaan, Rolf A. 2004. "The Immersed Experiencer: Toward an Embodied Theory of Language Comprehension." *Psychology of Learning and Motivation: Advances in Research and Theory* 44:35–62.

———. 2008. "Time in Language, Situation Models, and Mental Simulations." *Language Learning* 58 (1): 13–26.

Zwaan, Rolf A., Lawrence J. Taylor, and Mirte de Boer. 2010. "Motor Resonance as a Function of Narrative Time: Further Tests of the Linguistic Focus Hypothesis." *Brain and Language* 112 (3): 143–49.

6 Cycles of Narrative Necessity

Suspect Tellers and the Textuality of Fictional Minds

MARIA MÄKELÄ

A narratologist who happens to be mainly interested in literary fiction should not feel impeded by the cognitive turn and the ensuing erosion of disciplinary borders. On the contrary: now that we acknowledge the presence of narrative *everywhere* and embrace every social situation as a lesson in *mind reading*, it seems that reading literary narratives has come to be considered a privileged form of intercognitive activity. The study of fictional minds has been given a boost by theorists such as Monika Fludernik, David Herman, Uri Margolin, Alan Palmer, and Lisa Zunshine, who have blended literary analysis with "real-mind discourses" (see Palmer 2004, 4), and with most persuasive results. But beyond "drawing on tools from the cognitive sciences to develop new descriptive and explanatory techniques for the study of fictional mental functioning," literary narratologists are in a position to suggest how "more careful scrutiny of fictional minds can help illuminate the 'real minds' . . . on which specialists in the cognitive sciences have traditionally focused" (Herman 2003, 23). The literary minds of Richardson's Clarissa, Austen's Emma, and Nabokov's Humbert Humbert have thus ended up not just as subjects of cognitive-psychological vivisection but also as *illustrations* of actual human cognition as well as *tools* for understanding the mental processes of real minds. And why not? One of the goals of literary experimentation has been—at least from the early modernist to the late modernist era—to depict the mind "as it is," be it verbalized, streaming, intersubjective, unconscious, or fragmented.

Yet the recent use of ideas from the cognitive sciences to naturalize fictional minds departs from the emphases of early narratologists such as Käte Hamburger and Dorrit Cohn: for these scholars, the representation of fictional consciousness is precisely what distinguishes novelistic discourse from other kinds of discourse, narrative fiction being the only representational mode to grant us a look inside other people's heads (see Hamburger 1993, 81–89; Cohn 1978, 5–7, and 1999, 117–23). Alan Palmer's pathbreaking study on fictional minds critiques Cohnian notions of consciousness representation, claiming that structuralist analysis focused exclusively on the verbal aspects of fictional mind construction—to the exclusion of other, nonverbal aspects (Palmer 2004, 9–12). Making acquaintance with fictional characters may indeed bear more resemblance to a real-life cocktail party where everybody tries to figure out other people than to meticulous linguistic analysis where alleged thought-segments are classified as direct, indirect, and free indirect discourse. Palmer succeeds in broadening the notion of fictional minds from verbal to nonverbal mental functioning, and as such his theoretical arguments are more illuminating than reductive. Yet, despite the benefits of these new approaches to studying fictional minds, for me George Butte's response to Paul John Eakin's (2004) cognitive-psychological analysis of autobiographical writing still resonates: "Would improved knowledge of, say, the superior colliculus's communication with the thalamus . . . eventually clarify the functioning of free indirect discourse?" (Butte 2005, 300).

This chapter aims at a constructive critique of those "cognitivist"[1] developments in literary theory that—to my mind—may lead to reductive views on fictional consciousness representation. My concern is twofold. First, I believe that by reducing fictional minds to exempla of actual human cognition we miss the essential dynamics between verbal art and real-life experientiality. Second, if we assume that reading literary fiction requires the use of *exactly the same cognitive frames* we use when coping with our everyday lives, we will suffer serious literary-theoretical losses. At times the argumentation in this chapter may raise suspicions of a nostalgic plea for formalist notions of narrative art as autonomous and estranging in its relation to the real world and to actual human cognition. Indeed, in the context of the volume at hand, I wish to emphasize the peculiarly textual and constructed nature of *literary experientiality*. One does not necessarily have to embrace Cohn's (1999) somewhat uncompromising distinction between factual and fictional narratives to appreciate her earlier (1978) formulations concerning the unique nature of fictional minds: for Cohn, the same narrative techniques used to achieve the highest degree of psychological *vraisemblance* (such as free indirect discourse) are the most literary or, in a sense I discuss below, the most "unnatural" techniques. As Cohn puts it, "[i]n depicting the inner life, the novelist is truly a fabricator" (1978, 6). Thus the capacity for mimesis of the mind constitutes both the essence and the great paradox of novelistic discourse.

In what follows, I will argue for the distinctiveness of fictional minds by analyzing two literary texts in which making sense of the narrating protagonist's "cognitive mental functioning" (see Palmer 2003; Margolin 2003) presents a pressing interpretive challenge. My aim is not, however, to adduce alien modes of consciousness representation and thereby prove that, in the context of literary fiction, we are indeed dealing with something that is radically different from our own cognitive mental functioning. In other words, my purpose is not to add to the catalogs of types of "unnatural narration" being developed within the emerging field of "unnatural narratology" (see especially Richardson 2006; Abbott 2008; Alber et al. 2010; Alber and Heinze 2011; Hansen et al. 2011). Instead, my two test cases, both of them short stories by Richard Ford from the collection *A Multitude of Sins* (2002), are, at first glance, strikingly unexceptional; and this is precisely the reason for their choice as examples. Both narratives display textual and narrative techniques that are effective in evoking a sense of *both* cognitive familiarity *and* cognitive estrangement. Further, it is the dynamic interplay between naturalization and denaturalization—assimilation and estrangement—that I take to be the hallmark of readers' engagements with fictional minds.

In the collection's opening story, "Privacy," a first-person narrator confesses to having stalked—for a few times—a female neighbor undressing in an opposing window. The story is conveyed to us as the protagonist tries both to confess and to relive his past sensations. However, the narrator only hints at the consequences of his actions and enigmatically refers to these subsequent events as the "first cycle of necessity" in his life. In the other story, "Reunion," we encounter another first-person confessor: the protagonist tells a story of how—as he specifies, "before Christmas last year"—he happened to spot his ex-mistress's husband in the midst of a crowd at Grand Central station. Disturbingly, *both* the narrator *and* the experiencing I try to reconstruct this moment as the climax in a story that would otherwise remain just plain old adultery-turned-ennui.

These stories display narrative situations where the first-person narrators seem to operate within the "natural" frames of narrativization (as defined by Fludernik 1996) and reflect experientiality (Fludernik 1996, 12–13, 28–30; or "qualia," Herman 2007a, 256–57). However, at the same time, these narratives create an effect of *false* or *projected experiential-ity*, *displacement of agency*, and *displacement of narrative focus*, even to the point of questioning the narrators' authority as verisimilar "tellers." Instead of merely activating our theory of mind, these narrators disclose the textual and intentional designs of their minds. In Ford's stories, the illusion of subjective, unmediated experience is constantly undermined by the narrator's need to organize his story into a meaningful, coherent (even artistic) whole—and vice versa. What we end up with are conflict-ing cycles of narrative necessity: Whose hand actually draws the cycle of narrative coherence? Does the hand belong to the experiencing I, the nar-rating I, or the reader?

Ultimately, with these not-quite-naturalizable stories, I wish to ques-tion some of the premises of prototype-driven cognitive narratology, as well as some aspects of its emergent narratological counterforce, unnatu-ral narratology and its pronounced avoidance of the conventional. On the one hand, as cogently demonstrated by leading figures of unnatural nar-ratology (Alber et al. 2010), an interdisciplinary reliance on shared narra-tive schemata—along with the notion of naturally occurring narratives as the default (cf. Herman 2007a, 9; Ryan 2007, 24)—directs us away from the anti-mimetic (see also Mäkelä 2006). On the other hand, I am not convinced by the account of literary realism that the unnatural approach seems to presuppose; according to the argument of Alber et al. (2010), "ordinary realist texts" appear at the same end of the natural-unnatural axis as naturally occurring ("natural") narratives (114). This claim strikes me as a misreading of Fludernik's idea of a natural narratology, since the starting point of her theory is not the plausibility of the events presented in a given narrative (in contrast to the "physically and logically impossible" emphasized in Alber et al. 2010; see also Alber 2009) but instead the real-world anchoring experiential schemata shared by the teller and the reader. The point is made even clearer when we notice that one of the main cases treated by David Herman (see, e.g., 2007b, 6–7) is a *ghost* story, obviously "physically and logically unnatural," yet still evoking natural frames of sto-ry*telling*. At the same time, stories with realistic settings or, for that matter, novels of mainstream classical realism may well present the most unnatu-ral communicative and experiential situations whose thematic import is not affected by conventionalization. In fact, Alber et al. (2010) also point toward this possibility in the conclusion of their essay (131).

At the same time, researchers hailing from the camp of narrative psychology and sociology, instead of settling for the unproblematic prototype model of an integrational, coherence-driven, and firmly subjective narrative, have likewise directed their attention to increasingly problematic stories and narrative agencies (see especially Hydén and Brockmeier 2008; Hyvärinen et al. 2010). Combined with the considerations discussed in my previous paragraph, this work suggests that the distinction between naturally occurring and literary narratives is far from being clear-cut. This complex relationship between the natural and the literary will be one of the starting points of my analysis of Ford's two short stories, which point to the possibility of distinctive literary-textual mechanisms—mechanisms that foreground types of experientiality and narrative design different from those attaching to stories encountered in our social environment. Another point I would like to make through these analyses is that we do not have to resort to avant-garde literature to realize that the potential *unnaturalness*—or the peculiarly *literary* type of cognitive challenge—is always already there in textual representations of consciousness (see also Tammi 2008, 46); what makes it perceivable is the way making sense of fictional minds requires a to-and-fro movement between establishing and transcending natural frames of experience and narrativization.

Troublingly Natural Confessions?

What would be a more mundane narrative act than an intimate confession from one person to another? As Samuli Hägg remarks in his discussion of Fludernik's *Towards a "Natural" Narratology*, the first-person narrative situation, the form most easily graspable in the cognitive frame of "telling," should be the "'home-base' of Natural narrativity" (Hägg 2006, 181), the mode of narration most unlikely to cause cognitive estrangement. As Fludernik's theory of "natural narratology" has it, all storytelling and story processing is based on *experientiality*, "the quasi-mimetic evocation of 'real life experience'" (Fludernik 1996, 12). The narrative situation in the short story "Privacy" should thus be well tuned with our real-life cognitive parameters: it seems we have a troubled man confessing a chain of events and his own reaction to them, which resulted in failures both in his marriage and in his work as a writer. Already the title "Privacy," as well as the opening sentence—"This was at a time when my marriage was still happy"—call for interpretive strategies acquired in everyday oral narrative situations: this is something we could hear in a pub. After a while, the narrator-protagonist breaks off from the iterative description of his habitual married life of earlier days and goes back to the moment when he—for the first time—takes a pair of silver opera glasses from a drawer and yields to his nightly obsession.

> (1) I don't know all that I thought. Undoubtedly I was aroused. Undoubtedly I was thrilled by the secrecy of watching out of the dark. Undoubtedly I loved the very illicitness of it, of my wife sleeping nearby and knowing nothing of what I was doing. It is also possible I even liked the cold as it surrounded me, as complete as the night itself, may even have felt that the sight of the woman—whom I took to be young and lacking caution or discretion—held me somehow, insulated me and made the world stop and be perfectly expressible as two poles connected by my line of vision. I am sure now that all of this had to do with my impending failures. ("Privacy," 5)

The narration evokes the natural frame of retrospection—indicated by gaps in memory that are only to be expected. But, at the same time, we get an uncannily vivid description of the intense coldness and secrecy of the moment. The narrator distances himself by modalizing expressions ("It is also possible I even liked . . . may even have felt . . ."), doubts his memory, and shifts the focus to the moment of narration by alluding to the possibly severe consequences of his peeping activities. We are led to believe that these *consequences* are what prompt the narrator's confession, but we never actually hear about the "failures" he alludes to at the end of the passage.

Using classical narratological terms, we see here a peculiar combination of *dissonant* and *consonant* first-person narration: the narrator is both distancing himself from his earlier experience and reliving it. However, if we look closer at Cohn's original definitions of dissonance and consonance, we find that, in these terms, the narrator also *fails* at both strategies. With all his doubts and inconsistencies, he is *neither* "the enlightened and knowing narrator who elucidates his mental confusions of earlier days" *nor* "a narrator who closely identifies with his past self, betraying no manner of superior knowledge" (Cohn 1978, 143). Can the flash-like, illuminated—"enlightened"—vision be a product of the narrating I's superior interpretive ability? Or is it an impression already gained during the incident, perhaps only suppressed until the moment of recounting? Using Fludernik's cognitive angle, we end up with much the same result: there is some serious overlapping and ambivalence between prototype models of narrative mediacy. The frame of "telling" (somebody recounting what happened) triggered earlier starts to give way to the emerging cognitive frame of "experiencing" (deictic and psychological transition to the narrated past moment; reader's alleged access to "what is it like"). It seems that the passage quoted in (1) offers not one but *two* "models of the human mind at work" (see Margolin 1999, 165)—two cognitive mappings of the same situation—which, moreover, seem to be pulling the rug out from under each other. The narrator's insistence that he does not quite remember what he thought and the use of modalizing expressions build up into an interpretive dilemma: where does the experiential focus lie, in the retrospective act of the narrating I, or in the perceptions of the protagonist's earlier self?

And yet, this is still something we could hear in a pub. Or, depending on how we interpret the "impending failures" the narrator alludes to, perhaps during a police interrogation or a testimony. One of the established narratological reading strategies used to humanize fictional narrators is diagnosing them as unreliable. This strategy may well provide motivation for the dissonances in passage (1) and turn them into either a conscious (rhetorical) or an unconscious (psychological) strategy:[2] "A-ha! He remembers quite a lot, after all!" The thematic context of the narrative may even encourage such a diagnostic reading: the story is the first one in a collection of stories on adultery, thick with psychological undercurrents. However, condemning the narrator for unreliability—either for glossing over his "crime" or for self-denial—is, ultimately, just as unproductive an interpretation as condemning him for adultery. As Peter Brooks argues in his aptly titled work *Troubling Confessions*, both real and fictional confessions are verbal *performatives* that actually *create* the inwardness of the person confessing (Brooks 2000, 2). Passage (1) from "Privacy" could thus be read as a representative example of this process: the inwardness—or experientiality—is created by linguistic means, by a shift from doubtful modality into an illustrated report on the past sensation. In this manner, the narrator actually brings to mind the sorts of false confessions that Brooks discusses in the context of legal history. We may be prompted to ask questions similar to those raised by Brooks: Is the confessor creating his past or present inner states? And furthermore, is it the *language* that creates the criminal mind, retrospectively? Confession is just as much a fabrication, a *performance* (Brooks 2000, 21), as is the consequent "cognitive mental functioning" that we believe shows through this verbal act.

Ford's "Reunion" has the same air of confession, or of a personal reckoning. The story's narrative situation is framed by the narrator's attempt to recount his encounter with the man he has cuckolded, Mack Bolger, but as becomes evident, he has more than this to unload on his audience:

> (2) What went on between Beth Bolger and me is hardly worth the words that would be required to explain it away. At any distance but the close range I saw it from, it was an ordinary adultery. . . . Because it is the truth and serves to complicate Mack Bolger's unlikeable dilemma and to cast him in a more sympathetic light, I will say that at some point he was forced to confront me (and Beth as well) in a hotel room in St. Louis . . . with the result that I got banged around in a minor way. ("Reunion," 66)

The narrators of "Privacy" and "Reunion" both suggest the pertinence of Meir Sternberg's (2005) remarks about the "transmission-mindedness" of narrative agents: their discourse is very much audience-oriented. However, on reading example (1), although we could have been sitting in a pub or in a courtroom listening to an oral narrative, we had, or at least should have, an uncanny feeling of *double or constructed experientiality*. Example (2), for its part, makes even more explicit the connection between addressing an audience and constructing one's confession. The quoted passage reveals the narrator's self-reflexivity not just as a confessor who wants to tell the truth but also as a narrator who wants to cast *a particular kind of light* on his story—and moreover, on his *characters*. Later we learn that the protagonist's obsessive attempts to paint a psychologically "round" portrait of Mack Bolger—which would at the same time serve as a tribute to the deceived man and as an atonement for the betrayal—form one of the main thematic threads of the story. For now, however, suffice it to say that both examples suggest not just transmission-mindedness but *construction-mindedness*.

Projected Experientiality and Displacement of Agency

So far I have pointed out some conversational elements in my test cases that are likely to trigger natural frames of narrativization and mind reading. In the following I try to highlight the nature of literary narrative as a multi-level cognitive performance. Drawing on Fludernik's account of the dominating function of "consciousness" in narrative (Fludernik 1996, 49–50), I highlight one sentence I think holds especially true for narrative fiction: "this consciousness [i.e., the consciousness mediating the narrative] can surface on several levels and in different shapes" (1996, 49). The mediacy brought about by literary minds is different—if not radically different—from the real-world mediating functions of consciousness, since the processes of literary mediation and world-construction are necessarily multilayered. Consequently, it may prove impossible to separate transmission-mindedness from construction-mindedness. My two test cases demonstrate that the literary construction of experience disturbs our attempts to naturalize the minds of the protagonists as either tellers or subjects of experience. Their minds are ultimately private, and yet they reflect the features of literary communication. Thus the distinction in literary fiction between internal and external—or between experiencing, thinking, and speaking—turns out to be problematic.

When the protagonist of "Privacy" finally gets a closer look of the woman he has been peeping at, he finds out that this Chinese woman is surprisingly old.

> (3) When I stopped and looked at her she turned and gazed down the steps at me with an expression I can only think now was indifference mingled with just the smallest recognition of threat. She was old, after all. I might suddenly have felt the urge to harm her, and easily could've. But of course that was not my thought. . . . I said nothing, did not even look at her again. I didn't want her to think my mind contained what it did and also what it did not. ("Privacy," 7)

What sort of mediating consciousnesses are at work in this passage? This is the only instance in the story where the mind of the protagonist interacts with another mind and thus gives evidence of embodied mind reading, an aspect of fictional consciousness representation that has been the focus of recent research (see Zunshine 2006; Butte 2004; Palmer 2004; Mäkelä 2006). It also displays the same overlap among telling, experiencing, and (re)construction as in example (1). We can see how modalities ("Undoubtedly I was aroused," "may even have felt") turn, at the end of the story, into complete negation: the narrator reports what he *did not think.* But do we believe him? If we have a closer look at the sentence "I might suddenly have felt the urge to harm her, and easily could've," we can come up with at least three different interpretations: (1) the possibility of violence crosses the mind of the narrator only at the moment of recounting; or (2) the sentence *does* produce the past sensation of the experiencing I; this possibility is implied when the narrator says he did not want the woman to think what he was or was not thinking; or (3) we can read the sentence as a free indirect discourse-like approximation of the *woman's* thought (*that man may want to harm me and easily could*). This third interpretation, however, loops back into the other two: the narrator-protagonist *projects* his own violent and abusive obsessions into the woman's unnecessary fear.

The passage does not so much give an account of a true encounter with an other—of "deep intersubjectivity" (Butte 2004)—as it displaces the protagonist's own experience. In this connection, note that cognitively oriented studies on the interaction between literary minds are mainly interested in the horizontal relations between "cognizers." Less attention has been paid to vertical symmetries, contradictions, and overlaps in the cognitive mental functioning of characters, narrators, and their audiences. In this exemplary case, the main tension arises not from *social* relations (the real-life-like intersubjective communication on which, for example, Alan Palmer grounds some of his claims about fictional minds) but from the *textual* and *structural* interconnections among cognizers, as well as on their frames for producing and interpreting the narrative. The cognitive trick lies in the fact that in literary representation, telling, experiencing, and the construction of the fictional world and its agents all happen on the same level—that of narrative discourse. We have no 3-D model of embedded consciousnesses, but only a syntactic-linear display from which the reader's mind has to infer the relevant levels of mediation (see figs. 6.1 and 6.2).

Lisa Zunshine makes a very illuminating observation in claiming that narrative fiction tests and teases our mind-reading capacity by providing us with characters whose mental states we must infer from their behavior, or whose intentions we must "track down" from the representation by using our "metarepresentational capacity" (Zunshine 2006). Yet, instead of displaying all the levels of intention involved, like the *New Yorker* cartoon that Zunshine uses as her introductory example ("Of course I care about how you imagined I thought you perceived I wanted you to feel"

I might suddenly have
felt the urge to harm
her, and easily
could've.

Fig. 6.1. A textual representation of cognitive mental functioning. Created by the author.

[2006, 30]), narrative discourse in fiction more often than not *hides* the agencies behind cognitive activity, as suggested by example (3) above. Moreover, the task of "keep[ing] track of who thought, wanted, and felt what and when" (2006, 5) requires that the reader consider the *hierarchical* nature of narrative and thus the vertical relations between fictional agents: On which diegetic level are things perceived, experienced, processed, verbalized, constructed, or reflected? Does the cognitive agency manifest itself on the level of the former, experiencing I, on the level of the extradiegetic telling I, or on the level of the actual reader? And if the cognitive activities situated on different hierarchical levels overlap, what happens to processes of naturalization?

However, even after all the effort I have put into demonstrating how experientiality is defamiliarized in the story of the Peeping Tom and the old Chinese woman, the same pressing question, posed by natural narratology, remains: might we not hear this in a pub? It is one thing to claim that textual representations of intercognitive activity are not congruent with social dynamics between real human minds; it is another thing to prove that a fictional sequence narrated in the first person would be unimaginable as a sequence of conversational storytelling. Thus, to develop a model nuanced enough to capture the interplay between naturalization and defamiliarization in readers' engagement with fictional minds, instead of proposing a dichotomy between everyday minds and the minds created in literary fiction, I suggest the relevance of processes of *foregrounding*—in the sense specified in stylistics research. In other words, even the slightest deviances from cognitive verisimilitude generated by the textuality and narrative determination of fictional minds will inevitably call for reading strategies different from those applied in real-world social navigation.

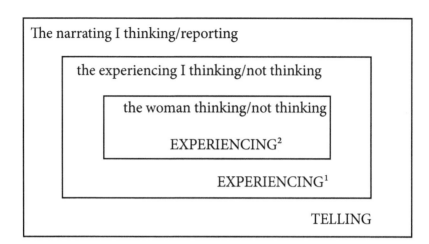

The narrating I thinking/reporting

the experiencing I thinking/not thinking

the woman thinking/not thinking

EXPERIENCING²

EXPERIENCING¹

TELLING

Fig. 6.2. Levels of intention (see Zunshine 2006) and "natural" frames of narrativization (see Fludernik 1996). Created by the author.

As Uri Margolin points out, "[t]hrough its use of nonstandard, often strongly deviant or deficient manners of narration, literature makes us aware *ex negativo* of the default clause, the standard or normal mechanisms and patterns of information processing" (2003, 277). Furthermore, for Margolin, it is precisely a "breakdown or failure" in fictional cognitive mechanisms that supplies the most effective "tool" for understanding the actual human mind (278). This formulation in many ways goes straight to the point, but still it seems that Margolin takes a shortcut from "manners of narration" to "our own mental functioning." Are we to be defamiliarized from conventions of thought or rather from conventions of writing? If we take another look at example (1), we may notice how defamiliarization works both ways. On the one hand, the passage's opening sentence, "I don't know all that I thought," violates not the natural frames of storytelling but the conventions of first-person narrative fiction, where we are likely to confront narrators with an extraordinary memory (see Cohn 1978, 162; Nielsen 2004, 135–36). Who in the world would remember *all* he thought, except for Marcel in *À la recherche du temps perdu*? But on the other hand, when the memory of the narrator starts to come alive miraculously and the experience of the narrator's past self is vivified in front of our eyes, we are situated in the realm of literary frames, inside which immediate access to another consciousness, no matter how distant in time, is something to be expected (see Fludernik 1996, 48). Thus example (1) both instantiates and departs from the conventions of literary narrative, and thereby both transgresses and conforms to conventions associated with everyday storytelling.

Despite Margolin's claims, however, this complex structure of norm-confirmation and norm-violation does not point to the deviant mental functioning of the protagonist. The deviance, rather, seems to be created in and by the narrative discourse: the fictional mind is diegetic and mimetic at the same time; experiencing and telling are *equally foregrounded* in the "flat" discourse of narrative prose. This textual effect is reinforced by passage (3) toward the end of the story, where experiential agency is radically displaced by negation. The thought of violence must have been experienced by the protagonist *at some point*; furthermore, what is the difference between what his mind "contained" and "what it did not"? The hypothesis of the woman's fearful thoughts, created with the help of the protagonist's theory of mind, reveals experientiality behind the words, even if it is of the embedded or of the projected type. In any case, the *discourse* encloses both what the mind contained and what it did not. Even while acknowledging this, we do not have to resort to diagnosing the protagonist as a schizophrenic.

All in all, "Privacy" may ask, via its themes and techniques, the same question we find at the core of cognitive science: what does it mean for a mind to contain something? Some additional questions, focusing on more literary issues, are raised as well: What is the relationship between a mind "containing" and a mind verbalizing, narrativizing, or constructing an experience? What is the relationship between cognitive and literary construction? These are the types of questions that we, as literary theorists, should be asking as well. The story further touches upon one fundamental difference between an experience lived and an experience read: literary experientiality is always, by nature, *projected*. In his confrontation with the old woman the protagonist seems to dwell on the same kind of second-degree experientiality as the reader when entering a fictional character's experiential plane.

The narrator of "Reunion" is more explicit in his construction-mindedness—in his urge to *create* experientiality. Consequently, the problematic relationship between mental and literary construction remains more foregrounded than it does in "Privacy."

(4) I was taken by a sudden and strange impulse—which was to walk straight across through the eddying sea of travelers and speak to him, just as one might speak to anyone you casually knew and had unexpectedly yet not unhappily encountered. And not to impart anything, or set in motion any particular action (to clarify history, for instance, or make amends), but simply to create an event where before there was none. And not an unpleasant event, or a provocative one. Just a dimensionless, unreverberant moment, a contact, unimportant in every other respect. ("Reunion," 67)

This passage displays telling, constructing, and experiencing not only as intermixed but also in a cognitively reverse order: narrative construction precedes the experience. The reader may be further puzzled by the motivation given by the narrator for his urge to create a signifying "reunion" between himself and Mack Bolger: *not* to "set in motion any particular action," and so on. This is, I would say, a very anti-cognitivist view of narrative dynamics: *not* to create sequences in order to approach something in terms of causality, "[b]ut simply to create an event where before there was none." The narrator's activity seems to come closer to that of an author or an auteur rather than that of a conversational storyteller. But, again, we may see the realistic psychological motivation showing through: the guilt-ridden ex-lover escaping into aesthetics and not clarifying what really should be clarified, not making the amends that should, perhaps, be made.

(5) Everything Beth and I had done was gone. All that remained was this—a series of moments in the great train terminal, moments which, in spite of all, seemed correct, sturdy, almost classical in character, as if this later time was all that really mattered whereas the previous, briefly passionate, linked but now-distant moments were merely preliminary. ("Reunion," 71)

When the protagonist, wandering through the grand terminal, really gets his machinery for narrativization going, he seems to substitute his former non-causal conviction for a new kind of causality that allows the narrative weight of adultery to be diminished in favor of the "classical" scene he himself will create. As indicated in example (2), the protagonist's narrative urge extends itself also on the character of Mack Bolger, who—at least for a while—becomes the protagonist's creation: "as though in a peculiar way the man I saw was not Mack Bolger but a good-looking effigy situated precisely there to attract my attention" (66).

In both stories, our own frames for reading are further complicated by the *self-reflexive* construction-mindedness of the narrators. Both are anything but ignorant of the artistic dimensions of framing. In "Privacy," the narrator peeps through a pair of opera glasses like some Nabokovian hero. Furthermore, example (1), with its Kandinsky- or Mondrian-like abstractions of perception and space, foregrounds the narrator's capability for self-conscious framing. On a thematic level, both stories can also be read as narratives of artistic failure. In "Reunion" the protagonist ultimately *fails* in creating a "moment," whereas in "Privacy" the "impending failures" that the narrator alludes to—apart from clearly referring to marital problems—can also be interpreted as his bankruptcy as a writer. The narrators' narrativization of their own experience by projecting and reframing comes close to the work of a fiction writer, but it also weakens their agency both as "centers of consciousness" in the narrated world and as *tellers*.

The feelings of not exactly being there, of not exactly telling or experiencing, may be familiar to most of us. The stories analyzed here reflect such perceptual, emotional, verbal, and narrative displacement, but they appear to achieve those effects *through their textual design*. I now move on to discuss these macro-structural displacements in both stories and their effects on readers' attempts to naturalize the narrators' experiences and their (subsequent?) acts of telling.

After Closure

"Privacy" and "Reunion" seem to evoke a sense of failure, not only in marital, social, or psychological terms but also in terms of the characters' construction of their experiences in narrative terms. In a way, those shortcomings might suggest the kind of "breakdown or failure" in cognitive mechanisms that Margolin regards as essential for cognitive estrangement in literature. Yet these effects cannot be properly analyzed without considering the way the stories are structured *as fictional narratives*. How does the outer cycle define the inner one, the author's textual design comprehend and structure the character-narrator's act of telling?

A sample of three sentences gives us an overall view of "Privacy"; the narrative, like a canopy, is stretched between these three sentences.

(6A) [the opening sentence:] This was at a time when my marriage was still happy. ("Privacy," 3)

(6B) [the approximate middle of the story:] I am sure now that all of this had to do with my impending failures. ("Privacy," 5)

(6C) [the closing sentence:] . . . my life entering, as it was at that moment, its first, long cycle of necessity. ("Privacy," 7)

These are the sentences that really frame the whole narrative—and they all point *outside* its own "cycle." The dominant feeling after reading this story is that you *never actually got the chance to hear it*. The real story concerns the cycles of necessity that follow from the narrated events. It seems that as readers we are victimized by the nature of the fictional universe as a closed system. A police interrogator, or even a random acquaintance in a pub, would not drop the matter here but ask further questions; for the reader, the cycle closes. Something similar happens in "Reunion" when we learn that the hero fails to create a climax in his encounter with Mack Bolger at the railway station.

(7) "Nothing happened today," Mack Bolger said. "Don't go away thinking anything happened here. Between you and me, I mean. *Nothing* happened. I'm sorry I ever met you, that's all. Sorry I ever had to touch you. You make me feel ashamed." ("Reunion," 73; emphasis in the original)

(8) I had, of course, been wrong about the linkage of moments, and about what was preliminary and what was primary. It was a mistake, one I would not make again. None of it was a good thing to have done. Though it is such a large city here, so much larger than, say, St. Louis, I knew I would not see him again. ("Reunion," 74)

In example (7) we read Mack Bolger *absolutely refusing* to play the part that the other man has constructed for him: "Nothing happened today," he says. "Don't go away thinking anything happened here." Example (8) is the closing chapter of the story, showing us how the narrator admits being mistaken about the narrative dynamics and causalities. He also mentions St. Louis in passing—the setting, as the reader may well remember, for the truly significant encounter during which he "got banged around in a minor way" in a hotel room. Finally, it seems he ends up telling us something that he ultimately considers *not worth telling*. But why has the *narrating I* not revised his version of "the linkage of moments"? He is, after all, telling something that, as he says himself, happened "before Christmas last year," and so he has had all that time to revise his account.

So finally, what we end up with are conflicting cycles of narrative necessity—and by those I mean conflicting aspirations toward *narrative closure*, in the sense defined by H. Porter Abbott: as "the satisfaction of expectations and the answering of questions raised over the course of any narrative" (2005, 65–66). In both stories, it is as if some narrative pullback mechanism kept returning the focus from the narrated events to the moment of narration. This process may reinforce our impression of the narrators as confessors with an audience in mind. But, then again, both narrators end up telling something that does not illustrate their own positions. Nor do their stories create narrative causality in any conventional sense. Indeed, these stories seem to be following a kind of *ex negativo* principle, since (1) the experiential impulse for narration seems to come from *outside* the narrated events, and (2) the reader has the same kind of nagging feeling about both narrators: *this is not what they would tell us—or anyone—if they had a choice.*

These narrators are very likely to possess a narrative urge to mold their lived experiences into well-formed stories with a satisfying closure. Yet as we read their stories it seems that they violate precisely such a cognitive-scientific ideal of narrative functioning as a recovery formula. Galen Strawson (2004) has expressed his vehement objection to the "psychological narrativity thesis" (we all process our experiences into a narrative) as well as to the "ethical narrativity thesis" (narrative understanding of life as a prerequisite for self-understanding and morally sound behavior), and the critique, it seems, has hit some nerve in the body of contemporary narrative theory (see responses, e.g., by Phelan 2005 and Battersby 2006).

In a way, my chosen examples hit that same nerve by refusing "cognitive closure"; yet, at the same time, they attest to the role of the "ethical narrativity thesis" in the narrators' own self-narrations—though along with the narrative agency and focus, the "moral" of these stories also seems somehow misplaced. Unable to achieve any sort of atonement, the narrator of "Reunion" contents himself with admitting that "[n]one of it was a good thing to have done." As Pekka Tammi suggests, against the cognitive grain, this kind of questioning of narrative unity is precisely what narrative literature is for: "[Is it] not the capacity of literary fiction—unlike that of standard narratives evoked by theorists—to deal specifically with the *impossibilities*, the paradoxes and problems, of our human efforts to order experience?" (2006, 30; emphasis in the original).

But how conscious are the narrating characters of their narrative efforts, ultimately? Meir Sternberg (2005) has called narratologists' attention to a significant but largely ignored feature of literary representation: the ambivalent status of fictional agents as both mimetic entities and conveyors of representation. Indeed, we can imagine the protagonists of "Privacy" and "Reunion" shuttling on a scale ranging from highly self-conscious and context-conscious tellers to solitary introverts unself-consciously (perhaps unwillingly) exposing their secret or even suppressed inner selves (cf. Sternberg 2005, 33). Theoretically, we would be hard pressed to prove that in some particular segment of narration (e.g., in the sentence "I don't know all that I thought") we would have, either on linguistic, structural, or even "cognitive" grounds, an informed teller-person present, whereas in some other segment of the same narrative (such as in "I might suddenly have felt the urge to harm her, and easily could've") we appear suddenly to lose this teller. But even if it were possible, an analysis of this sort would only flatten the narrative dynamics produced by the "shuttling." It is the multi-level, multi-cognitive structure of literary representation that allows for the frames of "telling" and "experiencing" to prevail at the same time and so renders the shuttling possible. As readers, we get the uncanny feeling of being told and yet ignored by the teller at the same time. This ambivalence is already suggested by the title "Privacy," which can just as well refer to the privacy of a corner table as to the privacy of one's thoughts.

Sternberg's formulations come close to what Henrik Skov Nielsen (2004) has pointed out as *the impersonal voice in first-person narration.* Nielsen opposes the entrenched idea that in a narrative text, first-person reference as well as related deictic elements, expressive markers, and stylistic foregrounding necessarily presuppose a personified narrator-figure. To overcome this narratological *idée reçue*, Nielsen provides a powerful addition to theories of first-person narration by suggesting the possibility of an unnatural, distinctively literary voice "which can talk about the protagonist in the first person" but which "neither belongs to the narrating-I nor to the narrated-I" (2004, 139).

Yet if we reopen the case of the potentially "triple voiced" sentence "I might suddenly have felt the urge to harm her, and easily could've," we could, paradoxically, use Nielsen's concept to *naturalize* the inconsistencies: perhaps it is actually the (momentarily intruding?) impersonal narrative voice that is responsible for the evocation of a potentially violent atmosphere. This unattached voice may verbalize the thought of the old Chinese woman; and if that is the case, then it follows that neither the mind of the experiencing I nor that of his later self would necessarily "contain" any violent thought. Alternatively, the impersonal narrator may enunciate those thoughts of the experiencing I which, at the moment of recollection, seem alien to the protagonist. After all, he does not "remember all [he] thought," and neither is his mind or its contents what it used to be. A somewhat similar explanation is applicable to "Reunion": the impersonal narrative voice enables the protagonist's misguided "narrative project," even if none of it appears worth telling from the point of view of the later self (whose presence in the discourse is, however, indicated by a deictic expression like "before Christmas last year").

When interpreting these stories by Ford, I believe that, at least momentarily, "we are aware that as readers we read a narrative that need not ever take place on the level of the character" (Nielsen 2004, 143). However, Ford's stories highlight the fact that when discussing both cognition and literature, we should not drop the matter *here*. For Nielsen's arguments lead us to ask the next question: What does it mean for a narrative to "take place"? This is also what Ford's two stories seem to be asking. Does narrative presuppose intentionality, organization, communication—or simply the activation of a cognitive schema? This may sometimes be the key interpretive problem posed by a fictional narrative. *Construction(-mindedness) does not automatically suppose transmission(-mindedness)*, and I suggest that this fact is pointedly foregrounded in literary representations of cognitive mental functioning and experientiality. Unlike real-world confessors, fictional first-person narrators are not necessarily speaking for themselves, not even *to* themselves, but instead they demonstrate—in their involuntary discursivity—how the fictional mind is conditioned by verbalization and the communicative structure of the narrative text. The narrators of the two stories share the apparent tendency to self-reflexively construct and frame their own experiences—as well as those of other people—up to a point where their shaky sketches approximate literary construction. Yet the literary minds inhabiting fictional universes are hardly ever aware of how literary, constructed, and under public scrutiny they ultimately are, even if they were to show symptoms of mental exhibitionism.

Short Conclusion: On Missing the Point

So, why *do* we read fiction? Lisa Zunshine provides a persuasive answer in *Why We Read Fiction* (2006): to let fiction test and tease the same intersubjective skills (theory of mind) we use in our social reality. However, one aspect Zunshine's theory does not cover is the literary illusion of the mind as verbalizable. In one sense, the minds of narrating or experiencing fictional agents always merge the representation with the represented: the mind is simultaneously both the performer and the arena of performance. Such "schizoid" textuality, discussed at length here, may threaten the apparent connection between experience and narrative construction: in fact, many of the narrative strategies for representing consciousness seem to emphasize both the *simultaneity* and the *incongruence* between real-time experience and its processing into a meaningful whole.

By merging lived experience with the construction of experience, Ford's stories point to the fact that there is no fixed point of construction, no true moment of absolute insight in life. While conventionally retrospective, these first-person narratives also make the process of narrative revision visible in a manner reminiscent of some present-tense narratives such as Coetzee's *Waiting for the Barbarians*. To rephrase the concern of the narrator in "Reunion," the question of what is preliminary and what is primary in the course of our lives may ultimately be left unanswered, before the cycle closes.

Notes

1. Here I find Joseph Tabbi's distinction between "cognitive" and "cognitivist" approaches helpful: "The fears [of cognitive invasion in literary studies] are justified, but only so long as cognitive researchers remain inattentive to the particular language of literary works and their specific demands on readers. . . . Such a[n ignoring] view might be termed 'cognitivist' rather than cognitive" (2004, 168–69).
2. On the difference between conscious versus self-conscious (or audience-oriented versus self-oriented) unreliability in fictional narrators, see Marcus (2005; 2006).

References

Abbott, H. Porter. 2005. "Closure." In *Routledge Encyclopedia of Narrative Theory*, ed. David Herman, Manfred Jahn, and Marie-Laure Ryan, 65–66. London: Routledge.

———. 2008. "Unreadable Minds and the Captive Reader." *Style* 42 (4): 448–70.

Alber, Jan. 2009. "Impossible Storyworlds—and What to Do With Them." *Storyworlds* 1:79–96.

Alber, Jan, and Rüdiger Heinze, eds. 2011. *Unnatural Narratives—Unnatural Narratology*. Berlin: de Gruyter.

Alber, Jan, Stefan Iversen, Henrik Skov Nielsen, and Brian Richardson. 2010. "Unnatural Narratives, Unnatural Narratology: Beyond Mimetic Models." *Narrative* 18 (2): 113–36.

Battersby, James L. 2006. "Narrativity, Self, and Self-Representation." *Narrative* 14 (1): 27–44.

Brooks, Peter. 2000. *Troubling Confessions: Speaking Guilt in Law and Literature*. Chicago: University of Chicago Press.

Butte, George. 2004. *I Know That You Know That I Know: Narrating Subjects from "Moll Flanders" to "Marnie."* Columbus: Ohio State University Press.

———. 2005. "I Know That I Know That I Know: Reflections on Paul John Eakin's 'What Are We Reading When We Read Autobiography?'" *Narrative* 13 (3): 298–306.

Cohn, Dorrit. 1978. *Transparent Minds: Narrative Modes for Presenting Consciousness in Fiction*. Princeton: Princeton University Press.

———. 1999. *The Distinction of Fiction*. Baltimore: Johns Hopkins University Press.

Eakin, Paul John. 2004. "What Are We Reading When We Read Autobiography?" *Narrative* 12 (2): 121–32.

Fludernik, Monika. 1996. *Towards a "Natural" Narratology*. London: Routledge.

Ford, Richard. 2002. "Privacy." In *A Multitude of Sins*, 3–7. London: Vintage Books.

———. 2002. "Reunion." In *A Multitude of Sins*, 65–74. London: Vintage Books.

Hägg, Samuli. 2006. "FID and Other Narratological Illusions." In FREE*language* INDIRECT*translation* DISCOURSE*narration: Linguistic, Translatological, and Literary-Theoretical Encounters*, ed. Pekka Tammi and Hannu Tommola, 175–92. Tampere: Tampere University Press.

Hamburger, Käte. 1993. *The Logic of Literature*. Trans. Marilynn J. Rose. 2nd rev. ed. Bloomington: Indiana University Press. Originally published as *Die Logik der Dichtung* (1957).

Hansen, Per Krogh, Stevan Iversen, Henrik Skov Nielsen, and Rolf Reitan, eds. 2011. *Strange Voices in Narrative Fiction*. Berlin: De Gruyter.

Herman, David. 2003. Introduction. In *Narrative Theory and the Cognitive Sciences*, ed. David Herman, 1–30. Stanford: CSLI Publications.

———. 2007a. "Cognition, Emotion, and Consciousness." In *The Cambridge Companion to Narrative*, ed. David Herman, 245–59. Cambridge: Cambridge University Press.

———. 2007b. Introduction. In *The Cambridge Companion to Narrative*, ed. David Herman, 3–21. Cambridge: Cambridge University Press.

Hydén, Lars-Christer, and Jens Brockmeier, eds. 2008. *Health, Illness and Culture: Broken Narratives*. London: Routledge.

Hyvärinen, Matti, Lars-Christer Hydén, Marja Saarenheimo, and Maria Tamboukou, eds. 2010. *Beyond Narrative Coherence*. Amsterdam: John Benjamins.

Mäkelä, Maria. 2006. "Possible Minds: Constructing—and Reading— Another Consciousness as Fiction." In FREE*language* INDIRECT*translation* DISCOURSE*narration: Linguistic, Translatological, and Literary-Theoretical Encounters*, ed. Pekka Tammi and Hannu Tommola, 231–60. Tampere: Tampere University Press.

Marcus, Amit. 2005. "The Self-Deceptive and Other-Deceptive Narrating Character: The Case of *Lolita*." *Style* 39 (2): 187–205.

———. 2006. "Kazuo Ishiguro's *The Remains of the Day*: The Discourse of Self-Deception." *Partial Answers* 4 (1): 129–56.

Margolin, Uri. 1999. "Of What Is Past, Is Passing, or to Come: Temporality, Aspectuality, Modality, and the Nature of Literary Narrative." In *Narratologies: New Perspectives on Narrative Analysis*, ed. David Herman, 142–66. Columbus: Ohio State University Press.

———. 2003. "Cognitive Science, the Thinking Mind, and Literary Narrative." In *Narrative Theory and the Cognitive Sciences*, ed. David Herman, 271–94. Stanford: CSLI Publications.

Nielsen, Henrik Skov. 2004. "The Impersonal Voice in First-Person Narrative Fiction." *Narrative* 12 (2): 133–50.

Palmer, Alan. 2003. "The Mind Beyond the Skin." In *Narrative Theory and the Cognitive Sciences*, ed. David Herman, 322–48. Stanford: CSLI Publications.

———. 2004. *Fictional Minds*. Lincoln: University of Nebraska Press.

Phelan, James. 2005. "Who's Here? Thoughts on Narrative Identity and Narrative Imperialism." *Narrative* 13 (3): 205–10.

Richardson, Brian. 2006. *Unnatural Voices: Extreme Narration in Modern and Contemporary Fiction*. Columbus: Ohio State University Press.

Ryan, Marie-Laure. 2007. "Toward a Definition of Narrative." In *The Cambridge Companion to Narrative*, ed. David Herman, 22–35. Cambridge: Cambridge University Press.

Sternberg, Meir. 2005. "Self-consciousness as a Narrative Feature and Force: Tellers vs. Informants in Generic Design." In *A Companion to Narrative Theory*, ed. James Phelan and Peter Rabinowitz, 232–52. Oxford: Blackwell.

Strawson, Galen. 2004. "Against Narrativity." *Ratio* 17 (4): 428–52.

Tabbi, Joseph. 2004. "Matter into Imagination: The Cognitive Realism of Gilbert Sorrentino's *Imaginative Qualities of Actual Things*." In *The Work of Fiction: Cognition, Culture, and Complexity*, ed. Alan Richardson and Ellen Spolsky, 167–85. Aldershot: Ashgate.

Tammi, Pekka. 2006. "Against Narrative ('A Boring Story')." *Partial Answers* 4 (2): 19–40.

———. 2008. "Against 'against' Narrative (On Nabokov's 'Recruiting')." In *Narrativity, Fictionality, and Literariness: The Narrative Turn and the Study of Literary Fiction*, ed. Lars-Åke Skalin, 37–55. Örebro Studies in Literary History and Criticism 7. Örebro: Örebro University Press.

Zunshine, Lisa. 2006. *Why We Read Fiction: Theory of Mind and the Novel*. Columbus: Ohio State University Press.

PART 3 | Minds and Cultures

7 Other Stories, Other Minds

The Intercultural Potential of Cognitive
Approaches to Narrative

ROY SOMMER

> Proposals that human beings have a "theory of mind" that allows
> them to recognize the mental states of others, to adopt an inten-
> tional stance towards them, to attribute to them a folk psychol-
> ogy of beliefs, goals, and desires, are a black box, a theoretical
> stipulation, a magic wand, unless we indicate where, in cognition,
> we find the source of such an understanding of mental states to
> begin with. The source of that understanding is our own experi-
> ence and understanding of ourselves.
>
> TURNER 2008, 36

Introduction

In his seminal study *The Literary Mind* (1996) and subsequent works,
Mark Turner has developed a complex model of the mind that explains
how our own conception of the mental self is always the source of our
understanding of others. By forming analogical connections between "us"
and "them" and creating double-scope blends containing other minds, we
gradually "develop and learn more sophisticated double-scope integration
networks, according to which the other minds in the blend differ in content and cast from our own minds" (Turner 2008, 36). The encounter with
fictional worlds and minds represented in novels, plays, or films makes an
important contribution to this learning process, as stories allow readers or
viewers to engage emotionally as well as cognitively with other cultures.

Aesthetic experience thus helps to develop what one might call an
"intercultural mind," that is, a mind-set that seeks to overcome the limitations inherent in ethnocentric worldviews and works toward intercul-

tural dialogue and understanding. Like George Lakoff's (2008) notion of the political mind, the concept of an intercultural mind as proposed here is based on empathy, the ability and willingness to adopt, albeit temporarily, the other's point of view and to engage cognitively and emotionally with his or her perspective. Like the political mind, the intercultural mind cannot be taken for granted but may be developed and improved to the benefit of ourselves and of others.

Given the relevance of concepts such as mind reading and empathy for understanding others, it seems surprising that intercultural literature studies have so far paid little attention to cognitive approaches to narrative. As Suzanne Keen (2007) has convincingly argued, there is more (or maybe less) to empathy than is commonly assumed: the widespread "empathy-altruism" hypothesis, that is, the idea that reading fiction (or plays) has a direct bearing on one's ability to feel with others in the real world, is based on pedagogical assumptions rather than empirical evidence. Similarly, intercultural literary studies have not yet systematically explored how readers use their own knowledge of the world to make sense of texts from other cultures, and how misreadings may be used constructively to demonstrate how culture influences cognition, and vice versa.

This chapter aims to bridge the gap between literary theories built around concepts of culture and intercultural understanding, on the one hand, and those focusing on narrative and cognition, on the other, by showing how these two approaches can complement each other, both in literary criticism and in teaching literature. The interactions among culture, narrative, and cognition link this chapter with Bart Keunen's contribution to the present volume, while my attempt to seek out the pedagogical relevance of my findings will remind the reader of the chapter by Bortolussi and Dixon.

The term "intercultural narrative" as used in this chapter refers to novels, plays, narrative poems, films, or any other kind of fictional narrative that explicitly or implicitly stages intercultural encounters of characters from diverse cultural, ethnic, and religious backgrounds, or the clash of different, subculture-specific values and beliefs within a single cultural, ethnic, or religious community (e.g., between first- and second-generation immigrants in a multicultural society), and which do so in ways that foster intercultural understanding in the broadest sense. Intercultural narratives, then, construct cultural difference in fictional worlds in order to deconstruct, or rather encourage their readers to deconstruct, it. Intercultural reading experiences, in turn, may be defined as the aesthetic experience (with all the cognitive engagement and emotional responses this entails) of an intercultural narrative by a reader or viewer whose cultural background is significantly different from that of one or several characters in the narrative. From this approach to reading in the sense of comprehension one has to distinguish an intercultural reading, that is, an interpretation of a novel *as an intercultural novel* (obviously every reader is free to produce an interpretation that completely ignores cultural aspects even if these are foregrounded in a narrative).

What, then, are the theoretical and methodological implications of the intercultural mind for literary studies and the further development of an intercultural or postcolonial narratology (see Sommer 2007)? How can the insights of cognitive theory be applied to the analysis of literature from other cultures, and how can they improve our understanding of an intercultural reading experience? Conversely, what are the implications of narratological studies of world literature for cognitive theory, especially for future work on the distinction between strategic and ambassadorial empathizing, as proposed by Keen (2007)?

The first part of this chapter offers an analysis of Ayub Khan-Din's highly acclaimed play *East Is East* (1997), a polyphonic portrayal of gender trouble and generational conflict between a Pakistani immigrant, his English wife, and their six children, who embody incompatible states of mind: art versus the mosque, pragmatism versus fundamentalism, individual versus community. By focusing on dramaturgical strategies that enable readers or viewers to understand the play's most controversial character, first-generation immigrant and violent husband and father George Khan, the analysis gives an insight into the narrative construction of empathy. As will be shown, the play makes extensive use of the triangular constellation of protagonist, antagonist, and observer that Breithaupt (2009, 153 ff.) defines as an essential constituent of "narrative" empathy.

The second part of the chapter shows how research on aspects of cognition, such as inference and categorization, can provide tools for monitoring and evaluating reader responses in literature courses at both undergraduate and postgraduate levels. It illustrates how a "clash of metaphors" can be observed in reader responses to unfamiliar storyworlds, in this case Ben Okri's *The Famished Road* (1992), a novel deeply rooted in Nigerian culture and Yoruba cosmology. The chapter describes a reading experiment conducted with a group of students, based on the stylistic method of "sophisticated inferentialism" (Clark 2009). The experiment demonstrates how a lack of cultural knowledge can be compensated for by other cognitive resources, such as social knowledge structures or theoretical paradigms. It can be compared to another chapter in this volume, namely, Auyoung's analysis of readerly inferences based on minimal cues in Tolstoy's *Anna Karenina*. The didactic value of such experiments, it will be argued, lies in their ability to raise awareness of the limitations of reader perspectives and of the challenges we face if we wish to avoid misreading other cultures.

"You not understand my mind": Narrative Empathy in Ayub Khan-Din's *East Is East* (1997)

One way of approaching mind and narrative from an intercultural perspective is by analyzing how literary works or dramatic performances make use of empathy, either by representing empathic behavior or by creating scenarios that actively engage their audience's capacity for empathy. Social psychology defines empathizing as "the drive to identify another person's emotions and thoughts and to respond to these with an appropriate emotion" (Baron-Cohen 2008, 65), and it defines empathy itself as the set of skills required to satisfy this drive. These skills may vary across individuals; moreover, cognitive and affective components of empathy can be distinguished (cf. Baron-Cohen 2008, 65; for a comprehensive definition of the term empathy see Stueber 2008). The former can be equated with theory of mind or the (psychological) concept of mind reading, whereas the latter describe emotional responses to another person's mental state.

It is important to repeat in this context that "theory of mind" means different things in different contexts. Drawing on the discovery of mirror neurons in the macaque monkey premotor cortex in the late 1980s, the simulation theory of mind reading, developed by Gallese and Goldman (1998), proposes that "humans' mind-reading abilities rely on the capacity to adopt a simulation routine" (493) and suggests that "an action/observation matching system similar to that discovered in monkeys also exists in humans" (495). More recently, experimental studies in neuroscience and cognitive psychology have used methods such as TMS, EEG, eyetracking, and fMRI in order to investigate theory of mind in children (with and without autism), twins, women with Turner's syndrome, and patients with neurodegenerative disorders (cf. Saxe and Baron-Cohen 2007, vii). What they are aiming at is an explanation of other people's experiences, explanations that should, ideally, be generally applicable (or even relate to universal cognitive features to be found in all human beings). While theory of mind is thus something very fundamental in psychology, an ability that individuals either do or do not possess (hence the difference between neurotypical and autistic persons), in literary studies the concept needs to be adapted for other analytic purposes—since narrative comprehension *always presupposes* a reader whose theory of mind is sufficiently developed and who is capable of mind reading in the basic, cognitive-psychological sense of the term.

When talking about readers' or viewers' encounters with aesthetic objects such as fictional narratives, the focus is usually on emotional empathy, because cognitive empathy has to be regarded as a necessary precondition without which no literary or dramatic communication would be possible. Emotional empathy, in contrast, is an effect largely created by the text itself, the product of dramaturgical strategies and narrative techniques which ensure that readers of novels or plays, or audiences in the theater or cinema, take sufficient interest in fictional or dramatic characters to become involved in the interpretive activity called mind reading. As Grabes (2008) points out, the most important textual strategies in this respect are those that give the reader access to the inner life of human beings by representing the characters' feelings, thoughts, and consciousness: "it is this transparency of the fictional minds which makes the reading of literature so fascinating" (125).

There is, however, one significant difference between empathy in the psychological sense and literary empathy: whereas in everyday life we have sufficient motivation to read other people's minds, that is, to find plausible explanations for verbal or nonverbal behavior whose intentions are not communicated explicitly, novels or plays have to work hard to create characters that we find appealing enough to empathize or sympathize with. There are many narrative strategies to achieve this end, the most obvious one being character constellations working with binary oppositions—good versus evil. The resulting effect of polarization has been exploited in numerous Victorian novels where orphans or poor people are victimized by their superiors (examples are Oliver Twist, who is hit by the master with the ladle when asking for more, young Jane Eyre, who is harassed by her older cousin John in Charlotte Brontë's eponymous novel, or Thomas Hardy's Tess, who is a victim of misogynist Victorian moral standards embodied by Alec d'Urberville and Angel Clare). The effectiveness of such character constellations is underlined by their repetitive yet no less successful use in innumerable Hollywood movies in which a particularly likable character has to face an utterly despicable opponent.

Another, more subtle narrative strategy aimed at facilitating empathy is to create scenes that more closely resemble real-world scenarios, where good and evil are distributed more evenly. Maybe there is also less dualism in real life than traditional concepts of empathy, founded on the idea of identification with the other, imply. According to Breithaupt (2009), narrative empathy generally involves not two, but three or more individuals. The concept assumes an archetypal scenario in which an observer (in aesthetic experiences the reader of a novel, the spectator in the cinema, the audience of a play) witnesses a disagreement or conflict between two other individuals and speculates about possible causes, intentions, motivations, and consequences (cf. Breithaupt 2009, 12 ff.). He or she takes sides mentally, without necessarily taking action (cf. Breithaupt 2009, 152 ff.). Breithaupt's concept seems to be particularly well suited to the analysis of empathy in fiction or drama, as it is not based on the idea that readers or viewers *identify* with characters but merely presupposes that readers or viewers *observe* and *evaluate interactions* between characters. As such, it can also account for the ways in which we empathize with characters we do not really understand, an effect frequently exploited in multicultural fiction and drama.

Ayub Khan-Din's British Asian tragicomedy *East Is East*, first performed at the Royal Court Theatre in 1997, is a case in point. Set in the English town of Salford in the 1970s, the play focuses on the Khan family, a mixed-race couple with six children who have to cope with the tensions between a traditional British Pakistani way of life, characterized by cultural practices such as circumcision and arranged marriage, and the less constrained English or Western way of life. These tensions are represented in terms of gender and generational difference. George Khan, a Pakistani immigrant who runs a fish-and-chip shop with his English wife, Ella, is a devout Muslim who hopes that his sons will one day return to Islamabad to lead a better life. The couple's children represent the range of possible responses of second-generation immigrants to the challenge of forming an identity. Responses range from assimilation to the English way of life, on the one hand, to conforming to the cultural traditions of their elders, on the other. While Nazir, the eldest son, has left the family to work as a hairdresser, the younger son Maneer tries to please his father. His brothers Tariq and Saleem, the latter of whom is training to become an artist, are afraid of following Nazir's radical example, but at the same time they are unwilling to succumb to their father's plans. These include an arranged marriage with the daughters of a wealthy British Pakistani businessman, Mr. Shah. Sajit, the youngest son, reacts to the psychological pressure exerted on him (and the circumcision he is forced to endure) by developing psychological problems, whereas the sister, Meenah, manages to get by without openly confronting her father.

The conflict between George and Ella escalates toward the end of act 2, scene 2, when Ella openly insults her husband's Pakistani family and refuses to let him have his way with their children: "Yes, 25 years I've been married to you, George, I've sweated me guts out in your bastard shop, and given you seven kids as well, and I'll tell you this for nothing, I'm not gonna stand by and let you crush them one by one because of your pig bloody ignorance" (51). George's reaction to what he regards as an intolerable provocation is physical violence, as described in the stage directions: "George grabs Ella violently by her hair and pulls her to the ground. He kicks and beats her." After a series of verbal insults and threats ("You baster bitch! You call me pig, you pucker, you talk to me like this again and I bloody kill you bitch, and burn all your baster family when you sleep!"), George "storms out leaving Ella crying" (51).

The character constellation in the play is reminiscent of the triangular scenario of narrative empathy described by Breithaupt: the main source of conflict, the disagreement between George and his sons Tariq and Saleem, is observed and commented on by Maneer. George represents the archetypal immigrant who works hard to offer his sons a good education and ultimately a better start in life: "You bloody lucky to go to college. I come to this country with nothing" (12). For this reason he insists that Saleem wear a suit at college and have his hair cut in order to impress his tutors: "You better chance than me see, go a college. So you sees, if your hair is tidy, and you looking smart, teacher looking see. May be help find job after. Always plenty job for engineer. Lota job in Pakistan, do good business there. Buy house in Islamabad, very nice bungalow there" (12). As he points out to Maneer, George feels estranged in Britain. He is subjected to racist remarks despite the fact that he has been living there for more than forty years: "I love my family, but all time I have trouble with people, they not like I marry your mother. Always calling you mother bad name. That why I always try to show Pakistani way to live is good way, parent look after children, children look after parent" (42). Maneer's reaction to this shows that he is torn between taking sides with his father and realizing that he is fighting a losing battle: "I know what you're trying to say dad! (To himself.) It's the others you've got to convince" (42).

Another key aspect of George's character is his faith. He is sincerely worried for Sajit, when he accidentally discovers at the mosque that Ella—contrary to his belief—did not have his youngest son circumcised: "You know nothing about my religion, you no bloody care your children have no God. Your son no Muslim with this thing, when he die he go straight to hell!" (6). Again it is Maneer's rendition of the scene in his conversation with Saleem, Tariq, and Meenah that allows the reader to see that George's aggression really hides other emotions that let him appear more sympathetic: "He looked dead embarrassed in the mosque, I thought he were gonna cry" (10). His siblings, however, fail to be convinced by their father's misery, and like Ella they are not willing to take his point of view. Thus, when George accuses Ella of not understanding him—"You not understand my mind" (29)—he might just as well refer to his whole family, except Maneer, and English society as a whole. By embarrassing him in front of the mullah at the mosque, Ella has, from George's point of view, threatened to estrange him from those who *do* understand—the Muslim community in Salford.

As these examples show, George cannot be reduced to the stereotypical image of the dominant and brutal father (cf. 15, 30, 55) feared by his children (cf. 11), the violent husband, the ignorant Muslim. From a dramaturgical point of view, the character of Maneer functions as a counterpart to the other characters in the play (and many readers of the play) when he pleads for a more varied response to George, accuses Tariq of ignorance, and explains what it means to be a Muslim: "It's my choice, I like it, I wouldn't force it on anyone, I don't think me dad should either. He's wrong to do that. But being Pakistani is more than just a religion, Tariq, you hate me dad too much to see it" (45). The complexity of George's character is further enhanced by his anxiety for the safety of his relatives in Pakistan, who live in a war zone: "I have to take interest, you sees, family in Azad Kashmir, near bloody border. Bloody make me worry" (7). Most importantly, however, his violent behavior, first expressed in the scene described above, meets its due retribution within the play. Domestic violence escalates when George beats Saleem for asking why he married Ella if he really thinks that all English women drink and sleep around ("Saleem has hit a raw nerve. George grabs him, and pushes him on the ground and kicks and slaps him" [55]). Later, when Ella sides with her children ("You ought to be ashamed George, you're not getting these lads married, you're selling them off to the highest bidder. Who's gonna get Meenah? Someone with double glazing and a detached house!" [72]), he has another go at her: "George grabs Ella, and pushes her to the floor, he starts to hit her" (72).

This time, however, George does not get away with it. Abdul interferes, separates his parents, and threatens to retaliate: "Dad if you touch her again I swear I'll kill you!" (72). At this point George suffers a breakdown. He starts to cry and attempts to justify himself: "I only try to help you son, I no want bloody hurt you. I love my family" (72). When Abdul asks him to go to the shop, he leaves: "George looks at Ella and the others, he looks at Abdul. Ashamed and upset, he walks slowly out of the room" (73). George's exit marks his defeat, which is irreversible, as this is the last scene of the play and he will not be seen on stage again. Abdul's resistance has changed the hierarchy in the family: George has to realize that he has once and for all lost control over his children and wife.

As this analysis shows, the character constellation in Khan-Din's play echoes Breithaupt's triangular scenario of narrative empathy: the reader or viewer observes how a character in the play (Maneer) tries to understand another character (George) who is in conflict with others (Ella and the sons). This scenario differs in one significant way from the dramaturgical strategies and dichotomous character constellations frequently used, for example, in Victorian novels and Hollywood movies: it does not require the reader or member of the audience to identify with one perspective (i.e., the victim's) and condemn the other (i.e., the villain's); instead, the processes of understanding and misunderstanding are portrayed in a way that allows for a more detached distribution of empathetic responses.

Such instances of character constellations allowing for narrative empathy are, of course, not exclusive to multicultural plays or novels: there are numerous examples of other literary texts or art-house movies (even in Hollywood) that employ similar dramaturgical strategies in order to make a character's subjective—and controversial—point of view more accessible to readers and viewers. It is equally true, however, that in multicultural literature, for instance, Asian British or black British writing, such scenarios are widely used, as they allow writers to counter stereotypical or even racist representations of ethnic groups very effectively by means of "strategic ambassadorial empathy" (Keen 2007, 142). *East Is East* is a prime example of such narrative design. The play and its film adaptation by Damien O'Donnell (1999) encourage their audiences to engage with the other's mind (rather than dismiss it), with the result that George's resignation—"You not understand my mind"—might turn out to be unfounded.

These are the assumptions of pedagogical theories that aim to foster intercultural understanding in higher education. In Germany, multicultural plays, novels, and films such as *East Is East* or *Bend It Like Beckham* (Gurinder Chadha, 2002) are part of a curriculum that is designed to raise an awareness of multicultural issues as well as to improve students' media literacy and analytical competencies. So far there is hardly any empirical evidence supporting or countering the links between narrative empathy scenarios, empathetic reading, and real-world behavior. As an alternative to approaches relying solely on the assumed effectiveness of empathy, teaching analytical approaches to intercultural narratives involves understanding the relationships among culture, narrative, and cognition. Understanding how literary texts use strategic ambassadorial empathy in order to introduce readers to the minds of others is one option frequently used in intercultural literary studies. The following section discusses a complementary, experimental approach to cross-cultural reading experiences that uses cognitive stylistics as a tool to monitor, evaluate, and compare reader responses.

Cross-Cultural Reading Experiences: Categorization, Social Knowledge Structures, and Ben Okri's *The Famished Road* (1992)

African fiction in English has been characterized as "extremely culture-specific" (Soliman 2004, 149), as it relies heavily on local cultures, on African cosmology, and on oral tradition (Soliman 2004, 149). As a consequence, African novels are often regarded as inaccessible to readers who are not familiar with their underlying network of references, allusions, and contexts. An example of such a novel that introduces the majority of its readers to an unfamiliar storyworld is Ben Okri's Booker Prize–winning novel *The Famished Road* (1992). Set in Nigeria at the time of independence in the early 1960s, the novel is deeply rooted in Yoruba cosmology with its specific concept of rebirth and spirit-children (*abiku*), which separates the visible world of humans from the invisible world of spirits.

Sowande (2001) points out that this symbolic code and the narrative style of the novel draw on the tradition of oral narrative and a rich African literary heritage that includes novels by D. O. Fagunwa and Amos Tutuola as well as poems by Wole Soyinka and J. P. Clark. Their works provide "the canon of mythology by which modern man can find meaning to [sic] his life" (Sowande 2001, 73). What happens, however, if the reader is not aware of this "mythological canon" and not familiar with its imagery? How do readers unaware of this tradition make sense of Okri's metaphors, for instance, the complex metaphor of the road in the novel's title, an intertextual reference to Soyinka's poem "Death in the Dawn" (cf. 78)? How do readers unaware of the fact that "[t]he characterization of Azaro has already been crafted by the signature of the spirit-child in the contemporary Yoruba belief-system" (75) manage to form mental representations of the novel's protagonist?

Although such complex issues are difficult to address empirically, linguistic "inferentialism" (Clark 2009), a pragmatic approach, offers a simple yet effective means of monitoring and keeping track of readers' inferences. Based on the framework of relevance theory, inferentialism is a particularly useful pedagogic procedural tool for understanding how readers may process textual cues even if they lack the cultural background knowledge needed to contextualize the narrative. Clark acknowledges the crucial role of inference in the stylistic analysis of fictional narratives, claiming that "an account of inferential processes is in principle a vital part of any adequate account of how texts create effects, even though it is not always practical to offer a detailed account" (2009, 173).

According to Clark, four approaches to inferential analysis can be distinguished. While "hardline inferentialism" claims that "it is essential to explore all the inferential processes involved in understanding every text since all acts of interpretation involve inference" (2009, 182), the opposite view, designated as "casual inferentialism," holds that "it is not important to explore inferential processes since we can all see what inferences we make without having to develop an explicit account for each one" (183). Between these extreme positions, one can situate two further, closely related approaches: "occasional inferentialism"—"the view that an account of inferential processes is important in cases where there is something unusual or marked about the inferential processes we go through when understanding a text" (184)—and "sophisticated inferentialism": "On this view . . . it is in principle always worth exploring all of the inferential processes involved in understanding a text, but it is not practical to do so" (184). Clark's description of this fourth position probably best fits the stance of the majority of cognitive literary theorists as well: "Where analysts notice something marked or unusual about an interpretation, this calls for an analysis of the inferential process. . . . It will be up to the analyst to decide in each case whether and where to develop an account of inferential processes" (184).

Clark's method thus entails a close reading, sentence by sentence, of selected passages of a given text. Using a table with three columns to organize his data (the opening scene of William Golding's *The Inheritors*), Clark (2009, 204 ff.) records for each sentence just read (column 1) all "current hypotheses" (column 2)—in other words, all mind-reading activities; that is, all assumptions made on the basis of the linguistic information in the sentence, including mental state ascriptions and explanations of characters' behavior. Column 3 then adds "unresolved questions," that is, questions whose answers cannot be hypothetically inferred from the textual information. Such a chart provides a basis for evaluating the reading process, as it allows the critic to monitor step by step how his or her understanding of the text in question unfolds.

In principle, then, this method works by making explicit what happens in the reading process. It allows the critic to see very clearly how and when unresolved questions are finally answered and how primacy and recency effects actively contribute to the process of sense-making. However, if this method of tracking inferences is used in an experiment with a larger group of readers, such as students in a literature class, some methodological problems will arise. First, in Clark's example the reader is an expert in stylistics who is specifically trained to perform the task at hand with minute attention to detail. Less experienced readers, who are only vaguely familiar with cognitive linguistics (among other relevant areas of inquiry), will produce less-well-structured and less-coherent results.

Second, in the experiment described below the majority of readers were not familiar with the novel to be analyzed. This explains why the opening sequence had to be selected, as no background information could be provided (after all, the point was to find out how readers compensated for a lack of contextual knowledge). Finally, the quality of response will vary, with some readers taking more time and care than others. Although these issues present certain difficulties for evaluating the results of the study to be reported here, they do not wholly undercut the validity of the method used in the study. Though the method used does need to be supplemented by more rigorous quantitative empirical research, it nonetheless provides interesting evidence that can be correlated with existing theoretical models of the reading process (e.g., Schneider 2001).

For present purposes, then, the method of "sophisticated inferentialism" seems to be sufficiently precise. A group of forty-four German students of English literature taking part in a lecture on postclassical narrative theory ("Narrative Theory and Literary History II: Storyworld Design") at the University of Wuppertal were asked to read the first thirteen sentences of Okri's novel and to specify their current hypotheses and unresolved questions, using a chart similar to the one provided by Clark (2009). The tests were conducted and evaluated in June 2010 (a sample chart can be found in the appendix). In the description of the experiment that follows, "S" stands for "sentence"—thus "s1" designates the first sentence of the passage the student participants read. Four students had read *The Famished Road* before, while for the remaining forty it was their first encounter with the novel. None of the students had any particular knowledge of Nigerian literary traditions or the Yoruba belief system. All of them, however, were familiar with stylistic methodology as proposed by Clark, which had been discussed in the course. They were allowed sufficient time (most of them completed the task within thirty minutes, while some took almost an hour), and participation was voluntary (and, of course, anonymous).

As was to be expected, there was some variation in individual response. Some students merely paraphrased the content of the sentences. Only one participant offered current hypotheses which showed that he or she had either completely missed the point or—more likely—did not wish to take the exercise seriously (s4, current hypothesis: "Setting must be a region with many rivers—Finland?"). Despite the variation, however, most responses fell into one of three groups. The first group tried to understand the text by establishing the literal meaning of each sentence and interpreting this in the light of preceding and subsequent sentences, a procedure one might call a "linguistic approach" or close reading. Those responses were frequently concerned with establishing whether the text had to be understood metaphorically, as in the "unresolved questions" prompted by s2 ("Real river or a metaphor?"; "Metaphorical language use? River = road?"), and with figuring out the precise implications of the text (e.g., s7: "How can terrors be beautiful?" or "What are the 'beautiful terrors of eternity'?"). In general, this group seemed to make very few assumptions and tried to stick to the actual text as closely as possible.

The second group adopted a "generic" approach. The opening sentence reminded them of the Bible ("Sounds like the beginning of the Bible") or, more specifically, the book of Genesis ("Genesis-like story"). This initial hypothesis or generic framing then seemed to structure the interpretation of subsequent information; thus s4 was regarded as confirmation of the initial hypothesis ("Process of world creation is described" or "'land of beginning' = the Garden of Eden"), as was s6 ("A place like heaven is described → Christian mythology"). Variations of the "generic" approach included references (mainly in the "unresolved questions" column) to fantastic elements, magic or magical realism, utopian writing, or, in one case, science fiction; one student simply asked in his or her response to s2: "Which genre?" Those who had initially grounded their reading in the generic biblical hypothesis later expressed doubts (s7: "Are we confronted with Hindu religion or a Christian religion in which eternity has another meaning?").

The third group opted for a "narratological" approach, analyzing the narrative structure of the novel's beginning. They used critical terminology (setting, story, plot, chronological order, narrator) and tried to establish the type of narrative situation (s3: "Who is telling the story?"). Following s5, nine of the students who adopted the narratological approach pointed out that a first-person narrator or "we narrator" is being introduced, two simply noted "homodiegetic narrator," and one, "omniscient narrator." This is hardly surprising, as the experiment was conducted with participants in my lecture course on narrative theory who were familiar with narratological concepts and terminology. Thus, this kind of reader response was clearly due to the context in which the experiment was carried out. For this reason it is not surprising that, while the "linguistic" and "generic" approaches appeared to be mutually exclusive alternatives—one might describe them as predominantly "textual" or "text-oriented" on the one hand as opposed to "contextual" or primarily context-oriented on the other—traces of a "narratological" approach could be found in the other two groups as well.

The experiment showed a number of things. For one thing, existing models of narrative comprehension throw light on the full range of responses. For instance, using Schneider's (2001, 618) model, one can clearly see that different types of knowledge structure—social and literary—were activated by participants in the experiment. Second, participants seemed to stick to interpretive hypotheses they had adopted initially, that is, to focus on the type of information that was relevant within the framework established by their first hypothesis. Only if (or when) the text provided new information that was clearly no longer compatible with the initial hypothesis, that is, when the recency effect proved stronger than the primacy effect, were initial assumptions called into question or abandoned altogether. This was more likely to happen when strong assumptions—such as generic framing in terms of biblical narrative—had been made and had then been subjected to revision (when, or rather if, the reader realized that the kingdom described here did not resemble Christian notions of paradise).

The third and most interesting finding, in the present context, is the fact that all readings were in fact meticulous protocols of *mis*readings: that is, students failed to understand, hermeneutically speaking, the meaning of the text. While the "linguistic" or text-oriented approach hardly managed to get beyond the literal meaning of these sentences (which is not particularly difficult to establish), the "generic" or "context-oriented" approach frequently led to wrong conclusions that had to be withdrawn. This confirms that without sufficient and relevant cultural knowledge any cognitive processing of textual information is destined to fail, regardless of the type of approach chosen (top-down or bottom-up).

The lack of culture-specific knowledge and sufficient experience with cross-cultural literary encounter is the norm rather than the exception—even experienced readers will initially find it difficult to come to terms with the narrative, as noted by Roy (2000): "Okri's encoding of his vision in a specifically Yoruba ontological framework erected through myths, riddles, rituals, and beliefs makes it only partially accessible to the alien reader while addressing his African audience through a mutually comprehensible symbolic code" (25). The most common reader reaction to such problems is either (1) recourse to preestablished critical or generic categories—for example, interpreting Okri within an exclusively postcolonial framework that, frankly, does not do justice to the complexity of the literary tradition in which his novel is embedded; or (2) simply surrendering efforts to understand the text in the face of incomprehensibility: the majority of students admitted they would not have continued reading the book (voluntarily), and, judging from the comparatively small number of articles discussing the novel, quite a few professional scholars seem to have drawn similar conclusions. This experimental method of monitoring, evaluating, and discussing our process of coming to terms with otherness may help to revalue such initially unsatisfactory reading experiences as part of an exciting, lifelong learning process—another step toward the development of an intercultural mind that is open to other stories and the seemingly incomprehensible mind-sets to which they provide access.

This is not to say, of course, that it is only intercultural texts that pose processing challenges. Such obstacles frequently occur in all kinds of fiction and drama, including mystery and detective writing (as discussed by Emmott et al. in this volume). However, the focus here is on cultural difference rather than, for instance, gender or class conflicts as the source of specific empathetic responses or misunderstandings. Nor am I arguing that other cultures are really incomprehensible: in the two examples discussed in this essay, cultural difference is an effect of strategic narrative design, including character selection, character constellations, characterization, and recourse to culture-specific symbols and metaphors. Both Khan-Din's play and Okri's novel construct cultural difference in such a way that it may be deconstructed by more or less experienced readers or viewers, thus adding an intercultural dimension to the aesthetic experience.

Conclusion

Both approaches to minds and narrative explored in this chapter—namely, the textual analysis of dramaturgical features designed to produce empathy and the monitoring and evaluation of reading processes and sense-making strategies—usefully extend ideas developed in cognitive narratology and have considerable pedagogical potential: they help to make readers more aware of how they react to fictional representations of other minds, and why they sometimes fail to make sense of other stories. These "other" stories may introduce us to "other" minds in ways that help us develop our own intercultural mind. Just as reading detective novels may allow for a pleasurable exercise of our meta-representational capacities (cf. Zunshine 2006, 125; Emmott et al. in this volume), intercultural novels may encourage readers to change perspective, to cope creatively with clashes of mind-set, metaphor, and belief, and to become more sensitive, as mind readers, to the variability of cultural norms and expectations. These considerations, pointing to the value of engaging with literature from other cultures, also provide an answer to an intriguing question prompted by the title of Lisa Zunshine's study: why we *teach* fiction at all.

Closely connected to this question, in turn, is the question of *how* we read fiction. The new critical paradigms established by research on minds and narrative open up alternatives to the widespread practice of predominantly thematic interpretation of intercultural drama and fiction, which concentrates on the representation of identities, races or racism, and cultural diversity or hybridity within the storyworld. Cognitive approaches are not, of course, to be considered as a mutually exclusive alternative to current critical practices in multicultural or postcolonial literature studies; rather, these paradigms should be regarded as complementary. Arguably, only a pluralist methodology, integrating political, thematic, linguistic, narratological, hermeneutic, cognitive, and historical perspectives, can do justice to the rich aesthetics of intercultural literary texts and to the complexity of an intercultural reading experience.

Appendix

Fig. 7.1. Table used to record reader responses to *The Famished Road*

	Sentence	Current hypothesis	Unresolved questions
S1	In the beginning there was a river.		
S2	The river became a road and the road branched out to the whole world.		

s3   And because the road was once a river it was always hungry.

s4   In that land of beginnings spirits mingled with the unborn.

s5   We knew no boundaries.

s6   There was much feasting, playing, and sorrowing.

s7   We feasted much because of the beautiful terrors of eternity.

s8   We played much because we were free.

s9   And we sorrowed much because there were always those amongst us who had just returned from the world of the Living.

s10   They had returned inconsolable for all the love they had left behind, all the suffering they hadn't redeemed, all that they hadn't understood, and for all that they had barely begun to

Sentence	Current hypothesis	Unresolved questions

learn before they were drawn back to the land of origins.

s11 There was not one amongst us who looked forward to being born.

s12 We disliked the rigours of existence, the unfulfilled longings, the enshrined injustices of the world, the labyrinths of love, the ignorance of parents, the fact of dying, and the amazing indifference of the Living in the midst of the simple beauties of the universe.

s13 We feared the heartlessness of human beings, all of whom are born blind, few of whom ever learn to see.

Created by the author.

References

Baron-Cohen, Simon. 2008. "Autism, Hypersystemizing, and Truth." *Quarterly Journal of Experimental Psychology* 61 (1): 64-75.

Breithaupt, Fritz. 2009. *Kulturen der Empathie*. Frankfurt am Main: Suhrkamp.

Clark, Billy. 2009. "Salient Inferences: Pragmatics and *The Inheritors.*" *Language and Literature: Journal of the Poetics and Linguistics Association* 18 (2): 173–212.

Gallese, Vittorio, and Alvin Goldman. 1998. "Mirror Neurons and the Simulation Theory of Mind-reading." *Trends in Cognitive Sciences* 2 (12): 493–501.

Grabes, Herbert. 2008. "Encountering People through Literature." In *The Literary Mind*, ed. Jürgen Schlaeger and Gesa Stedman, 125–39. Tübingen: Gunter Narr.

Keen, Suzanne. 2007. *Empathy and the Novel.* Oxford: Oxford University Press.

Khan-Din, Ayub. 1997. *East Is East.* London: Nick Hern Books.

Lakoff, George. 2008. The Political Mind. Harmondsworth: Penguin.

Okri, Ben. 1992 (1991). *The Famished Road.* London: Vintage.

Roy, Anjali. 2000. "Post-modern or Post-colonial? Magic Realism in Okri's *The Famished Road.*" In *The Post-colonial Condition of African Literature*, ed. Daniel Gover, John Conteh-Morgan, and Jane Bryce, 23–39. Trenton NJ: Africa World Press.

Saxe, Rebecca, and Simon Baron-Cohen. 2007. "Editorial: The Neuroscience of Theory of Mind." In *"Theory of Mind": Social Neuroscience*, ed. Rebecca Saxe and Simon Baron-Cohen, i–ix. Hove: Psychology Press.

Schneider, Ralf. 2001. "Toward a Cognitive Theory of Literary Character: The Dynamics of Mental-Model Construction." *Style* 35 (4): 607–40.

Soliman, Mounira. 2004. "From Past to Present and Future: The Regenerative Spirit of the Abiku." *Alif: Journal of Comparative Poetics* 24:149–71.

Sommer, Roy. 2007. "'Contextualism' Revisited: A Survey (and Defence) of Postcolonial and Intercultural Narratologies." *Journal for Literary Theory* 1 (1): 61–79.

Sowande, Bode. 2001. "The Metaphysics of Abiku: A Literary Heritage in Ben Okri's *The Famished Road.*" *Matatu: Journal for African Culture and Society* 23–24:73–81.

Stueber, Karsten. 2008. "Empathy." In *The Stanford Encyclopedia of Philosophy*, ed. Edward N. Zalta. http://plato.stanford.edu/archives/fall2008/entries/empathy/.

Turner, Mark. 1996. *The Literary Mind: The Origins of Thought and Language.* Oxford: Oxford University Press.

———. 2008. "The Mind Is an Autocatalytic Vortex." In *The Literary Mind*, ed. Jürgen Schlaeger and Gesa Stedman, 13–43. Tübingen: Gunter Narr.

Zunshine, Lisa. 2006. *Why We Read Fiction: Theory of Mind and the Novel.* Columbus: Ohio State University Press.

Plot, Morality, and Folk Psychology Research

BART KEUNEN

> What is a poet? . . . He is a man speaking to men: a man, it is
> true, endued with more lively sensibility, more enthusiasm and
> tenderness, who has a greater knowledge of human nature, and
> a more comprehensive soul, than are supposed to be common
> among mankind.
>
> WORDSWORTH, PREFACE TO THE *LYRICAL BALLADS*

The Endeavor of Commonsense Psychology

In his autobiography, Fritz Heider, a pioneer of social psychology and a
founder of folk psychology research (Bruner 1990, 37), offers some comments on the famous experiments he conducted together with Marianne Simmel during World War II (Heider and Simmel 1944). Heider's
comment from 1983 turned out to be prophetic in its anticipation of the
debates that would later guide the development of the "theory of mind"
hypothesis. By means of a film with moving objects (see http://www.you-
tube.com/watch?v=76p64j3H1Ng), the experiment demonstrated that
people are compelled "to perceive things as agents and ascribe intentions
and other mental states to them" (Malle and Ickes 2000, 204). Heider and
Simmel projected a small triangle and a circle that were made to interact
with a large triangle.

The main observation folk psychology theorists deduced from these
experiments was that the human brain possesses specific abilities to attribute mental states to persons (and even objects) in the external world. In
his autobiography, however, Heider emphasized the fact that a far more
complex socio-psychological skill is involved when observers attribute
intentions and emotions to projected objects: "as I planned the action of
the film, I thought of the small triangle and the circle as a pair of lovers

or friends and I thought of the big triangle as a bully who intruded on them" (1983, 148). While ascribing intentions and emotions to dynamic events (e.g., bullying someone), Heider seems to tell us, the observer never loses sight of the whole of the events. Intentionality and emotions are not simply projected onto the events, but are connected to a judgment within a communicative context; the observers saw the hand of a narrator (Heider) in the events and integrated this knowledge in their reflection on the intentions and emotions of the geometrical figures. In this sense, the test subjects perceived the events as part of a *story*. At the same time, the experimental situation turned into an instance of narrative communication: "the geometric shapes and their movements served as a kind of language in which Heider communicated a human interest story. How he translated this story into the language of moving geometric shapes is at least as intriguing as the fact that observers were able to infer the story from the movements" (Malle and Ickes 2000, 204). The nucleus of Heider's argument, in other words, is that narrative communication (i.e., communication by means of a series of causally linked observations and statements directed at solving a conflict or problem) is essential to the "commonsense psychology" of his test subjects.

The narrative nature of commonsense psychology, later called folk psychology, came as no surprise to Heider. While developing the presentation of his hypotheses, he had dedicated himself mainly to the study of literary sources. From his teacher Kurt Lewin, he had learned that predictions about behavior could be found in the work of such authors as Dostoyevsky. Moreover, the introduction to *The Psychology of Interpersonal Relations* tells us Heider believed "that the insights concerning interpersonal relations embodied in fables, novels and other literary forms, provide a fertile source of understanding" (Heider 1958, 7). Indeed, *stories*, according to Heider, are preeminent vehicles for the study of commonsense psychology; they show how people in everyday life handle interpersonal relations, and they reveal the emotions and judgments that go along with these relations. "In everyday life we form ideas about other people and about social situations. We interpret other people's actions and we predict what they will do under certain circumstances. Though these ideas are usually not formulated, they often function adequately" (Heider 1958, 5). With his narrative view on folk psychology, Heider anticipated a way of resolving the dispute between "theory theory" and "simulation theory" that has recently emerged in fields such as cognitive and developmental psychology and the philosophy of mind.

Theory theory claims that folk-psychological attributions (the attribution of specific mental states to others) are founded in principles and rules that can be compared to a theory (e.g., our ability to recognize anger on the basis of our theory about anger in general; see Ravenscroft 2004). Simulation theory, on the other hand, does not invoke theoretical knowledge to conceptualize our folk-psychological abilities, but refers to the procedural nature of our reflection on mental states; we are likely to simulate the processes we attribute to others when we want to interpret the mental states of others (e.g., our ability to simulate what it is to be angry in specific situations; see Gordon 2009). Both theories, Heider would say, formulate the problem in a reductionist manner. The question is not so much how the human brain works but rather how the human brain functions in a social environment. Studying the role of stories and storytelling in commonsense psychology will help us to further develop Heider's project "to develop a theory of social perception and to construct a theory of how people think about social behavior" (Heider 1958, 5).

To this end, my chapter builds on Heider's project as well as Daniel Hutto's more recent work on the narrative practice hypothesis (NPH). This hypothesis is directly related to Shaun Gallagher's interaction theory, and more specifically to his view that "[t]he understanding of the other person is primarily neither theoretical nor based on an internal simulation. It is a form of embodied practice" (Gallagher 2005, 208; cf. Kuzmičová's discussion of embodiment in this volume). The NPH leaves room for social and psychological reflection in the manner of Heider—given that it starts from "the underexamined idea that our interpretative abilities may well be socioculturally grounded" (Hutto 2008, x). By emphasizing the sociocultural basis of the commonsense psychology people employ and by stressing the pivotal role of narrative in sociocultural environments, my analysis ties up with Sommer's contribution to this volume and focuses on the function of narrative practices in everyday life, especially on the stories people attribute to the behavior of others.

Even though I endorse many aspects of Hutto's hypothesis, I would like to point out that implementing it without sufficient caution could lead to a new form of reductionism. Only when we succeed in meticulously determining the different ways in which narrative procedures are at the basis of the human epistemic faculties will we be able to turn the NPH into a workable theory that may prove fruitful in philosophical anthropology. David Herman has made an important contribution to this endeavor with his pilot study "Storied Minds: Narrative Scaffolding for Folk Psychology." Herman introduced the idea that stories, through the action models that they embed, structure our interpretations of others' behavior. In Herman's view, the action models employed by an observer are responsible for generating an understanding of the reasons for actions. These action models also determine the procedure for attributing these reasons to actors. Herman manages to concretize Hutto's concept of "narrative practice" by characterizing the "narrative-enabled modelling procedures" (2009, 65) that help us to account for our own and others' actions.

Following directly from his argument, my contribution seeks to apply the NPH in the richest manner possible by asserting that we need to take into account the full range of "narrative practices" in order to produce evidence for Hutto's account of the folk-psychological basis of human knowledge. Herman pays little attention to an important aspect of the human epistemic faculty, namely, our tendency, as far as our social interaction is concerned, to deal with the behavior of others in terms of systems of moral norms.[1] Hutto does not take moral norms into account either, for that matter. Yet the literary tradition in the Western world compellingly shows that human beings are fascinated by stories in which moral qualities are ascribed to the behavior of people. Some heroes are brave and honest (e.g., James Bond), others are mean and treacherous (e.g., the villains in gothic novels and fairy tales). It is striking to see the frequency with which "thick moral concepts" (to use a term discussed in my next paragraph) appear in traditional stories—fairy tales, adventure stories (from the Hellenistic variants via those of the Middle Ages to the popular modern-day and contemporary variants), and picaresque stories—in order to enrich those stories with a moral lesson.

The notion of "thick moral concepts" was first introduced by British moral philosopher Bernard Williams (1985, 140–43; see also Bennett 1998) to distinguish relatively abstract moral concepts, such as "right" and "good," which he calls "thin," from other, more richly specified concepts such as treachery, loyalty, usury, and courage, which he labeled "thick." Such thick moral concepts play the leading part in Western literary history. Interestingly, these concepts are also prominent in the everyday intersubjective sphere. As we all know from personal experience, moralistic judgments—that is, judgments of others' conduct in terms of systems of moral norms—often constitute the basis for attributing motivational drives behind the others' actions. Such moral judgments play a determining role in situations in which we demonstrate our talent as folk psychologists. In other words, we tend to read others' minds by way of motives for action that are based on *thick* moral concepts. Hence moral judgments and moral reasoning, which can be linked to Herman's ideas about "modeling procedures," need to be taken seriously in the development of the NPH.

Thick moral concepts, I argue, go hand in hand with a specific narrative logic. Stories about treachery and courage, for example (think of Chrétien de Troyes and Ian Fleming), evoke an implicit or even explicit morality—they introduce normative concepts to qualify the behavior of the story's characters. In constructing this moralistic pattern of narration, readers and writers employ a fairly rigid action model. Such narrative models, and the moral judgments that they enable, are exemplary for specific folk-psychological attitudes. Those evoked by Heider's experiment, for example, closely resemble the attitudes adopted by readers and writers in their (re)construction of a story structured in terms of clearly defined moral oppositions. At issue is how readers construct a storyworld on the basis of a holistic action pattern that sometimes moves away from a moral ideal and sometimes moves toward it. In short, thick moral concepts are a key facet of action models; to a greater or lesser degree, they give shape to the folk-psychological capabilities of human beings.

In what follows, I first discuss the way in which action models featuring thick moral concepts contrast with the action models that are central to the thought of Herman and Hutto. Next, I situate the narrative procedures grounded in such thick moral concepts against the backdrop of developments in modern literature. These developments provide an additional context for investigating the narrative practices discussed by Herman and Hutto. Throughout the argument, my main focus is on the diversity of moral attitudes displayed by people when engaging in folk-psychological reasoning about their own and others' conduct.

Minimalist Causality Attribution

One of the most important arguments Daniel Hutto discusses in his attempt to rethink previous approaches to folk psychology (i.e., theory

theory and simulation theory) is concerned with the problem of causality: "proficiency in making isolated propositional attitude ascriptions—attributing certain goals, desires, thoughts and beliefs—is not the same as knowing how these combine to become reasons. This stronger condition must be satisfied if one is to be a folk psychologist" (2007, 52–53). It is not enough to ascertain that the observed person displays certain mental states to understand his or her behavior. Implicitly inspired by Donald Davidson's highly influential reflections on actions, reasons, and causes (e.g., 1963, 9), Herman and Hutto believe that a more sophisticated cognitive operation is needed, one that involves causality. In turn, because causality is one of the fundamental conditions of narrativity, it is fair to say that an experienced folk psychologist needs to have insight into stories. Attributing reasons for others' behavior requires training in narrative practice. It requires the ability, acquired through experience, to use stories to make sense of the conduct of both self and other.

As I said before, this new view on folk psychology can be considered an important breakthrough in the development of folk psychology theory. I follow Hutto when he states that folk psychology research needs to start from the study of narrative practices—the study of "stories about protagonists who act for reasons" (2008, xii)—and when he claims that a person only becomes a folk psychologist when he or she is able to ascribe reasons for the actions of others. I also follow David Herman's complementary argument that the knowledge of causal relations needed for folk-psychological insights can be founded narratologically. Narrative practices, as Herman concludes from his reading of Hutto, precede the cognitive operations human beings use in their attempts at interpreting each other's behavior: "ascriptions of beliefs, desires, goals, and other mental states emerge from . . . storylines, rather than providing the basis for them" (2009, 65).

But Hutto's and Herman's accounts are fairly general, and I would like to refine them by introducing concepts from moral theory. I consider the question of morality to be an important element in reflections about the narrative nature of folk-psychological phenomena, because the attribution of reasons for acting is most clearly observable in moral judgments. "In making moral judgments," says Geoff Sayre-McCord, "we seem to be making a claim that, if true, establishes that someone or other has a reason to act or be a certain way" (2007). In order to refine Hutto's and Herman's insights I would like to explore the kind of moral judgments that are involved in the narrative practices that underlie our folk-psychological inclinations; more specifically, I will introduce a distinction between two types of "moral" causality that I consider to be crucial. A story that is used to account for the behavior of another person may vary according to the degree of complexity of the causal rationale applied for this purpose. It makes a difference whether a folk psychologist wants to understand individual intentions or whether he or she attempts to map collectively embedded goals. The reasons a person may have to act as an individual are subject to other factors and contingencies than those bearing on a person guided by collective objectives. The individual's reasons, and the effects of those reasons, will be much more heterogeneous ("rhizomatic") than the reasons associated with collective goals and norms. Consequently, the action models that underlie stories about individual behavior will necessarily be more complex than the models employed for group-determined or group-oriented behavior. If a person acts on the basis of moral traditions or on the basis of collective motivations of action, simple, stereotypical action models can suffice; the observer does not need to give a maximalist description of the motivating reasons for action, but can limit the description to a minimal set of reasons for action.

A fine illustration of this contrast can be found in the way Flaubert's contemporaries reacted to Emma Bovary's mental state. Even if Emma's reasons for action are essentially heterogeneous (or at least are depicted as such by Flaubert), the bourgeois community that put Flaubert and his publisher on trial, on the basis of moral judgments, reduced the psychological complexity of the character (together with the complex motivation that inspired the author of the novel) to a minimal set of reasons for action. From this discrepancy we can conclude that Flaubert's maximalist attitude contrasts with the minimalist attitude of his prosecutors in court. In the rest of this chapter, I will use the terms "maximalist causality attribution" and "minimalist causality attribution" to refer to these contrasting attitudes or contrasting narrative strategies for attributing reasons for action. The first covers the attribution of reasons that are connected with individual intentionality (personal goals, desires, or insights), while the latter covers the attribution of reasons that are related to collective goals (socially relevant societal ideals and other thick moral concepts).

Generally speaking, these two types constitute the poles between which every folk psychologist's narrative practice must oscillate. Moreover, and this would be my modest contribution to the folk psychology debate, maximalist and minimalist causality attribution go together with two ways in which stories can be used to make sense of observed behavior. One way to "read" the behavior of other persons seems to be modeled after an interpretation strategy that dominates our reading of traditional texts—chivalric romances, but also adventure stories that follow the James Bond format and the Christopher Vogler recipes, or love romances from the Hellenistic period to contemporary dime novels. Another way to deal with "reasons for action" involves more complex reading strategies that were developed to tackle modern literature—that is, the literary tradition since the rise of the "realistic" novel in the eighteenth century and the subsequently acquired taste for psychological realism in novels.

Although both reading strategies can be used for both types of literature, readers will be prompted by traditional stories to adopt well-structured and fairly simple action models to make sense of the characters' conduct. They will, on the other hand, broaden their scope toward more complex action models when confronted with, say, a psychological novel. Before I discuss in more detail these two opposing action models generated by Western narrative culture, let me turn to the way minimalist causality attribution emerges in the case of an actor who is driven by thick moral concepts or who projects such concepts onto the behavior of others.

A first form of minimalist causality attribution can be found in mythical patterns of thought. One of the peculiarities of mythical thought is the magical interpretation of others' behavior. Note that the actor's intentionality, which is the central object of attention in Hutto's philosophy, is not decisive in the case of magical interpretation of behavior. Nevertheless, (quasi-)magical thinking is fairly pervasive even today. In our culture, few people would readily throw a wedding ring into a river without having a bad feeling about it or experiencing some presentiment of doom. Nor would I be inclined to disfigure a picture of my mother without being forced to do so. Rather than instigating a quest for intentions, observing this sort of behavior (or non-behavior) involves a quest for the observed person's worldview. The question raised by magical behavior is a question about values (in both examples, it would be the thick moral concept of loyalty) that make a person refrain from acting in a certain way. Granted, this kind of belief in magical forms of causality may not be comparable to behavior that is characterized by extensive psychological deliberation.

Still, it equally springs from reasons and therefore equally belongs to folk psychology's toolkit. Significantly, Fritz Heider maintained that an explanation of behavior "must deal with common sense psychology regardless of whether its assumptions and principles prove valid under scientific scrutiny. If a person believes that the lines in his palm foretell his future, this belief must be taken into account in explaining certain of his expectations and actions" (1958, 5). In order to understand how the magical interpretation of behavior goes hand in hand with what David Herman (2009, 65) calls "narrative-enabled modelling procedures," we may consult the observations on mythical thought gathered in cultural philosophy and anthropology by Ernst Cassirer in the 1920s.

Cassirer presented his findings in the second part of his magnum opus, *The Philosophy of Symbolic Forms*. Cassirer explains that the essence of mythical thought is to be found in its concept of causality: "mythical thinking is by no means lacking in the universal category of cause and effect, which is in a sense one of its very fundamentals" (1975, 43). In mythical cosmogonies and theogonies he discovers a narrative practice that is based on a temporal and spatial logic that differs radically from the logic of other worldviews. The "narrative" consecration of an original temporal and spatial state is of crucial importance to these kinds of myths. Myths categorically distinguish between an eternal *inside* world enclosing the original sacred forces and an *outside* world consisting of empirical, fleeting events (1975, 130). As such, mythical thought expresses the conviction that eternal forces govern the cosmos; implied in it is the belief that the seemingly chaotic forces of nature have a stable center and eternally preserve their harmonious rhythm. Keeping this worldview in mind, we can easily explain how minimalist causality attribution works in mythical and magical thought. When a certain behavior is observed, the observer will try to connect the facts from the empirical "outside" world with the logic of the mythical "inside" world.

It goes without saying that this connection between the actual behavior of mythological figures and suprapersonal reasons for events has little in common with ascribing complex intentions to an actor in everyday social interaction. Similarly, it should come as no surprise that Hutto barely takes into account such minimalist causality attributions. As I have said before, Hutto sees causal explanations based on more complex individual intentions as more important.[2] This is obvious, for example, from his claim that certain cultures do not attach any causal meaning to intentional actions: "It is far from given that all cultures make sense of intentional actions in terms of reasons" (2008, 188). With the causal reasonings of mythical thought in mind, we could restate this sentence in order to arrive at a more accurate account of the scope of action logic: "It is far from given that all reasons for action must be considered as the result of an individual intention." A person thinking in mythical fashion does not interpret certain kinds of behavior as the result of an individual intention, but rather as spontaneous effects of the divine or animistic forces that obey the norms of an original world. Such interpretations are concerned with the impersonal ("Foucauldian") power exercised by institutions and social groups through tradition-driven discursive practices.

Hutto does not take into account these forms of psychology. At this point, he allows research from the field of moral theory and cultural anthropology to overrule his philosophy. S. N. Balagangadhara, for example, believes it to be typical of Western societies that behavior is interpreted in terms of individual intentions. To this tendency he opposes other concepts of morality that involve a phenomenon we could call "orthopraxis." Many cultures, and even Western culture when it is involved in certain ideological, magical, or moralistic practices, do not always rely on individual reasons for action (which we could call "orthodoxy"). Instead, they conceptualize behavior in terms of good practices and good habits, in terms of pregiven norms and concepts of normality:

> To be moral, in the West, is to follow some or other moral principle. The relation is between an individual, isolated subject and some injunction or the other. . . . By contrast, [in] a culture dominated by mimesis (like India) the relation is *between* individuals (be they the really existing community or the fictitious individuals portrayed in the stories). A moral individual, in other words, presupposes a moral community. . . . One of the basic beliefs in the Western tradition is that human action is goal oriented action, and that this constitutes an *intrinsic* property of human actions. . . . But mimesis, as a subintentional learning that involves the ability to execute actions, does not require the presence of goals. Practical activity, practical knowledge is not intentional and it is not goal-directed. (Balagangadhara 1987, 90, 93)

It follows that a different type of folk psychology must be taken into account, namely, a psychology that attributes causality on the basis of a pregiven worldview. Because of this reductionism, I choose to call this folk-psychological concept of causality "minimalist."

A second form of minimalist causality is active in patterns of thought found in the simply structured, moralistic stories from the period preceding the rise of the novel, as well as in many forms of popular narrative culture. Such stories, in my view, prove that the process of ascribing reasons for action in post-mythical times can still recruit from a pregiven worldview. The worldview of a *roman de geste*, for example, or of a Hellenist romance is characterized by a rigid action model that barely leaves room for the attribution of complex psychological reasons to the observed behavior. On the contrary, this behavior is first and foremost placed in the service of a higher goal, namely, the affirmation of collective values.

The clearest proof of the power of collective values in our narrative practices is found in the use of an action model with a pronounced *happy ending* or, by contrast, with a distinct refusal of happy endings (as in tragic stories). Such endings confer a clear moral meaning on the storyworld; no wonder that the moral of the story is explicitly inserted as a coda in some stories. Indirectly, these story endings are responsible for putting the protagonists' behavior into a straitjacket of thick moral concepts. Jurij Lotman is right in claiming that our fondness for happy endings can be linked to this tendency toward a moralistic interpretation: "that's why a good or bad ending is so significant for us: it attests not only to the conclusion of some plot, but also to the construction of the world as a whole" (1977, 216). A moralizing conclusion to a story gives a mythical touch to the interpretation of the protagonists' behavior, as the story's dynamics are modeled after a voyage through an "outside" world that ends in (re-) gaining access to an "inside" world, where the community's collective values emerge in full glory.

From an evolutionary psychological and folk-psychological perspective, David Geary has described similar narrative practices as "perfect world simulations":

A perfect world is one in which the individual is able to organize and control social (e.g., mating dynamics), biological (e.g., access to food), and physical (e.g., shelter) resources in ways that would have enhanced the survival or reproductive options of the individual and kin during human evolution. The evolved function of the simulation is to enable the use of problem solving, reasoning, attributions, and so forth, to devise behavioral strategies that can be used to reduce the difference between one's current situation and this perfect world. (2005, 494–95)

In these "traditionalist" fictional works, however, a perfectly balanced mythical world is rarely explicit. Our narratives bear witness to our tendency to address those facts that distance us from the mythical state of harmony, reflecting our desire to confront the negative. Narratives confront us with the non-mythological state, with an imperfect world. This confrontation does not derive from a masochistic desire but rather from the same longing for happiness and perfection we find in mythological thought (Hogan 2003, 221). In order to tell us of deprivation and hope, these stories not only adumbrate the perfect world we wish for but also focus on the vicissitudes that keep us from reaching this world. Evocations of contingencies are absolutely vital to the "traditionalist" narrative practices, because stories are only interesting ("tellable"; D. Herman 2002, 84) inasmuch as they contain a picture of the imperfect world that haunts us (D. Herman 2005, 83; D. Herman 2009, 48).

Initially, one would expect the protagonists' confrontation with the contingencies of the imperfect world to render their behavior more unpredictable and the causality attribution more complex. Yet this is only partially the case. To a certain extent, the protagonists in adventure stories have a degree of freedom to take initiative (and to have personal reasons for their behavior). Intentional states such as believing, desiring, intending, and grasping a meaning (the most obvious proofs of a self-conscious mind; see Bruner 1990, 8) are manifestly present in these stories. The protagonists' intentions, however, are overshadowed by a fairly rigid worldview and by the norms (i.e., thick moral concepts) and concepts of normality that characterize this worldview.

My point is that, in "premodern" and "popular" narrative practices, we are inclined to read the intentions of the protagonists by reducing them to moral traditions and social habits. The intentional state of an adventurer in a Chrétien de Troyes novel, for instance, becomes more meaningful if his intentions are interpreted as part of a well-structured narrative whole, in the same manner applied to the protagonists in the story Heider and Simmel used in their experiments. The courageous or loyal intentions of the hero (based on thick moral concepts) are best expressed when they are linked to a plot-overarching causal framework; the desire to make the world perfect again and the belief that the forces of good will overcome the forces of evil are only meaningful within a plot structure in which the equilibrium of the world is a self-evident given. For these "traditionalist" narrative practices, the remark of narratologist Gerald Prince is a fundamental law: "Many narratives can be viewed as teleologically determined. Narrative often displays itself in terms of an end which functions as its (partial) condition, its magnetizing force, its organizing principle" (1982, 157).

The Narrative Practice Hypothesis and the Diversity of Narrative Action Models

My contribution to the NPH focuses on the tendency toward minimalist causality attribution, which I described above as inherent to traditional narrative practices. More broadly, Western narrative culture shows that at least two types of causality attribution can govern our narrative practices. One could argue that the minimalist way of reading and writing was dominant until the maximalist way gradually gained in importance, in response to (and as a cause of) wider changes in the surrounding culture. The differences in causality attribution indicate two models of reading, two strategies for interpreting events in stories viewed from one or the other action model.

The same models of reading return in two traditions in narratology, classical formalist and structuralist narratology on the one hand, and postclassical narratology on the other. Both types, however, are more than mere methods of reading. In what follows, I argue that, from the perspective of folk-psychological research, these reading methods can also be seen as distinct modeling procedures that govern the ways of moral thinking that accompany our narrative practices.

The schemas drawn up by structuralist narratologists to plumb the depths of plot mechanisms (e.g., Vladimir Propp's list of narrative functions or A. J. Greimas's actantial scheme) are particularly suitable for the more traditional texts discussed above. Todorov (who at the end of the 1960s developed a "grammaire du récit," or narrative grammar, in his seminal works; see Todorov 1968 and 1969) and Bremond (1981) have generalized this schema by pointing out that a narrative in its elementary state generates a story arc: it stretches from a state of balance to a situation of imbalance, which at the end of the narrative bends back to a new or renewed state of balance. Jurij Lotman briefly recapitulates the definition of traditional narrative practices by simultaneously contrasting them with Mikhail Bakhtin's view of the modern novel.

> In Propp's description, a text gravitates toward panchronic equilibrium: . . . there is only an oscillation around some homeostatic norm (equilibrium—disruption of equilibrium—calmoration of equilibrium). In Bakhtin's analysis, the inevitability of movement, change, and destruction is latent even in the static state of a text. . . . For Propp, the natural domain of a text is the folk tale, but for Bakhtin it is the novel and the play. (1981, 39)

Not only Bakhtin, but many literary theorists in recent decades have sensed that the definition given by structuralist semiotics failed to cover the variety of narrative practice in Western literatures. They found that applying formalist schemas to the modern novel, for instance, has never really been a successful method of analysis (L. Herman and Vervaeck 2005, 54). Some tend to seek the reason for this deficiency in the fact that the modern novel possesses properties intrinsically different from other text types. José Ortega y Gasset discusses this issue in his *Notes on the Novel* (1927) when he addresses the topic of the "disappearance of the plot" (Ortega 1948, 63) in modern literature. "Epics, romances of chivalry, adventure stories, dime novels, serials" are, according to Ortega, based on an action "which moves as fast as possible toward a conclusion" (1948, 80–81). The modern novel, on the other hand, proceeds from quite different principles: "The essence of the novel—that is to say, of the modern novel with which alone I am here concerned—does not lie in 'what happens' but precisely in the opposite: in the personages' pure living, in their being and being thus, above all, in the ensuing milieu" (87).

Indeed, the action models constructed in order to understand the modern novel of psychological realism are entirely different from the more limited, restrictive models employed when minimalist causality attribution is involved. Drawing on the Bakhtinian concept of "dialogic thought," Alan Palmer submits (largely in keeping with my own insights on this matter; see Keunen 2007 and Keunen 2011) that it is possible to describe modern narrative practices in a more adequate way. In *Fictional Minds*, Palmer argues in favor of a narratology that takes into account "the dialogic nature of characters' embedded narratives and the nature of the fictional storyworld as a battleground within which the thoughts and actions of individuals contend and clash" (2004, 152–53). Indeed, Bakhtin's work on narratives of psychological realism (such as Dostoyevsky) suggests that these stories can very well be thought of as experiments of complex folk psychology.

In such stories, neither characters nor readers can fall back on prefabricated action models and worldviews. Rather, they are faced with more complex and individualized psychological constructions that have to be created *in situ* by means of what Patrick Hogan has called "situational empathy." For Hogan, "situational empathy" is a psychological attitude that is composed of "fusion or mapping with a perspectival shift" by means of which the observer "maps his/her memory onto the current situation, but his/her perspectival place in the memory is now taken by the other person" (2003, 142).[3] Situational empathy is an indispensable tool in reading modern novels, for an obvious reason: the protagonists' behavior is so crucially central that, to a great extent, the story's meaning comes to depend on the manner in which "reasons for action" are ascribed to protagonists. In Dostoyevsky's world, says Bakhtin (1984, 7), characters are no longer objects ("fixed elements in the author's design"). The overall action model (or plot-space; cf. Lotman 1979, 168) is no longer a combination of "finalized images of people in the unity of a monologically perceived and understood world" but rather a "plurality of equally-valid consciousnesses, each with its own world. In Dostoyevsky's novels, the ordinary pragmatics of the plot play a secondary role and perform special and unusual functions. The ultimate clamps that hold his novelistic world together are of a different sort entirely; the fundamental event revealed through his novel does not lend itself to an ordinary pragmatic interpretation at the level of the plot" (Bakhtin 1984, 7). It is Alan Palmer's belief that Bakhtin's work "provides part of the theoretical basis for a new approach toward the analysis of presentations of fictional minds in novels" (Palmer 2004, 156–57). According to Palmer, Bakhtin's views on modern fictional action models constitute a first step toward a theory that emphasizes "the social basis of thought" (157). As such, Palmer anticipates both Hutto's NPH and the stance David Herman adopts toward Ian McEwan's *On Chesil Beach*. In his analysis, Herman emphasizes that the writing and reading of fictional texts boils down to a complex manipulation of the temporal awareness of the novel's characters. The novel's subject ("the central conflict . . . between Edward's and Florence's attitudes toward the wedding night and all that it entails"; D. Herman 2009, 61) can only be reconstructed if readers and writers take into account the ways in which "the motivations, structure, and consequences of actions" are connected with "multiple positions in time" (2009, 56). As far as modern literature is concerned, Herman shows, the art of interpreting is mainly a construction of complex action models that map "how one action entails others over time" and show that "an action performed at one temporal location can generate reasons for acting that are distributed across time" (2009, 59).

As Herman's comments on McEwan's novel indicate, the network of moments in a modern plot-space is in need of a concept of time that differs from the holistic awareness of time inherent in minimalist causality attribution. Modern literature is in need of a completely different concept of plot and a different form of thematics. The teleological reconstruction of a linear timeline does not match with the development of time in the modern novel. Modern novels undergo a Kantian revolution. This revolution implies a new conceptualization of time—to put it in the words of Arthur Schopenhauer: "Before Kant we were in time; now time is in us" ("Vor Kant waren wir in der Zeit, seit Kant ist sie in uns") (1969, 424). Bakhtin seems to mirror this view of the Kantian revolution when he characterizes the construction of the novel of emergence: "Changes in the hero himself acquire plot significance, and thus the entire plot of the novel is reinterpreted and reconstructed. Time is introduced into man, enters into his very image, changing in a fundamental way the significance of all aspects of his destiny and life" (1986, 21). In the modern novel, characters and their dialogue with their environment (social forces as well as the psychological forces that are inherent to the character) are indeed central. As a result, the "closure," the teleological focus on a final resolution of the story, is devalued. Teleology is still possible, yet this principle no longer dominates the composition. In the modern novel, change on the level of the plot becomes a matter of relations between states of consciousness. Consequently, this type of novel will focus on more complex, maximalist causality attributions.

The shift in temporal awareness—from a linear emplotment obsessed with the magnetic force of "the perfect world" to a network of variously characterized, experienced moments in time—also goes hand in hand with a change in the moral load of the stories. My distinction between two types of folk-psychological tendencies of action modeling is supported by philosophical reflection in contemporary moral theory. According to Charles Larmore, the difference in moral reasoning that I have been discussing is a difference between modern and classical thinking about human action. The modern approach considers rational behavior from the point of view of a "sort of self-understanding that *ought* to be ours, namely, one in which we view our deepest commitments not as the objects of autonomous choice but rather as the expression of our belonging to a given form of life" (1996, 58). In classical moral thought (and within the kind of narrative intelligence found in older moralistic stories and in some strata of today's popular culture), the faculty of reason requires the agents "to stand back critically from their way of life as a whole, as though its ultimate aim were to view the world *sub specie aeternitatis*" (58). While protagonists in traditional and popular stories are straitjacketed in action models that are supported by a global idea about ways of living, characters in modern stories tend to apply a concept of reason directed toward the way in which human beings "are to go on within the terms of [a] way of life" (58). Only in situations of doubt and crisis does modern humankind seek for justifications for its moral beliefs: "not belief itself, but change of belief, forms the proper object of justification" (60).

My distinction between maximalist and minimalist causality attribution seamlessly fits in with Larmore's distinction. The impact of individual decisions is minimized because the interpretation reduces behavior to pregiven worldviews and is influenced by traditional thick moral concepts. Conversely, a maximal development of individual decisions will tend to question the pregiven schemas of interpretation. Clearly, narrative practices in Western culture operationalize both forms of interpretation simultaneously. In the same way, we can determine that the maximalist interpretation of behavior is closely tied up with the rise of modern culture. In "The Novel in Search of Itself," Thomas Pavel gives a fine outline of the options available to Western narrative culture in the sphere of morality:

> [T]he novel raises, with extraordinary precision, the philosophical question of whether moral ideals are inherent in this world, for, if

they are, why do they seem so remote from human behavior, and if they are not, why does their normative value impose itself so clearly on us? For the novel to raise this question is to ask whether, in order to defend their ideals, humans should resist the world, plunge in to try to defend moral order, or concentrate on trying to correct their own frailties. (2006, 3)

Pavel's distinction between moral ideals inherent in the world and those that lie hidden in human beings corresponds to the two kinds of narrative practices I introduced above, those evoking a minimalist and a maximalist causality attribution, respectively. In the first case, when moral ideals are intrinsic to the storyworld, we are dealing with external obstacles and with hero(in)es who are the incarnations of these moral values (Grendel versus Beowulf, e.g.). Narratives of this kind invariably end with "the moral of the story," sometimes explicitly, sometimes implicitly. Defending the moral order and a preestablished moral objective is the story's primary concern. Readers of these kinds of stories are thus invited to ascribe to the protagonists a restricted, minimal set of reasons (minimalist causality attribution).

Maximalist commonsense psychology may also contain moral ideals, but these are embodied by psychologized characters. The moral question in these narratives becomes, Why should we, and how can we, be moral? And also, How do I correct my own weaknesses? The overall action model (or plot-space) in this second case notably consists of crucial moments of interaction that pose moral problems to the characters' psychology. Readers of narratives of this kind are thus invited to search for a rich, maximal set of reasons (maximalist causality attribution). By inviting the observer to engage in maximalist causality attribution, modern narrative art is able to keep spreading specific moral messages, which are now attuned to post-mythical or even post-sacral times.

Although modern man or woman proves to be increasingly unable to deduce values from a "transcendental system of belief" (Brooks 1995, viii), he or she is still fascinated by the great conflict between good and evil. The difference between these more recent narratives and older, moralistic stories resides in how the characters deploy highly subjective and less rigorous teleological action lines. They are torn between moral choices that get entangled initially yet go on to form a larger whole that rounds up events.

Together with the desacralization of morality, teleological plot models and explicit moralism are relegated to the background. Peter Rabinowitz states that "one of the primary targets for many nineteenth- and twentieth-century novelists has been closure itself. . . . I would argue that many realistic writers prefer endings in which the full consequences of the events portrayed . . . are neither worked out nor clearly implied" (2002, 307). Not only does he detect this process in *Crime and Punishment*, and in *Pelléas et Mélisande*, but also—and this is in keeping with Peter Brooks's analyses in *The Melodramatic Imagination*—in the novels of Balzac and James, which truly excel at "unresolved endings." Each of these novels stages personalities and psyches, and most of the suspense is created by the relationships of tension *between* and *in* the characters. To be sure, the characters are uninterruptedly involved in problem solving and intentional, goal-directed action, perhaps even more than ever in Western narrative culture. Yet their projects only very rarely reach a conclusion. Modern literary men and women simply detest well-rounded lives.

Concluding Remark

In the preceding paragraphs, I focused on moral attitudes as an element of folk psychology. Literature provides the ideal training and testing ground because it is based on "the awareness, shared by author and readers, that the story being told belongs to a special kind of cultural artifact that debates (either figuratively or allegorically) the normative dilemmas and the value conflicts of actual and invented beings alike" (Pavel 2000, 535–36). The current narratological approach to folk psychology likewise maintains that fiction provides insight into human processes of thought, especially into our ability to search for "reasons for action"; yet curiously, the debates start from the assumption that these reasons are situated at a level "beyond good and evil," that all stories propagate a post-Nietzschean lifestyle. In my contribution to the discussion, I have brought a specific *kind* of reasons for acting to the fore, namely *moral* ones. An "ethical turn" as advocated by Thomas Pavel is capable of reshaping research by pointing out that fiction demonstrates the manner in which the human brain handles the gap between the empirical world and the world of human desires: "the poet and the reader must also know how to distance themselves from the world of 'is,' the empirical realm, in order to explore its dependence on the world of 'ought,' the realm of norms, and the world of 'praise,' the realm of values" (2000, 532).

Acknowledgments

This chapter has greatly benefited from valuable comments by Sofie Verraest, Tom Claes, Freddy Mortier, Geert Vandermeersche, and Lars Bernaerts. I would like to thank Jo Smets for translating the original Dutch text into English.

Notes

1. In fact, Herman himself points out the importance of such models in Western narrative culture: "Admittedly, in folktales and (some) myths the lines between villainy and heroism may be starkly drawn; in these contexts narrative representations of action embody the simplifying and idealizing functions standardly attributed to models" (D. Herman 2009, 53). Yet, he does not appear to put much trust into research taking this direction.

2. The fact that Hutto does not discuss peripheral models of causality should not be taken to mean that he denies their possibility. "The NPH," he writes, "predicts that if cultures diverge in significant ways in the profile of their narrative practices, we can expect to find different local tendencies and proficiencies in the use of folk psychology" (2008, 188). Other theorists (e.g., Thomas 2001) equally extend folk-psychological research by describing anthropological differences. In these studies, however, NPH's essential component, the belief that folk psychology is based on narrative action models, is neglected.

3. Minimalist causality attribution in its turn may be associated with what Hogan, following Duckitt's empirical work, calls "categorial empathy": "When people 'are given the opportunity to discriminate' against outgroups, they 'show increased self-esteem' (Duckitt 1992, 85). It is, of course, just this sort of collective self-definition that provides the basis for the social prototype of happiness as group domination. In this prototype, the group is, in effect, a version of oneself, an in-group with whom one shares a definitive categorical identity. It is also this sort of group definition that provides a ground for the ethics of group protection, for the group to be protected is the in-group (national, religious, or whatever). Empathy based on this sort of identification, I will refer to as 'categorical empathy'" (Hogan 2001, 18; Hogan 2003, 141).

References

Bakhtin, Mikhail M. 1984 [1929]. *Problems of Dostoevsky's Poetics*. Ed. and trans. Caryl Emerson. Manchester: Manchester University Press.

———. 1986. "The Bildungsroman and Its Significance in the History of Realism." In *Speech Genres and Other Late Essays*, ed. Caryl Emerson and Michael Holquist, 10–59. Austin: University of Texas Press.

Balagangadhara, S. N. 1987. "Comparative Anthropology and Action Sciences: An Essay on Knowing to Act and Acting to Know." *Philosophica* 2:77–107.

Bennett, Jonathan. 1998. *The Act Itself*. Oxford: Oxford University Press.

Bremond, Claude. 1981 [1966]. "La logique des possibles narratifs." In *L' analyse structurale du récit (Communications 8)*, ed. Roland Barthes et al., 66–83. Paris: Seuil.

Brooks, Peter. 1995 [1976]. *The Melodramatic Imagination: Balzac, Henry James, Melodrama, and the Mode of Excess*. New Haven: Yale University Press.

Bruner, Jerome. 1990. *Acts of Meaning*. Cambridge: Harvard University Press.

Cassirer, Ernst. 1975 [1925]. *The Philosophy of Symbolic Forms*. Vol. 2, *Mythical Thought*. New Haven: Yale University Press.

Davidson, David. 1963 [1980]. "Actions, Reasons, and Causes." In *Essays on Actions and Events*, 3–19. Oxford: Clarendon Press.

Duckitt, John H. 1992. *The Social Psychology of Prejudice*. New York: Praeger.

Gallagher, Shaun. 2005. *How the Body Shapes the Mind*. Oxford: Oxford University Press.

Geary, David C. 2005. "Folk Knowledge and Academic Learning." In *Origins of the Social Mind*, ed. Bruce J. Ellis and David F. Bjorklund, 493–519. New York: Guilford. http://web.missouri.edu/~gearyd/FolkKnowledgePDF.pdf (accessed April 26, 2010).

Gordon, Robert M. 2009. "Folk Psychology as Mental Simulation." *Stanford Encyclopedia of Philosophy*. http://plato.stanford.edu/entries/folkpsych-simulation/ (accessed April 26, 2010).

Greimas, Algirdas Julien. 1966. *Sémantique structurale*. Paris: Larousse.

———. 1981 [1966]. "Eléments pour une théorie de l'interprétation du récit mythique." In *L' analyse structurale du récit (Communications 8)*, ed. Roland Barthes et al., 34–65. Paris: Seuil.

Heider, Fritz. 1958. *The Psychology of Interpersonal Relations*. Hillsdale NJ: Erlbaum.

———. 1983. *A Life as a Psychologist: An Autobiography*. Lawrence: University Press of Kansas.

Heider, Fritz, and Marianne Simmel. 1944. "An Experimental Study of Apparent Behavior." *American Journal of Psychology* 57:243–49.

Herman, David. 2002. *Story Logic: Problems and Possibilities of Narrative*. Lincoln: University of Nebraska Press.

———. 2005. "Conflict." In *The Routledge Encyclopedia of Narrative Theory*, ed. David Herman, Manfred Jahn and Marie-Laure Ryan, 83. London: Routledge.

———. 2009. "Storied Minds: Narrative Scaffolding for Folk Psychology." *Journal of Consciousness Studies* 16 (6–8): 40–68.

Herman, Luc, and Bart Vervaeck. 2005. *Handbook of Narrative Analysis.* Lincoln: University of Nebraska Press.

Hogan, Patrick Colm. 2001. *Literary Universals.* http://litup.unipa.it/docs/story.htm/ (accessed April 26, 2010).

———. 2003. *The Mind and Its Stories.* Cambridge: Cambridge University Press.

Hutto, Daniel D. 2007. "The Narrative Practice Hypothesis: Origins and Applications of Folk Psychology." In *Narrative and Understanding Persons,* ed. Daniel Hutto, 43–68. Cambridge: Cambridge University Press.

———. 2008. *Folk Psychological Narratives: The Sociocultural Basis of Understanding Reasons.* Cambridge: Cambridge University Press.

Keunen, Bart. 2007. *Verhaal en Verbeelding: Chronotopen in de Westerse verhaalcultuur.* Gent: Academia Press.

———. 2011. *Time and Imagination: Chronotopes in Western Narrative Culture.* Evanston: Northwestern University Press.

Larmore, Charles. 1996. *The Morals of Modernity.* New York: Cambridge University Press.

Lotman, Jurij. M. 1977 [1970]. *The Structure of the Artistic Text.* Trans. from the Russian by Gail Lenhoff and Ronald Vroon. Ann Arbor: University of Michigan.

———. 1979 [1973]. "The Origin of Plot in the Light of Typology." *Poetics Today* 1 (1/2): 161–84.

———. 1981 [1972]. "Text within Text." *Soviet Psychology* 26 (3): 32–51.

Malle, Bertram F., and William Ickes. 2000. "Fritz Heider." In *Portraits of Pioneers in Psychology,* ed. Gregory A. Kimble and Michael Wertheimer, eds., 4:182–213. London: Routledge.

Ortega y Gasset, José. 1948 [1929]. *The Dehumanization of Art and Notes on the Novel.* Princeton: Princeton University Press.

Palmer, Alan. 2004. *Fictional Minds.* Lincoln: University of Nebraska Press.

Pavel, Thomas. 2000. "Fiction and Imitation." *Poetics Today* 21 (3): 521–41.

———. 2006. "The Novel in Search of Itself: A Historical Morphology." In *The Novel,* vol. 2, *Forms and Themes,* ed. Franco Moretti, 3–31. Princeton: Princeton University Press.

Prince, Gerald. 1982. *Narratology: The Form and Functioning of Narrative.* Berlin and New York: Mouton.

Rabinowitz, Peter. 2002. "Reading Beginnings and Endings." In *Narrative Dynamics: Essays on Time, Plot, Closure and Frames,* ed. Brian Richardson, 300–312. Columbus: Ohio State University Press.

Ravenscroft, Ian. 2004. "Folk Psychology as a Theory." *Stanford Encyclopedia of Philosophy*. http://plato.stanford.edu/entries/folkpsych-theory/ (accessed April 26, 2010).

Sayre-McCord, Geoff. 2007. "Metaethics." *Stanford Encyclopedia of Philosophy*. http://plato.stanford.edu/entries/metaethics/ (accessed April 26, 2010).

Schopenhauer, Arthur. 1969. "Appendix: Criticism of the Kantian Philosophy." In *The World as Will and Representation*, vol. 1. New York: Dover Press.

Todorov, Tzvetan. 1968. "La grammaire du récit." *Languages* 12:94–102. http://www.persee.fr/web/revues/home/prescript/article/lgge_0458-726x_1968_num_3_12_2355/ (accessed April 26, 2010).

———. 1969. *La grammaire du Décaméron*. La Haye: Mouton.

Williams, Bernard. 1985. *Ethics and the Limits of Philosophy*. London: Fontana.

Afterword

Narrative and Mind: Directions for Inquiry

DAVID HERMAN

The present volume grows out of an international conference on "Minds and Narrative" that was held at Katholieke Universiteit Leuven, in Leuven, Belgium, in June 2009. The invigorating diversity of the book's contents reflects the many perspectives and interests that were in evidence at the conference itself.[1] Thus, assembling essays written by authors from Belgium, Canada, Germany, Italy, Scotland, Sweden, and the United States, and outlining a similarly wide range of strategies for exploring areas of intersection between storytelling and the sciences of mind, the volume suggests something of the scope and variety of the research methods, analytic goals, and corpora that now fall within the domain of mind-oriented scholarship on narrative. At the same time, the book outlines questions that are relevant for narrative-oriented scholarship on the mind.

Characterized broadly, the essays gathered here share a common focus on mental capacities and dispositions that provide grounds for—or, conversely, are grounded in—narrative experiences. Yet in examining these interfaces between story and mind, the contributors use a range of methods—from empirical studies of text processing (and memory for text) based on informants' responses to constructed as well as naturally occurring narrative examples; to a deep, reflexive engagement with individual stories, used as the basis for hypotheses about the structure and functions of narrative gaps, about how narratives invite imaginative engagement with represented worlds, or about the way encounters with fictional minds at once ground themselves in and estrange readers from everyday assumptions concerning the nature of the mental; to wide-scope investigations of how cultural differences, and storytelling traditions from different epochs, may impinge on readers' capacity for empathetic identification with characters or affect inferences about why fictional individuals act in the way they do. These and other analytic methods used by the contributors suggest the rich possibilities for research on the nexus of narrative and mind, as do other studies being conducted in the field—studies drawing on ecological-, evolutionary-, and social-psychological approaches, on neuroscientific findings, and on cross-cultural investigations of emotion.[2]

In their introduction to the volume, the editors have already provided helpful synopses of individual essays, along with an overview of the purpose and aims of the volume as a whole. I would thus like to use this brief afterword as an occasion to highlight five broader questions raised by the studies included in this book. Taken together, these open questions suggest directions for inquiry in the field; they also underscore that, when it comes to research on the interplay between narrative and mind, researchers have only begun to develop strategies for engaging with (some of) the relevant issues.

> 1. In investigations of the mind-narrative nexus, what are the prospects for integrating quantitative, empirical research and qualitative research based on the analyst's intuitions about particular narrative case studies?

The different methods of inquiry used in the contributions to part 1 grow out of two broad approaches to the interfaces between narrative and mind—and suggest the benefits of working to integrate or at least reconcile those approaches. In social-scientific parlance, the two approaches at issue can be classified as qualitative and quantitative. To draw on Barbara Johnstone's (2000) account, qualitative methods, which can also be called "phenomenological" or "intuition-driven," address questions about *how* and *why* data have the particular character that they do. By contrast, quantitative—or "empirical" or "data-driven"—methods address questions about *how much* (the degree to which) and *how often* (the frequency with which) the data of interest display a given property or set of properties.[3]

The qualitative approach, used by Elaine Auyoung in part 1 as well as by other contributors to the volume, is grounded in what might be called the phenomenology of reading.[4] In this approach analysts consult their own readerly intuitions, which are in turn made possible by the nomenclatures and structural categories that derive from the collective intuitions of a larger community of expert readers (Toolan 2001, 22). On the basis of these individual and collective intuitions, analysts propose hypotheses concerning how specific kinds of textual cues prompt interpreters to draw particular kinds of inferences about the structure, content, or effects of a given story—with the aim of making it possible to extrapolate from the example narrative to narratives in general. In this qualitative approach, goodness-of-fit between hypotheses and data stems from the overall ecological validity of the hypotheses in question—that is, from the extent to which the analyst's model can be mapped onto how readers tend to engage, in everyday settings, in the process of interpreting naturally occurring narratives, whether literary texts, newspaper stories, cinematic narratives, web-based hypertexts, or other modes of storytelling. The logical end point of the qualitative approach would thus be a theory that captures or emulates the experience of reading a particular narrative, in all its individual richness and complexity.

By contrast, the quantitative approach used by Bortolussi and Dixon, as well as by Emmott, Sanford, and Alexander (see also Sommer's contribution to part 3), trades ecological validity for increased generalizability. This approach draws on methods used in a number of disciplines (including studies of text processing, artificial intelligence research, and corpus and computational linguistics) that have developed techniques for gathering, sorting, counting, and analyzing empirical data—whether through questionnaires, the measuring of readers' response times vis-à-vis questions about the text, or the coding and analysis of identifiable textual structures.[5] The logical end point of the quantitative approach is a theory of some core set of cue-inference correlations underlying all narrative processing, no matter what kind of story is under examination—whether it is experimentally constructed or naturally occurring.

Collectively, the essays assembled in the present volume raise the question of how to accommodate, if not overcome, this basic tension between ecological validity and generalizability in research on the mind-narrative nexus. In investigating cue-inference relationships, how can the intuition-driven methods of humanistic inquiry, based on a deep engagement with particular texts, be reconciled with data-driven methods premised on a wider-scope but shallower analysis of large narrative corpora?[6] This question remains an open one, but restating the issues involved may point to strategies for moving forward. To adapt Kant's account of the relationship between concepts and intuitions: in the absence of empirical, quantitatively based testing, the process of (re)formulating hypotheses about narrative and mind may prove to be empty; but by the same token, if they are not qualitatively anchored—phenomenologically grounded in narrative experiences—the use of empirical, quantitative methods in this area of inquiry could turn out to be blind.

> 2. What is the best way to foster genuine dialogue or interaction between scholarship on narrative and the sciences of mind—as opposed to a unidirectional borrowing, by narrative scholars, of ideas from the cognitive sciences?

Up to now, the "direction of fit" between narratology and the sciences of mind has largely run from the latter to the former—with narrative scholars working to enrich classical, structuralist models of narrative with ideas about human intelligence that were unavailable to early analysts such as Roland Barthes, Gérard Genette, A.-J. Greimas, and Tzvetan Todorov. Thus, scholars such as Alan Palmer (2004) and Lisa Zunshine (2006) have used cognitive, social, and evolutionary psychology as the source domain for concepts they seek to map onto the target domain of narrative inquiry—with work in discourse analysis, cognitive linguistics, categorization theory, and other fields also being used, by other commentators, for this same purpose (see, e.g., Herman 2009). As Meir Sternberg (2003) has emphasized, however, if research on narrative and mind is to become a bona fide interdiscipline, theorists need to move beyond unidirectional borrowing and engage in genuine dialogue and exchange. In turn, for dialogue of this sort to be initiated and sustained, analysts need to establish the relevance of traditions of narrative inquiry—the pertinence of ideas developed by scholars of story—for research on the mind (see Herman 2013 for further discussion).

A number of the contributors to this volume lay important groundwork for this enterprise, with Maria Mäkelä, for example, underscoring how literary narratologists studying fictional minds can contribute importantly to discussions of the mind more generally. Likewise, Bart Keunen suggests how study of the world's narrative traditions can illuminate the changing methods that people use to reason about their own and others' reasons for acting—and also why different ways of engaging in such folk-psychological reasoning might be in circulation in different (sub)cultures at the same time. To use terms that I develop in my contributions to another study (Herman, Phelan, Rabinowitz, Richardson, and Warhol 2012), Mäkelä and Keunen both explore how *model persons* or individuals-in-storyworlds can at once shape and be shaped by broader *models of persons*, or schemes for understanding persons that emerge from prior encounters with stories and other kinds of texts, as well as everyday social encounters (see also Eder, Jannidis, and Schneider 2010; Herman 2013; Jannidis 2004, 2009; Schneider 2001). This focus thus provides a strategy for exploring ways in which scholarship on narrative can inform, and not just be informed by, research on the mind. Other, complementary strategies need to be developed in order to foster dialogue across the multiple fields of study that are relevant (or rather required) for engaging with the mind-narrative nexus.

> 3. With a view to establishing true reciprocity between narrative theory and the cognitive sciences (per question 2), how can the ideas from different (inter)disciplines concerned with the mind be brought into relationship both with one another and also with traditions of narrative inquiry?

At the closing roundtable session of a conference on "Literature and Cognitive Science" held at the University of Connecticut in 2006, the cognitive psychologist Richard Gerrig noted one of the perils of unidirectional borrowing of the kind criticized by Sternberg. Specifically, Gerrig pointed out that scholars of literature, when adopting ideas from fields such as psychology, sometimes do so in an eclectic, even haphazard manner, because they remain unaware of larger debates in the fields from which they are importing novel concepts. Thus, Gerrig pointed out that among cognitive psychologists the "theory of mind" concept remains subject to dispute, to a degree that some of the literary-narratological work on fictional minds has not fully registered.[7] This sort of problem is only intensified when, as is the case with research on stories that seeks to engage with the broader umbrella field of cognitive science, scholars in the humanities draw on concepts and methods from multiple disciplines, each with distinct traditions of inquiry. Thus, contributors to the present volume bring scholarship on narrative into dialogue with work in psychology, linguistics and stylistics, the philosophy of mind, ethnography, and other fields. The question is how to promote familiarity with best practices in all of these fields, and hence best practices when it comes to establishing an interdiscipline situated at their meeting point.

One strategy may be to develop mechanisms for collaborative authorship as well as cross-disciplinary vetting of the resulting research. In this connection, Bortolussi and Dixon and Emmott, Sanford, and Alexander set an important precedent in their contributions, given that the members of these author teams draw on different areas of disciplinary expertise and report findings made possible by their shared engagement with complex, multidimensional issues of narrative and mind. More generally, however, the present volume outlines a number of key research problems, including the fundamental question of how readers imagine or experience narrative worlds (see Caracciolo's essay), that teams of authors based in different fields might productively work to address.

> 4. When studying issues of narrative and mind, what is the best way to take into account the relationship between theory and corpus— that is, the way one's understanding of the mind-narrative nexus will be shaped by the kinds of narrative practices one considers?

In her essay in this volume, Anežka Kuzmičová suggests that theories of reader response, which have been skewed toward contemporary ways of engaging with narrative texts, can benefit from a fuller engagement with the history of reading practices—and a fuller consideration of how those practices relate to changing methods of storytelling. Kuzmičová's analysis raises broader questions about the relationship between accounts of the mind-narrative nexus and the specific narrative corpora used as the basis for theory building in this domain.

In general, analysts have come to recognize the need to diversify the corpus of narrative texts—the range of storytelling practices—on the basis of which they seek to develop accounts of what stories are, how they work, and what they can be used to do. To quote a formulation by Gerald Prince (1995), in his discussion of the impact a focus on female-authored texts might have on work in narratology, "it can be argued that a modification of the narratological corpus [e.g., an inclusion of more texts by women] . . . may affect the very models produced by narratology; and, should it turn out that such a change does not lead to an alteration of the models, the latter would be all the more credible, all the less open to negative criticism" (78). Along the same lines, as Kuzmičová's essay suggests, analysts of narrative and mind need to consider how the stories they consider shape the models they build. How might the choice of stories from different periods, genres, or cultural traditions affect the way theorists characterize the mental capacities and dispositions that provide grounds for—or are grounded in—narrative experiences? For that matter, how do issues of medium-specificity come into play in this same connection? How might models developed with reference to monomodal or single-channel narratives need to be adjusted to accommodate multimodal storytelling via film, conversational interaction, digital environments, or comics, in which the interplay between different semiotic channels presents different opportunities and challenges for narrative sense making?

These last remarks build on a previous study (Herman 2011), in which I argue that taking multimodal narratives into account requires recalibrating the approaches to narrative and mind developed by literary narratologists. But conversely, traditions of inquiry growing out of the study of literary narratives promise to enrich the models of narrative comprehension—and the accounts of how stories are used to build models of the world—that have been developed for example by researchers analyzing storytelling in everyday interaction (e.g., Ochs and Capps 2001).

> 5. What difference does this area of research make when it comes to interpreting particular stories—or should it make a difference? In other words, to what extent can (or should) studies of storytelling vis-à-vis the sciences of mind be translated into strategies for interpreting specific narratives?

This final question brings me back, full circle, to my first question, which concerned the relationship between the in-depth study of individual narratives and wider-scope analysis of broader narrative patterns revealed through quantitative methods. Here, however, the issue is exactly how—and whether—a focus on narrative and mind might shape theorists' engagement with specific narratives. After all, it does not go without saying that the value of mind-oriented approaches should be judged according to the criterion of hermeneutic productivity, or their ability to generate strategies for interpreting particular stories.

Indeed, in his pathbreaking 1991 study *Reading Minds*, Mark Turner characterized his approach as cutting against the grain of what he described as default assumptions, both in the humanities in general and in literary studies in particular, about the importance of generating readings of specific works. Turner suggested that practitioners should shift from producing ever more sophisticated readings of individual texts to developing an account of the basic and general principles underlying the process of reading itself. At issue is a reprioritizing of reading over readings, a reassessment that places systematicity over nuance; common, everyday cognitive abilities over ostensibly unique or special capacities bound up with literary expression; and unconscious sense-making operations over what falls within the (narrow) domain of conscious awareness.

In this respect, Turner's approach harkens back to that of the structuralist narratologists, who likewise insisted that narratology was not (or should not be) a handmaiden to interpretation. The structuralists claimed that, just as the Saussurean linguist studies the system of language (*langue*) rather than the individual messages made possible and intelligible by that system (*parole*), narratologists should study *how* narrative in general means, rather than *what* particular narratives mean. But though Saussure emphasized code over message—that is, though he foregrounded the structural constituents and combinatory principles of the semiotic system of language over situated uses of that system—in the years since structuralism convergent research developments across multiple fields, including discourse analysis, philosophy, psychology, and narrative theory itself, have revealed the importance of studying how people deploy various sorts of symbol systems to refer to, and constitute, aspects of their experience. Further, as a number of contributors to the present volume underscore, storytelling affords methods—arguably, serves as a primary resource—for such acts of world modeling and world creation. In turn, a key question for future inquiry is how a focus on the mind-narrative nexus might illuminate the structure and functions of these situated storytelling acts.

The idea here is not to reprioritize readings over reading, and thus undercut Turner's critique of the literary-critical status quo. The idea, rather, is to explore how any general account of the reading of narratives requires attending to the specificity of particular story designs—and to the way such designs both emanate from and trigger identifiable sense-making operations. Multiple issues relevant for the study of narrative and mind are at stake in this connection, including the manner in which story designs cue tentative, defeasible ascriptions of authorial intention—ascriptions to story creators of the reasons for acting that (probabilistically) account for why a given text has the structure it does. At issue, too, are how narrative designs prompt interpreters to co-construct storyworlds and to draw inferences about the mental lives of the characters who inhabit the worlds in question. Though fuller investigation of these issues[8] remains a task for future research, the present volume affords a richly suggestive starting point. More accurately, the volume provides important foundations for further inquiry in the field—for the ongoing attempt, by theorists across a range of disciplines, to make sense of narrative sense making. *Stories and Minds* promises to deepen as well as widen the conversation among the theorists engaged in this attempt, allowing them to formulate new insights—and, just as important, new questions—as they continue to develop strategies for exploring the nexus of narrative and mind.

Notes

1. The conference (http://www.narratology.ugent.be/minds.html) was generously co-sponsored by the FWO (Research Foundation-Flanders), the international research group OLITH (https://olith.ned.univie.ac.at/de/node/13886), and the University of Antwerp, Ghent University, and Katholieke Universiteit Leuven.
2. For work developing ecological, evolutionary, and social-psychological approaches, see, e.g., Easterlin (2012), Mellmann (2010), and Brockmeier (2012), respectively. For studies incorporating neuroscientific findings, see Richardson (2010) and Young (2010). Hogan (2011), meanwhile, takes into account cross-cultural research on emotion.
3. See Herman (2005) for further discussion of these two approaches, as well as strategies for integrating quantitative approaches, in particular, into narrative inquiry.
4. By "reading" I mean, more broadly, "narrative interpretation," whether the story in question is written, literary narrative, a film, or a radio narrative. Here I flag issues of medium-specificity discussed in connection with question 4 below.
5. See Short (2001) for a helpful overview of some of the relevant techniques for measurement and analysis.
6. See Moretti (2009) for a discussion of some of the fundamental issues.
7. In the same connection, see Hutto (2009).
8. I explore these and related issues under the heading of "narrative worldmaking" in my contributions to Herman et al. (2012) and also in Herman (2013).

References

Brockmeier, Jens. 2012. "Narrative Scenarios: Toward a Culturally Thick Notion of Narrative." In *The Oxford Handbook of Culture and Psychology*, ed. Jaan Valsiner, 439-67. Oxford: Oxford University Press.

Easterlin, Nancy. 2012. *A Biocultural Approach to Literary Theory and Interpretation*. Baltimore: Johns Hopkins University Press.

Eder, Jens, Fotis Jannidis, and Ralf Schneider. 2010. "Characters in Fictional Worlds: An Introduction." In *Characters in Fictional Worlds: Understanding Imaginary Beings in Literature, Film, and Other Media*, ed. Eder, Jannidis, and Schneider, 3-64. Berlin: de Gruyter.

Herman, David. 2005. "Quantitative Methods in Narratology: A Corpus-based Study of Motion Events in Stories." In *Narratology beyond Literary Criticism*, ed. Jan Christoph Meister (in cooperation with Tom Kindt, Wilhelm Schernus, and Malte Stein), 125–49. Berlin: de Gruyter.

———. 2009. *Basic Elements of Narrative*. Oxford: Wiley-Blackwell.

———. 2011. "Storyworld/Umwelt: Nonhuman Experiences in Graphic Narratives." *SubStance* 40 (1): 156–81.

———. 2013. *Storytelling and the Sciences of Mind*. Cambridge: MIT Press.

Herman, David, James Phelan, Peter Rabinowitz, Brian Richardson, and Robyn Warhol. 2012. *Narrative Theory: Core Concepts and Critical Debates*. Columbus: Ohio State University Press.

Hogan, Patrick Colm. 2011. *Affective Narratology: The Emotional Structure of Stories*. Lincoln: University of Nebraska Press.

Hutto, Daniel D., ed. 2009. *Narrative and Folk Psychology*. Exeter, UK: Imprint Academic.

Jannidis, Fotis. 2004. *Figur und Person: Beitrag zu einer historischen Narratologie*. Berlin: de Gruyter.

———. 2009. "Character." In *Handbook of Narratology*, ed. Peter Hühn, John Pier, Wolf Schmid, and Jörg Schönert, 14-29. Berlin: de Gruyter.

Johnstone, Barbara. 2000. *Qualitative Methods in Sociolinguistics*. Oxford: Oxford University Press.

Mellmann, Katja. 2010. "Voice and Perception: An Evolutionary Approach to the Basic Functions of Narrative." In *Toward a Cognitive Theory of Narrative Acts*, ed. Frederick Aldama, 119–40. Austin: University of Texas Press.

Moretti, Franco. 2009. "Style, Inc. Reflections on Seven Thousand Titles (British Novels, 1740–1850)." *Critical Inquiry* 36:134–58.

Ochs, Elinor, and Lisa Capps. 2001. *Living Narrative: Creating Lives in Everyday Storytelling*. Cambridge: Harvard University Press.

Palmer, Alan. 2004. *Fictional Minds*. Lincoln: University of Nebraska Press.

Prince, Gerald. 1995. "On Narratology: Criteria, Corpus, Context." *Narrative* 3 (1): 73–84.

Richardson, Alan. 2010. *The Neural Sublime: Cognitive Theories and Romantic Texts*. Baltimore: Johns Hopkins University Press.

Schneider, Ralf. 2001. "Toward a Cognitive Theory of Literary Character: The Dynamics of Mental-Model Construction." *Style* 35 (4): 607-40.

Short, Michael. 2001. "Epilogue: Research Questions, Research Paradigms, and Research Methodologies in the Study of Narrative." In *New Perspectives on Narrative Perspective*, ed. Willie Van Peer and Seymour Chatman, 339–55. Albany: State University of New York Press.

Sternberg, Meir. 2003. "Universals of Narrative and Their Cognitivist Fortunes (I)." *Poetics Today* 24:297–395.

Toolan, Michael J. 2001. *Narrative: A Critical Linguistic Introduction*. 2nd ed. London: Routledge.

Turner, Mark. 1991. *Reading Minds: The Study of English in the Age of Cognitive Science*. Princeton: Princeton University Press.

Young, Kay. 2010. *Imagining Minds: The Neuro-Aesthetics of Austen, Eliot, and Hardy*. Columbus: Ohio State University Press.

Zunshine, Lisa. 2006. *Why We Read Fiction: Theory of Mind and the Novel*. Columbus: Ohio State University Press.

Contributors

Marc Alexander is a lecturer in English language at the University of Glasgow. His work primarily focuses on cognitive and corpus stylistics, digital humanities, and the semantic development of the English language. He is director of the STELLA Project and associate director of the *Historical Thesaurus of English*, both at the University of Glasgow.

Elaine Auyoung is a Mellon Postdoctoral Associate in the English Department at Rutgers University, where she teaches Victorian literature. She received her PhD in English from Harvard University in 2011, and specializes in nineteenth-century British literature and culture, the history and theory of the novel, and cognitive and aesthetic approaches to the arts. She is completing a book currently titled "Missing Fiction: The Feeling of Realism."

Lars Bernaerts is a professor of literary theory at the Free University of Brussels and a postdoctoral researcher of the Research Foundation Flanders (FWO) at Ghent University, Belgium. He is the editor of several books on Dutch literature and has authored a narratological study of mad first-person narrators.

Marisa Bortolussi is a professor in the Department of Modern Languages and Cultural Studies at the University of Alberta. She is the coeditor of *Directions in Empirical Literary Studies* (2008) and coauthor of *Psychonarratology* (2003) with Peter Dixon.

Marco Caracciolo is a postdoctoral fellow at the research center "Arts in Society" of the University of Groningen in the Netherlands. He is mainly interested in cognitive approaches to literature and in literary aesthetics. He has been a visiting scholar at the Ohio State University (Project Narrative) and at the University of Hamburg (Interdisciplinary Center for Narratology). His work has appeared in journals such as *Poetics Today, Storyworlds, Phenomenology and the Cognitive Sciences*, and *Partial Answers*.

Dirk De Geest is a professor of Dutch literature and literary theory at KU Leuven, Belgium. He has authored, coauthored, and coedited numerous volumes on literature and narratology in Dutch.

Peter Dixon is a professor of psychology at the University of Alberta. He is the coauthor of *Psychonarratology* (2003) with Marisa Bortolussi and has published on a wide variety of topics in cognitive psychology.

Catherine Emmott is a senior lecturer in English language at the University of Glasgow. She is the author of *Narrative Comprehension: A Discourse Perspective* (1997) and *Mind, Brain and Narrative* (with A. J. Sanford, 2012). She was text and stylistics editor for the *Encyclopedia of Language and Linguistics* (2006) and is currently assistant editor of the journal *Language and Literature*. She is director of the STACS (Stylistics, Text Analysis and Cognitive Science) Project at the University of Glasgow.

David Herman, based at Ohio State University, is currently pursuing several projects that explore intersections among narrative studies, cognitive science, and critical animal studies. His book *Storytelling and the Sciences of Mind* will be published in 2013.

Luc Herman is a professor of American literature and narrative theory at the University of Antwerp, Belgium. He has coedited *The Cambridge Companion to Thomas Pynchon* (2011) and coauthored *Handbook of Narrative Analysis* (2005) with Bart Vervaeck.

Bart Keunen is a professor of comparative literature at Ghent University, Belgium. He is the author of *Time and Imagination: Chronotopes in Western Narrative Culture* (2011), *Literature and Society: The Function of Literary Sociology in Comparative Literature* (with Bart Eeckhout, 2001), *The Urban Condition: Space, Community and Self in the Contemporary Metropolis* (with the Ghent Urban Studies Team, 1999), and several books in Dutch.

Anežka Kuzmičová is completing a doctoral dissertation at Stockholm University on mental imagery in the reading of literary narrative. Her articles have appeared in *Semiotica* and *Samlaren*. She is also one of the contributors to *Mimesis: Metaphysics, Cognition, Pragmatics* (ed. Gregory Currie et al., 2012).

Maria Mäkelä is a university lecturer in comparative literature at the University of Tampere in Finland. She coedited *Narrative, Interrupted: The Plotless, the Disturbing and the Trivial in Literature* (with Laura Karttunen and Markku Lehtimäki, 2012). She has published on classical, postclassical, and "unnatural" narratology, consciousness representation, intermediality, literary romance and adultery, and realism.

Anthony J. Sanford is an emeritus professor at the University of Glasgow and an Honorary Senior Research Fellow at the Institute of Neuroscience and Psychology. He is a cognitive psychologist with a special interest in human understanding and the psychology of language. He has published numerous scientific papers and several books on these topics. With Catherine Emmott, he is the author of *Mind, Brain and Narrative* (2012), in which they jointly develop a theory describing how emphasis and focus works in narrative comprehension.

Roy Sommer is a professor of English at the University of Wuppertal in Germany, where he is a founding member of the interdisciplinary Center for Narrative Research. He has edited, coedited, and authored numerous books, among them, with Sandra Heinen, *Narratology in the Age of Cross-disciplinary Narrative Research* (2009).

Bart Vervaeck is a professor of Dutch literature at Ghent University, Belgium. He is the coauthor of *Handbook of Narrative Analysis* (2005) with Luc Herman.

Index

Brooks, Peter, 135, 193
Brooks, Rodney, 87
Bruner, Jerome, 10, 65
Butte, George, 130

Camera (Toussaint), 119–20, 124
Caracciolo, Marco, 15–16, 81–100
Carmichael, L., 25
Cassirer, Ernst, 183
categorization, 17, 157, 164–65, 202
causality, 184, 186; maximalist attribution of, 181–82, 190, 192; minimalist attribution of, 181–82, 183, 185, 187, 188–89, 191–92; and narrativity, 179–80
Chabris, Christopher, 86
characters, narrative, 45–46, 50
Chrétien de Troyes, 179, 186
Christie, Agatha: *Sad Cypress*, 51–53; *Sparkling Cyanide*, 47–49; "The Tuesday Night Club," 51
Clark, Billy, 165–67
Clark, J. P., 165
closure, 16, 145, 190, 193
Coetzee, J. M., 148
cognition, 1, 100, 116, 129, 130, 156, 157; grounded and situated, 115; of readers, 2–3, 41, 157; of verbal and perceptual cues, 64
Cognitive Poetics (Stockwell), 10
cognitive theory, 9–10, 13
cognitivist approach, 8–9, 130, 148n1, 156; opportunities in, 12–13; threats to, 10–12
Cohn, Dorrit, 129, 130–31
commonsense psychology. *See* folk psychology
communication, 107; and language, 108–9; narrative, 176
concept-driven approach, 71–72, 76n4

confessions, 135–36
consciousness: and experience, 83, 96; and imagination, 15, 90–91, 94–96; mediating functions of, 137; of reader, 84, 85, 93; representation of, 81, 84–85, 130
Consciousness Explained (Dennett), 2–3
consonance, 134
construction-mindedness, 136, 137, 141, 143, 147
Courtès, Joseph, 6
Crane, Tim, 85
Crime and Punishment (Dostoyevsky), 193
cues, 201; limited and minimal, 60, 64–66, 73–74; perceptual, 64, 66; representational, 60, 66, 71–72; textual, 9, 15, 62, 76n4, 121, 165, 200; verbal, 60, 63, 64
Culler, Jonathan, 6

Dahl, Roald, 50
Darwinism, literary, 12
Davidson, Donald, 180
defamiliarization, 7, 73, 140. *See also* estrangement, cognitive
De Geest, Dirk, 1–18
Demetrius, 122
Dennett, Daniel, 2–3, 10, 97
depth of processing, 39, 40–41
determinacy, 59, 71
Dewey, John, 69
direct presence: and bodily movement, 114, 116–18, 123; localization of, 121; and motor resonance, 114–16; multimodal, 118–20; and verbal presence, 108, 110–11, 112–13, 123–25
dissonance, 134, 135

distal-coherence puzzle, 32–33
distractors, 48–49
Dixon, Peter, 7, 9, 14, 23–36, 121, 201, 204
Doležel, Lubomir, 2
Dostoyevsky, Fyodor, 189, 193
Dreaming by the Book (Scarry), 62, 90
Dunbar, Robin, 109

Eakin, Paul John, 130
East Is East (Khan-Din), 157, 160–64
The Embodied Mind (Varela, Thompson, and Rosch), 86
embodiment, 115; and imagery, 94; and language, 94; readerly, 16, 123
Emmott, Catherine, 14–15, 39–54, 66, 82, 201, 204
empathy: categorical, 194n3; narrative, 17, 157, 158–60, 161, 163–64; situational, 189
empathy-altruism hypothesis, 156
enactivism, 15, 81; and experience, 86–87, 99–100; philosophy of perception of, 82, 86–87
estrangement, cognitive, 16, 131, 133, 143, 157. *See also* defamiliarization
ethical narrativity thesis, 145
experiences, 10, 95, 98, 124; and consciousness, 83, 96; construction of, 136, 148; enactivist view of, 85–90, 99–100; and imagination, 89–90; and perception, 85, 88, 91
experientiality, 15, 16, 91, 123; constructed, 130, 136, 148; of gap-filling, 92–93; narrative texts and, 82–83, 90, 92, 95–96, 100, 109, 132; projected, 132, 141–42; and representation, 83, 94, 95, 101n2; and storytelling, 133, 135; and verbal art, 130

Expositional Modes and Temporal Ordering in Fiction (Sternberg), 7–8

Fagunwa, D. O., 165
false reconstructions, 50–53
familiarity, cognitive, 16, 131
The Famished Road (Okri), 157–58, 165–70
Fictional Minds (Palmer), 188–89
first-person narration, 33, 131, 133, 140, 168; and bodily movement, 108, 114, 116, 117; dissonant and consonant, 134; impersonal voice in, 146–47
Flaubert, Gustave, 113, 114, 117, 118–19, 123, 181
Fleming, Ian, 179
Fludernik, Monika, 7, 11, 82–84, 101n2, 109, 129
folk psychology, 178, 183, 189, 191, 192; and causality, 179–81, 185; and fiction, 193; and morality, 17, 180–81, 193; narrative nature of, 17, 176–77, 180, 187, 193, 194n2; sociocultural basis of, 17, 177
Ford, Richard, 131–32; "Privacy," 133–36, 137–39, 141, 143–44; "Reunion," 136, 141–43, 144–45
foregrounding, 7, 32, 40, 139; devices, 41, 44, 49–50
Freedgood, Elaine, 62–63

Gadamer, Hans-Georg, 5
Gallagher, Catherine, 71
Gallagher, Shaun, 177
Gallese, Vittorio, 116, 158
gap-filling: cognitivist approach to, 2–3, 8–9; experientiality of, 92–93; hermeneutic tradition on, 4–6; reading as, 59–60; structuralist approach to, 4–7

minimal cues: advantages of, 65–66; in daily experience, 64–65; and style, 73–74; in Tolstoy, 66–73

minimalist causality attribution, 181–82, 183, 185, 187, 188–89; and maximalist causality attribution, 191–92

model persons, 202–3

morality, 184, 185; and folk psychology, 180–81, 193; and narrative culture, 191–93; and thick moral concepts, 17, 178–79

Morrow, Daniel G., 33

motivation, 142, 159, 179, 181; and naturalization, 6–7

motor imagery. *See* sensorimotor imagery

motor resonance, 114–15, 116

Mukařorvsky, Jan, 7

Multitude of Sins (Ford), 131–32

Myin, Eric, 86

mystery and detective fiction, 41, 47–53

myths, 182–84

Nagel, Thomas, 83

Narayanan, Srini, 93

Narrative Comprehension (Emmott), 82

narrative practice hypothesis (NPH), 177–78, 187–93, 194n2

narrativization, 10, 84–85, 142, 180; and continuations, 45–47; dissonance and consonance in, 134; and gaps, 1, 2–3; narrators and, 124, 143; natural frames of, 131, 133, 136

narratology, 189; as approach, 109, 168–69; and cognitive theory, 9–10; and mind, 202; natural and unnatural, 131, 132–33; postclassical, 4, 167, 187; structuralist, 187–88, 206

naturalization, 6–7, 16, 131, 139

natural narratology, 132, 133

Nielsen, Henrik Skov, 132, 146

Noë, Alva, 86, 87, 93, 116–17

Notes on the Novel (Ortega y Gasset), 188

"The Novel in Search of Itself" (Pavel), 191–92

novels, 61, 182, 190; discourse in, 62, 129, 131; empathy in, 159–60, 163; French, 113, 119, 123, 124; information in, 23, 59; intercultural, 157, 164–65, 171; modern, 17, 188, 189, 190; reading of, 34, 124; realism in, 132, 182, 188

O'Donnell, Damien, 164

Okri, Ben, 157–58, 165–70

Olde, Brent, 33

Oliver Twist (Dickens), 159–60

On Chesil Beach (McEwan), 189–90

Ong, Walter J., 123

O'Regan, Kevin, 86, 87

Ortega y Gasset, José, 188

pain, 98–99

Palmer, Alan, 2, 13, 129, 130, 188–89, 202

paralipsis, 2, 6

Pavel, Thomas, 191–92, 193

Pelléas et Mélisande (Maeterlinck), 193

perception, 75; and action, 117; and bodily movements, 93, 116; enactivist account of, 82, 84, 86–87; and experience, 69, 85, 88, 91; and imagination, 82, 89, 90, 91; partial, 64–66

Perfetti, Charles A., 27

performance, 135–36, 137

phenomenal presence. *See* presence